Multiracial Identity in Children's Literature

A must-read and resource for elementary and middle-grade teachers, librarians, parents and scholars, *Multiracial Identity in Children's Literature* expands the field of multicultural literature far beyond black and white and provides a timely "critical multicultural analysis" of contemporary mixed race children's literature.

—Laura Kina, Vincent de Paul Professor of Art,
Media, and Design at DePaul University, USA

Racially mixed children make up the fastest growing youth demographic in the U.S., and teachers of diverse populations need to be mindful in selecting literature that their students can identify with. This volume explores how books for elementary school students depict and reflect multiracial experiences through text and images. Chaudhri examines contemporary children's literature to demonstrate the role these books play in perpetuating and resisting stereotypes and the ways in which they might influence their readers. Through critical analysis of contemporary children's fiction, Chaudhri highlights the connections between context, literature, and personal experience to deepen our understanding of how children's books treat multiracial identity.

Amina Chaudhri is Assistant Professor of Teacher Education at Northeastern Illinois University, USA.

Routledge Research in Education

For a full list of titles in this series, please visit www.routledge.com

177 **Vocationalism in Further and Higher Education**
Policy, programmes and pedagogy
Edited by Sai Loo and Jill Jameson

178 **Children's Creative Music-Making with Reflexive Interactive Technology**
Adventures in improvising and composing
Edited by Victoria Rowe, Angeliki Triantafyllaki and Francois Pachet

179 **Community-based Media Pedagogies**
Relational Practices of Listening in the Commons
Bronwen Low, Chloe Brushwood Rose, and Paula Salvio

180 **Reclaiming Discipline for Education**
Knowledge, relationships and the birth of community
James MacAllister

181 **The Politics of Differentiation in Schools**
Martin Mills, Amanda Keddie, Peter Renshaw, and Sue Monk

182 **Language, Race, and Power in Schools**
A Critical Discourse Analysis
Edited by Pierre W. Orelus

183 **Teacher Educators' Professional Learning in Communities**
Linor L. Hadar and David L. Brody

184 **Spirituality, Community, and Race Consciousness in Adult Higher Education**
Breaking the Cycle of Racialization
Timothy Paul Westbrook

185 **Multiracial Identity in Children's Literature**
Amina Chaudhri

Multiracial Identity in Children's Literature

Amina Chaudhri

Routledge
Taylor & Francis Group
NEW YORK AND LONDON

First published 2017
by Routledge
711 Third Avenue, New York, NY 10017

and by Routledge
2 Park Square, Milton Park, Abingdon, Oxon, OX14 4RN

Routledge is an imprint of the Taylor & Francis Group, an informa business

© 2017 Taylor & Francis

The right of Amina Chaudhri to be identified as author of this work has been asserted by her in accordance with sections 77 and 78 of the Copyright, Designs and Patents Act 1988.

All rights reserved. No part of this book may be reprinted or reproduced or utilised in any form or by any electronic, mechanical, or other means, now known or hereafter invented, including photocopying and recording, or in any information storage or retrieval system, without permission in writing from the publishers.

Trademark notice: Product or corporate names may be trademarks or registered trademarks, and are used only for identification and explanation without intent to infringe.

Library of Congress Cataloguing-in-Publication Data
A catalogue record for this book has been requested

ISBN: 978-1-138-86017-9 (hbk)
ISBN: 978-1-315-71672-5 (ebk)

Typeset in Sabon
by Apex CoVantage, LLC

For Reza, who will write his own stories.

Contents

	Preface	ix
	Acknowledgements	xiii
1	Introduction	1
2	Multiracial Identity in the United States: Historical and Current Discourse	11
3	Multiracial Stories in Picturebooks	22
4	Multiracial In/Visibility: The Legacy of Pathology in Contemporary Fiction	37
5	Multiracial Blending: The Post-Racial Myth in Contemporary Fiction	51
6	Multiracial Awareness: Power and Visibility in Contemporary Fiction	69
7	Voices of the Past: Multiracial Identity in Historical Fiction	93
8	Hidden Identities: Whiteness and Passing	115
9	Teaching and Learning with Multiracial Fiction	136
	Appendix A	142
	Appendix B	144
	Appendix C	146
	Appendix D	148
	Appendix E	149
	Appendix F	150
	Index	151

Preface

Multiracial Identity in Children's Literature pushes at the boundaries of multicultural children's literature to invite exploration of how current publications for elementary-age readers depict multiracial experiences through text and image. The historical background in Chapter 2 provides a trajectory of perspectives that have influenced how we think of mixed race identity in the U.S. today. Early scientific interest disseminated notions about biological "purity" and "impurity" of races, categorizing people into discrete groups and positing the mixing of racial groups as genetically precarious and socially undesirable. Over time, as it became gradually understood that race is a social construct, laws and instruments such as the Census and other official tracking methods changed to allow people to self-identify in a variety of ways, thus expanding the ways race is constructed. Mixed race studies research shows that context, geography, language, immigration, migration, policy and numerous other factors play a role in how multiracial Americans are viewed and view themselves.

This book draws on Rudine Sims Bishop's (1982) foundational study of African American experiences in children's literature. In *Shadow and Substance: Afro-American Experience in Contemporary Children's Fiction*, Sims Bishop categorized books to show the patterns of representation that were occurring in the body of children's literature that included African American characters. She describes the books in her study in three broad categories. The "social conscience books" presented the problem of racial segregation with one dimensional or secondary African American characters who needed to be brought into the fold of mainstream (white) society. In "melting pot" books, race was descriptive but not functional in the stories. The third was a set of "culturally conscious" books that portrayed African American life in rich, authentic and complex ways. Organizing a corpus of similar books into smaller sets based on shared themes enables detailed analysis and discussion of those themes within an historical context. In *Multiracial Identity in Children's Literature* I unite contemporary and historical fiction published since the Census change in 2000 that includes multiracial content. Authors of fiction are invested in creating believable characters in settings that closely resemble their temporal, albeit fictional reality, that engage readers on multiple levels and perhaps transform them in some way. Having identified a corpus of picture books and novels, I modified Bishop's framework and grouped titles broadly based on their treatment of multiracial identity. In Chapter 3, Multiracial Stories in Picturebooks, I unite a corpus of books for very young readers (preschool—early elementary grades) that combine image and text in their portrayal of biracial identity. A number of picturebooks are intended for biracial readers to see themselves represented in loving, happy contexts with affirming messages about being proud to be mixed. Others include the tension of being expected to choose between one racial group or another, debunking the need for children to do that. Still others make no mention of racial identity, but images of families allow young readers to see themselves represented in interesting stories, in caring communities, and in full color.

Chapter 4, Multiracial In/Visibility: The Legacy of Pathology in Contemporary Fiction examines books in which multiracial characters struggle with who they are. Their racial identity is a source of internal conflict and intense pain that dominates all aspects of their lives. Characters come from broken or dysfunctional families and have internalized painful ideas about the impossibility of belonging anywhere because they are mixed race. The protagonists are simultaneously highly visible for being biracial, and made invisible, marginalized, because of it. Chapter 5, Multiracial Blending: The Post-Racial Myth in Contemporary Fiction, looks at books in which racial identity is not the main source of conflict. Blending books depict a variety of ways of understanding biracial experiences. Some characters are described as being biracial simply as a descriptive detail that might easily be overlooked by the reader. In other Blending books authors take care to establish characters' identity with significant description and occasional ramifications for the characterization. In still other books, mixed race characters racially blend in with the presumably-monoracial people around them. A smaller subset of Blending books is those in which characters' lives are equally shaped by both their racial identities forming new selves. In Chapter 6, Multiracial Awareness: Power and Visibility in Contemporary Fiction, characters are neither troubled by nor oblivious to their racial heritage. Instead they have a secure, dynamic understanding of who they are and how they are connected to their communities. Moreover, in Awareness books, characters successfully confront prejudiced characters and make them realize the consequences of their racist ways.

Chapters 7 and 8 examine racial identity construction in historical fiction. These books require an analysis that situates them within their specific historical contexts. In Chapter 7, Voices from the Past: Multiracial Identity in Historical Fiction, I look at ways in which biracial subjectivity is constructed in the context of colonial expansion and war. Although prevalent racial attitudes of the times often resulted in the children of interracial unions being rejected by both sides, the treatment of racism in some books is uncritical, contributing to a normalcy that excuses rather than critiques. Another set of recent publications, however, posits multiracial characters who actively resist prejudice and transform their surroundings rather than passively accept oppression. These counterstories interrupt the readers' tendency to view oppression as a predictable inevitability with the oppressed subject having little or no agency. Chapter 8, Hidden Identities: Whiteness and Passing, tackles the issues of whiteness as an ethnic construction which is separate from whiteness as a privileged norm with a history of racism. The contemporary fiction analyzed in this section depicts biracial characters who learn about their ethnic white heritage as opposed to their nonwhite heritage—a rare occurrence in the existing corpus of literature. The section on passing juxtaposes several treatments of historical fiction in which protagonists pass for white. The analysis reveals opportunities for readers to critique authors' renderings of the experience of passing when it is presented as an easy choice for some, and a matter of daily peril for others. Chapter 9, Teaching and Learning with Multiracial Fiction, recaps the importance of including mixed race mirrors and windows in classroom literature so that fewer children grow up experiencing the marginalizing effects of microaggressions—seemingly innocuous questions and comments—that, over time, wear away at a child's sense of self. Some of the contemporary publications about mixed race characters are ideal for teaching and learning about the internal and external forces in the construction of identity.

Acknowledgments

This book is for the many students and teachers who have inspired me over the years. Countless conversations with colleagues about children's literature shaped many of the ideas here. I am grateful to Northeastern Illinois University for awarding me a summer research stipend, and to Susan Chaudhri and Nadia Chaudhri for their encouragement. I owe so much to Lourdes Torres and Henry Fukawa for being my most constructive critics and constant companions—thank you.

1 Introduction

During my time as an elementary school teacher in a Chicago public school, I relied on children's literature in all areas of the curriculum to reach my students on deeper levels than textbook learning allowed. Stories inspired and motivated as well as provided insight into life experiences that were similar to or different from their own. I shared with my fourth graders the metaphor that we can think of literature as a mirror that enables us to see our own lives reflected, and as a window through which we can view different experiences (Bishop 1990). The metaphor resonated deeply with my students and inevitably became an integral part of our discussions. Books such as *Because of Winn Dixie* (DiCamillo 2000) encouraged us to talk about different types of friendships and ways in which we tend to be judgmental; *Kira Kira* (Kadohata 2006) brought up the topics of sibling relationships, racism, and loss. *The Watsons Go to Birmingham-1963* (Curtis 1995) was a window into the Jim Crow south. For many of my students, that kind of racism was something that happened to other people in another time, but became a less distant concept when we connected *Watsons* to current events. Immigration stories such as *Lupita Mañana* (Beatty 1981) hit home in very immediate ways as almost everyone had their own immigration story to tell. One year a student noted that she had never read any stories that mirrored who she was—"Chinese and American." Others agreed, and I looked around and realized that at least six of my students were biracial (as far as I could tell). And they were right. Not one of us could think of a story that depicted a multiracial protagonist. Moreover, I recalled that I had once had a similar realization decades earlier, when I read a book that mirrored my own Pakistani and English heritage. I remembered the awe and disbelief that smatterings of that author's life matched mine. It was in that moment that this project was born and I set out to find fiction for young readers that depicted multiracial experiences. Where were these stories? Who was telling them? What kinds of mirrors and windows would they provide?[1]

Literature for children that includes multiracial characters is not easy to identify. In her study of literature for young adults, Nancy Reynolds (2009) comments on the variety of responses to her query in search of books with multiracial content. Respondents suggested titles that were about nonwhite characters, or written by writers of color, but not necessarily about multiracial experiences. My own experience was similar. I received suggestions of books about white and nonwhite characters overcoming racial differences, such as Jacqueline Woodson and E. B. Lewis's (2001) *The Other Side,* or of books with diverse casts of characters such as some of Uma Krishnaswami's novels (*Naming Maya* 2004, *Many Windows* 2008), or simply books by nonwhite authors. Like Reynolds, I found that purveyors of children's books who I approached understood the terms "mixed race," "biracial" and "multiracial" vaguely, the way that the term "diverse" is used as a catch-all label that includes everyone and avoids naming race. Fortunately, the Library of Congress (LoC) uses the subject heading "racially-mixed people" and offers a searchable online catalog that identifies relevant titles. In my search, I found that library databases and lists created by individual readers and bloggers on sites such as Goodreads.com and Amazon.com overlapped with the LoC lists for the most part. Additionally, I was able to find other books if, by chance, reviewers for publications such as The Horn Book, The Bulletin of the Center for Children's Books, and Booklist, made mention of multiracial characters. Sometimes, however, the label is used arbitrarily so that a search through a database for books using the terms "mixed race" or "multiracial" might refer to books with multiple characters of different racial backgrounds such as *The Misadventures of the Family Fletcher* (Levy 2014), which features four adopted brothers of gay fathers, two of whom might be white, and two might be black (one has to infer based on fleeting descriptions). Conversely, some books are not labeled and do not come up in many searches for mixed race children's books. Pam Muñoz Ryan's (2004) middle grade novel, *Becoming Naomi León* does not bear the LoC subject keyword, though it is most certainly about a character whose parents are white and Mexican, and her search for identity, as the title declares, involves her learning about her Mexican heritage. Neither does *My Basmati Bat Mitzvah* (Freedman 2013) which features a protagonist who is very much connected to her Indian and Jewish cultures. Blue Balliett's (2013) novel, *Hold Fast* comes up in online searches for mixed race books although there is nothing in the novel to lead readers to believe the family is interracial or the protagonists biracial. The determination appears to have been made from this description: "The father is pale, the mother dark, the kids cocoa and cinnamon. Eyes in this family are green, amber, and smoky topaz" (5). The identification of books as having multiracial content appears to dependent on the keyword choices decided upon by authors and publishers, and by book reviewers who may or may not notice or choose to comment on racial identity. The absence or presence of these keyword tags plays a role in the accessibility of the books for readers who might be intentionally seeking stories featuring multiracial experiences. This project unites contemporary and historical fiction (and some narrative non-fiction picturebooks) intended for beginning and middle grade readers and contextualizes depictions of multiracial identity within a historical framework. Essentially, *Multiracial Identity in Children's Literature* responds to the question: what recent publications feature multiracial lives, and what are they saying about the experiences of being multiracial?

Arnold Adoff and Emily McCully's (1973) *Black Is Brown Is Tan* is considered the first children's book featuring multiracial people. It is a picturebook, published shortly after the Supreme Court decision in Loving v. Virginia (1967) overturned antimiscegenation laws in the United States. Adoff and his wife, Virginia Hamilton were themselves an interracial couple for whom the law and society's judgmental views about interracial marriage must have had implications, so they understood the impact of laws on public perception and personal experience. Indeed, their son, Jaime Adoff is the author of three of the books with biracial primary characters. *Black Is Brown Is Tan* was significant for drawing attention to racial diversity in children's books at a time when there was little, if any affirmation of children of color in literature. Twenty years later, in 1993, Marguerite Davol and Irene Trivas's *Black, White, Just Right* doubled the number of books depicting multiracial children to two. The 1990s saw an average of two publications per year, with a sharp increase in 1999, the year before the U.S. Census change allowed people to "mark all that apply" among racial categories. To date, the Library of Congress lists 214 titles for children with the subject keyword "racially mixed people." It is possible that more books exist that have not been labeled, and finding these becomes a task of serendipity. Given that about 5,000 children's books are published annually, 214 books with multiracial content over the course of nearly four decades is a small number indeed. In a quantitative study, Chaudhri and Teale (2013) found that over the course of ten years, fiction for intermediate and middle grade readers with multiracial content comprised a mere 0.2 % of all publications. Another salient finding of the Chaudhri and Teale study is that 87% of the titles identified were about white and nonwhite biracial stories, with nonwhite mixes comprising only 13%. Representation is not only scarce overall, but limited in the ways multiracial identity is perceived and disseminated in the literary world. Critical multicultural analysis includes the consideration of the production aspect of children's books. With regard to multiracial books we should ask questions about how and why certain books are identified as multiracial, and when and why they are promoted. Over the years, other scholars have also commented on the dearth of mixed race literature (Sands-O'Connor 2001; Smith 2001; Yokota and Frost 2003). All this is to say that taken as a whole, the "slipperiness of language" (Reynolds 2009, xi), the shortage of books, and the absence of critical attention, suggest a national blind spot in the view of the current racial terrain. Clearly, there are not enough multiracial mirrors for today's rapidly growing multiracial population.

Multiracial Identity and Children's Literature: The Need for Mirrors and Windows

A key tenet of the multicultural education movement is to ensure that historically marginalized groups are represented in literature and curriculum. The Cooperative Children's Book Center (CCBC) at the University of Madison reports annually on the racial breakdown of books by and about people of color. CCBC librarians review approximately 3,500 books per year and the data shows that only around 10% are by and about people of color. Multiracial content is not reported separately and is probably folded into the general 'multicultural' realm. This is a woefully inadequate number that makes it hard for teachers and parents to find a variety of books for young readers beyond the heavily marketed award-winners. The need for an awareness of the contributions and struggles of people of color, immigrants, LGBTQ, and differently-abled Americans has given rise to a slow but significant presence of quality literature by writers such as Christopher Paul Curtis, Sherman Alexie, R. J. Pallacio, Alex Sanchez, Rita Williams-Garcia, and Ami Polonsky, to name a few. As issues of civil and human rights have become more prominent on our cultural landscape, the influence of identity-based movements has been felt in many realms, including literature. Visibility is a critical starting point. Maria P. P. Root (1992) reminds us, "in essence, to name oneself is to validate one's existence and declare visibility." (7) As a key factor in identity construction, literature is examined for how it contributes to positive, negative, or complex perceptions of marginalized people. Authors make intentional choices in the characters they create and their fictional representations may resonate with readers in profound ways. When children see themselves represented in the books in their classrooms, libraries and bookstores in positive ways, they understand that who they are matters enough to be in a book. The educational benefits to this are tremendous and have been documented by many research studies that attest to an increase in self-concept, motivation, comprehension and literacy development (Brophy 2008; McNair 2013; Flemming et al. 2015) Children experience literature in deeply aesthetic and personal ways that contribute to the development of personal values that necessarily influence how they interact with other people (Galda and Cullinan 2000). Thus, literature for children who are not biracial can serve as windows and provide insight into what those experiences might be like. In the increasingly racially-mixed world of today, it is significant that multiracial identity is being represented in a small body of literature, being received by readers, and playing a role in shaping a perception of what it means to be multiracial. Critical readings of these texts can contribute new ways of thinking about racial identity, breaking away from the "binary caste system" (Reynolds 2009, xiv) consisting of white and nonwhite people.

Multiracial people are not a recent phenomenon, but the claiming of a multiracial identity is relatively new practice. The "mark one or more" option in the 2000 U.S. Census was a turning point in American history that permitted individuals to choose multiple racial categories for the first time. As a result, 2.4% of the population, 6.8 million people, identified themselves as multiracial. The 2010 Census results showed that 3%, or 9 million people identified as belonging to two or more races. The symbolism of this emergent shift in self-identification is significant and is discussed in greater detail in Chapter 2. That millions of people reject the white/nonwhite categorization that is the legacy of the "one-drop rule" in recognition of the racial and ethnic multitudes in their heritage speaks volumes about the changing attitudes about racial identity in North America. How this racial identity manifests itself is at once a matter of individual self-perception and national social construction. *Multiracial Identity in Children's Literature* explores the ways multiracial experiences are portrayed in children's contemporary realistic and historical fiction against the backdrop of discursive and social practices that have defined mixed race identity for centuries.

Theoretical Framework

Western interest in children's literature is as old as the idea of childhood itself. Seth Lerer's (2008) book *Children's Literature: A Readers' History from Aesop to Harry Potter*, and Leonard Marcus' (2008) *Minders of Make Believe: Idealists, Entrepreneurs, and the Shaping of American Children's Literature*, are two recent publications that document the scholarly and public examination of what children read. More so than adult or even young adult literature, children's literature has come under the scrutiny of all manner of "minders" who regulate, prescribe, censor and advocate the content and quality of literature that ends up in the hands of young readers. No matter which end of the ideological spectrum, adults in charge of children agree that stories can have an impact on emerging identities. The literate child, as Lerer (2008) points out, is "made through texts and tales." (1)

This national awareness of the shaping powers of literature and the political, financial and ideological interests of the publishing world are intricately related (Marcus 2008), so it is not surprising that as in the realms of art, film and music, literature, too, tends to reflect dominant cultural sentiments. Efforts to have literature become more representative of diverse experiences in the United States led to the emergence of multicultural literature in the 1960s with the growing awareness of the deleterious effects on children of school and social segregation. A significant moment occurred in 1965 with the appearance of Nancy Larrick's review of more than 5,000 children's trade books in the *Saturday Review*. Published in the wake of critical events in the civil rights movement, Larrick's article revealed "an all-white world of children's literature" and sparked rigorous scholarship in the field of multicultural children's literature by researchers who were invested in highlighting themes and topics in quality books, as well as critiquing persistent problematic depictions of marginalized groups. Another foundational study, and one on which this book draws was Rudine Sims Bishop's (1982) analysis of representations of African American experiences in children's fiction in *Shadow and Substance* followed by a second study in 2007. *Free Within Ourselves: The Development of African American Children's Literature*, is a comprehensive historical overview documenting a rich tradition of children's literature that harkens back to the Harlem Renaissance. Because of the historical context from which it emerged, this now substantial body of literature is "purposeful, intended to serve functions that have not been expected of the larger body of American children's literature." (xii) In other words, Bishop posits, literature for, by, and about African Americans is suffused with an ideological intentionality that sets it apart from mainstream literature. These stories offer perspectives shaped by the shared and individual experiences of being African American and challenge hegemonic ideas of what it means to be American in a "parallel culture" (274). They offer readers access and affirmation. Bishop's work is foundational in describing thematic connections between books in relation to the historical settings in which they were written. Her work provides a template for exploring how other "parallel cultures" are represented in children's literature. Outside of the academy, insightful critical attention is being paid to issues in multicultural children's literature on websites such as the We Need Diverse Books campaign, and blogs by scholars, writers and activists such as Debbie Reese's website "American Indians in Children's Literature," and "Reading While White," which is maintained by a collaboration of librarians.[2] Several children's literature authors participate in conversations about multicultural books on their own websites: Monica Brown, Mitali Perkins, Zetta Elliott, and Uma Krishnaswami (to name a few).[3] Currently the body of books by and about multiracial Americans is not nearly as robust as it needs to be, and one goal of *Multiracial Identity in Children's Literature* is to highlight the dearth of mirror stories for biracial readers and window stories for their peers.

As I mentioned at the start, this book was inspired by my 4th grade students who pointed out the invisibility of their own identities in fiction. They also made me realize that my preparation as a teacher had not equipped me to bring up multiracial matters in the classroom. I would have to teach myself, and the learning curve was steep. I know from my own life that being biracial means constantly having to explain my name, my accent, my appearance and that was likely to be the experience of my students as well. But there had to be more to it. Unless teacher preparation programs actively and consistently engage preservice teachers in metacognitive critical analysis of children's literature, our ways of thinking remain predictable, and so will our students'. Now I teach at the university level and undergraduate and graduate students in my children's literature courses are initially predictable in their approaches, comfortable with discussing literary elements, but not ideological perspectives. They struggle with the seeming absurdity of using a feminist lens to analyze *Esperanza Rising* (Ryan 2000) to think about the protagonist's agency in terms of the male characters' influence on her life. My students think I expect them to teach their future elementary students about feminism (which I don't deny!) and it takes a while for them to realize that critical analysis, using any lens, is simply a way of expanding ways of observing and thinking about stories and recognizing the invisible work of ideology. In this book I have selected a set of texts to analyze to show how their subject positions invite readers to think about mixed race identity. I have selected texts that adhere to, resist, and negotiate paradigmatic ideas about multiracial identity in various ways. The focus is on deconstructing literary depictions of mixed race identity construction, for which I draw on three fields of research: mixed race studies, critical race theory, and critical multicultural analysis.

Mixed race studies crosses many disciples–sociology, literature, art, history–and offers many perspectives about the historical construction of multiraciality which I discuss in detail in Chapter 2. Critical race theory (CRT) comes from the field of law, but has found expression in other fields, especially in education (Ladson-Billings and Tate 1995; Rogers and Wetzel 2006; Brooks 2009; Hughes-Hassell, Barkley and Koehler 2009). Critical race theorist, Richard Delgado (1995) delineates several tenets of CRT, among which, the following are relevant to discussions of mixed race identity. One is that that racism is ubiquitous in our society, "it looks ordinary and natural" (xiv) which means it is essentially invisible. Another is that CRT challenges racism through storytelling whereby writers highlight the "invisible" operations of oppression and exposes them by telling a "counterstory." (65) Several multiracial novels can be read as counterstories for the ways in which authors bring the everyday racism faced by biracials to the fore, and challenge readers to recognize it. Maria José Botelho and Masha Kabakow Rudman (2009) articulate a theory of critical multicultural analysis (CMA) that moves beyond the celebratory tendency of conventional multiculturalism to look at intersections of power across race, culture, gender, and class. CMA recognizes that literature is a cultural artifact, imbued with the ideology of its context. Readers can accept or resist the encoded messages if they are taught that they have agency in how they make meaning of text and image (3). *Multiracial Identity in Children's Literature* uses CMA to ground readings of fictional, literary, multiracial identity construction in the historical perceptions that form current ways of thinking about mixed race.

About Language

There is no clear consensus about what term "children" means among those of us who study child-related work. For the purpose of this books, I refer to children's literature as those texts that would be read to very young non-readers, all the way through to the early teen years. These age parameters include books with protagonists no older than sixteen because conventional wisdom in the teaching field agrees that children tend to be interested in books with protagonists who are up to two years older than they are, and I was interested in books for middle school and younger students. Thus my use of the term "children's literature" imagines an audience of age four through eight for the picturebooks, and age nine through fourteen for the tradebooks.

In the search for books for this project I used the terms "mixed race," "mixed heritage," "multiracial," "biracial," and a number of combinations of racial and cultural labels in order to cast as wide a net as possible to unite a corpus of titles. All have different implications and their use is as varied as the people themselves. There is no national consensus among multiracial Americans about a preferred label and many move between racial identities depending on time, context and personal preference. In this book I use the three terms "mixed race", "multiracial" and "biracial" interchangeably to refer to fictional characters whose parents are described as belonging to different racial groups. Using three terms instead of one lends itself to the pragmatics of writing and calls attention to the arbitrary nature of racial categories. When referring to specific texts I adhere to the language used by the author.

Notes

1 For quantitative findings on the content of mixed race fiction for middle-grade readers see Chaudhri, Amina, and William H. Teale. 2013. "Stories of Multiracial Experiences in Literature for Children Ages 9–14." *Children's Literature in Education* 44, no. 4: 359–76.
2 "American Indians in Children's Literature." https://americanindiansinchildrensliterature.blogspot.com/
   "Reading While White." http://readingwhilewhite.blogspot.com/
3 These authors maintain websites and blogs in which they write about their own publications and comment on current events in the world of children's literature.
   Monica Brown: http://www.monicabrown.net/, Zetta Elliott: http://www.zettaelliott.com/, Mitali Perkins: http://mitaliperkins.com/, Uma Krishnaswami: https://umakrishnaswami.org/blog-writing-with-a-broken-tusk/

References

Adoff, Arnold, and Emily Arnold McCully. 1973. *Black Is Brown Is Tan*. New York: Harper & Row.
Balliett, Blue. 2013. *Hold Fast*. New York: Scholastic Press.
Beatty, Patricia. 1981. *Lupita Mañana*. New York: Morrow.
Bishop, Rudine Sims. 1982. *Shadow and Substance: Afro-American Experience in Contemporary Children's Fiction*. Urbana, IL: National Council of Teachers of English.
———. 1990. "Mirrors, Windows, and Sliding Glass Doors." *Perspectives* 1, no. 3: ix–xi.
———. 2007. *Free Within Ourselves: The Development of African American Children's Literature*. Westport, CT: Greenwood Press.

Botelho, Maria José, and Masha Kabakow Rudman. 2009. *Critical Multicultural Analysis of Children's Literature: Mirrors, Windows, and Doors*. New York: Routledge.
Brooks, Wanda. 2009. "An Author as a Counter-Storyteller: Applying Critical Race Theory to a Coretta Scott King Award Book." *Children's Literature in Education* 40, no. 1: 33–45.
Brophy, Jere. 2008. "Developing Students' Appreciation for What Is Taught in Schools." *Educational Psychologist* 43, no. 3: 132–41.
Chaudhri, Amina, and William H. Teale. 2013. "Stories of Multiracial Experiences in Literature for Children Ages 9–14." *Children's Literature in Education* 44, no. 4: 359–76.
Curtis, Christopher Paul. 1995. *The Watsons Go to Birmingham—1963*. New York: Delacorte Press.
Davol, Marguerite W., and Irene Trivas. 1993. *Black, White, Just Right*. Morton Grove, IL: A. Whitman.
Delgado, Richard. Ed. 1995. *Critical Race Theory: The Cutting Edge*. Philadelphia: Temple University Press.
DiCamillo, Kate. 2000. *Because of Winn-Dixie*. Cambridge, MA: Candlewick Press.
Flemming, Jane, Susan Catapano, Candace M. Thompson, and Sandy Ruvalcaba Carillo. 2015. *More Mirrors in the Classroom*. Place of Publication Not Identified: Rowman & Littlefield.
Freedman, Paula J. 2013. *My Basmati Bat Mizvah*. New York: Amulet Books.
Galda, Lee, and Bernice E. Cullinan. 2000. "Children's Literature." In *Handbook of Reading Research*, edited by Gwynne Ellen Ash, 361–79. Mahwah: Erlbaum Associates.
Hughes-Hassell, Sandra, Heather A. Barkley, and Elizabeth Koehler. 2009. "Promoting Equity in Children's Literacy Instruction: Using a Critical Race Theory Framework to Examine Transitional Books." *School Library Media Research* 12: 1–20.
Kadohata, Cynthia. 2006. *Kira-Kira*. New York: Atheneum Books for Young People.
Khan, Rukhsana, Elisa Lynn Carbone, and Uma Krishnaswami. 2008. *Many Windows: Six Kids, Five Faiths, One Community*. Toronto: Napoleon Pub.
Krishnaswami, Uma. 2004. *Naming Maya*. New York: Farrar Straus Giroux.
Ladson-Billings, Gloria, and William F. Tate, IV. 1995. "Toward a Critical Race Theory of Education." *Teacher's College Record* 97, no. 1: 46–62.
Larrick, Nancy. 1965, September 11. "The All White World of Children's Books." *Saturday Review*, 63–85.
Lerer, Seth. 2008. *Children's Literature: A Reader's History, From Aesop to Harry Potter*. Chicago, IL: University of Chicago Press.
Levy, Dana Alison. 2014. *The Misadventures of the Family Fletcher*. New York: Yearling.
Marcus, Leonard S. 2008. *Minders of Make-Believe: Idealists, Entrepreneurs, and the Shaping of American Children's Literature*. Boston: Houghton Mifflin.
McNair, Jonda C. 2013. "I Never Knew There Were So Many Books about Us: Parents and Children Reading and Responding to African American Children's Literature." *Children's Literature in Education* 44: 191–207.
Reynolds, Nancy Thalia. 2009. *Mixed Heritage in Young Adult Literature*. Lanham, MD: Scarecrow Press.
Rogers, Rebecca, and Melissa M. Wetzel. 2006. "Racial Literacy in a Second-Grade Classroom: Critical Race Theory, Whiteness Studies, and Literacy Research." *Reading Research Quarterly* 41, no. 4: 462–95.
Root, Maria P. P. 1992. *Racially Mixed People in America*. Newbury Park, CA: Sage Publications.
Ryan, Pam Muñoz. 2000. *Esperanza Rising*. New York: Scholastic Press.

———. 2004. *Becoming Naomi León*. New York: Scholastic Press.
Sands-O'Connor, Karen. 2001. "Why Are People Different? Multiracial Families in Picturebooks." *The Lion and the Unicorn* 25, no. 3: 412–26.
Smith, Cynthia L. 2001. "Interracial Children's and Young Adult Novels." *Library Talk*, January, 14–16.
Woodson, Jacqueline, and Earl B. Lewis. 2001. *The Other Side*. New York: Putnam's.
Yokota, Junko, and Shari J. Frost. 2003, December. "Multiracial Characters in Children's Literature." *Book Links*, 51–57.

2 Multiracial Identity in the United States
Historical and Current Discourse

The election of President Obama in 2008 rekindled media interest in mixed race America. Prior to this, articles in *Time* and *Newsweek* in 1997 (White) and 2000 (Clemetson; Leland and Beals), along with Tiger Woods' proclamation that he was "Cablinasian" (Caucasian, black, Indian, Asian) became hugely popular among multiracial youth who could relate, and among conservatives who used his success and novel racial identification to call for an end to affirmative action and other civil rights measures. Critical mixed race studies scholar, Rainier Spencer (2014) argues that the mainstream media has a significant role in promoting discourse about multiraciality that focuses on issues of identity affirmation and color-blindness rather than the struggle for racial justice. Mainstream reporting choices, Spencer asserts "highlight particular people in their articles, a nearly ubiquitous feature of mixed-race stories . . . [behind which] is the presumption that mixed-race individuals, especially young people, are leading us to our postracial destiny." (164). Another impression the media attention has created is that multiracial people are a recent component of the U.S. population. Embedded in this double message about "newness" (new population, new racial consciousness) are two misconceptions. The first is that multiraciality is a new phenomenon, which the brief history of mixed race studies research included here will discredit. The second is that the growing numbers of mixed race Americans means that racial issues will soon become a thing of the past. The latter idea parallels the naïve assertion that the election of President Obama symbolizes racial equality for African Americans. Race will matter as long as there is racism and the significance of the country's first African American (or biracial, depending on who you ask) president must be recognized but not manipulated. These views are typically held by conservatives who are interested in preserving the existing racial paradigm. A different view, particularly among activists, is that an increase in the number of people identifying as multiracial corresponds to a decrease in the numbers in populations that have been institutionally marginalized for whom a reporting of greater numbers means the possibility of more resources being allocated. Still others worry about the "whitening" of America with biracial people distancing themselves from their nonwhite histories and assimilating. The extent to which this is even an option varies; for some groups this is simply not possible. The one thing that all these positions suggests is that discourse about mixed race identity requires a recognition that race is a social and political construct with boundaries that are much more permeable than often believed. It raises complicated questions: if race is not biological, how can we talk about a person being half this or a quarter that? How are race and culture different? Can people be more or less of something and if so what does that mean? Isn't everybody multiracial? Does that mean we are all the same? Do mixed race people have to hail from the ends of the racial binaries—white and nonwhite? Is someone whose parents are Korean and Thai mixed race? If so, are "Korean" and "Thai" races? Nationalities? Cultures? Many Native Americans do not consider themselves people of color or even think of themselves in terms of race, preferring tribal ancestry. Yet there is literature and language about people who are Navajo and white[1] or Crow, Chumash, Filipino and Mexican.[2] Even while the arbitrariness of racial categories is exposed by the questions, we only have language that reinscribes racial categories as stable entities. To describe myself as biracial implies that my parents must be of two races—two distinctly separate races. Does "mixed" refer only to the immediate generation in question or does it go far back up the genealogy tree?[3] None of these questions have simple answers but an understanding of historical perspectives around mixed race identity in the U.S. can provide some context as a starting point. In this chapter I draw on research in mixed race studies. Current discourse is shaped by the use of the Census as a taxonomic tool for sorting people; early scientific and sociological research gave us the language and concepts we negotiate today; and later efforts to redefine racial identity through law and practice.

Theorizing Multiracial Identity

In the United States, race has been an institutionalized concept since the earliest days of colonial contact when the separation of people was necessary in order to justify the subjugation and enslavement of indigenous peoples and slaves. Race was used as a category on the very first U.S. Census in 1790. This practice of placing people in discrete categories started centuries ago had implications for policy and cultural attitudes that persist today. Silence around certain racial issues (such as white privilege) is as much a part of our cultural discourse as those issues that do get discussed. Until recently, people of mixed race heritage have been rendered invisible by the Census. Initially, the Census counted individuals identified as mulattoes, octoroons and quadroons, for purposes relating to slavery. This ended after 1890 and with it any classification of mixed race people. Scientific and anthropological interest in people of mixed heritage, however, was robust, and it is relevant to look to early scholarly treatises as they provide a backdrop that explains contemporary perceptions of multiracial identity.

Ifekwunigwe (2004) calls the time period in which such research was being produced the "age of pathology" (9) and Thornton (1996) describes this research approach as the "problem approach" (108) because of the consistent focus on the purportedly genetic "problem" of the multiracial subject. In the late 19th century, scientists and sociologists such as Robert Knox (1850), Joseph Gobineau (1853), and Charles Darwin (1871) studied and wrote about what they believed was an inherent weakness in the 'species' created by black and white interbreeding. Gobineau was particularly influential for his treatises asserting the perfection of the white race above all other groups measured by degrees of "beauty" (cited in Spickard 2001). The conviction of these men about the irretrievable incongruity of black and white unions is echoed in the personal narratives shared by interviewees documented by Lee and Bean (2012) more than a century later. These narratives share experiences in which biracial children of black and white parents find themselves under public scrutiny when seen with their white parent. Indeed, the very language with which we currently grapple stems from research that used scientific terms of genetics and quantity in reference to race: "dilution," "hybridity," "crossing," "pure bred," "half breed." (Darwin 1871; Delany 1879; Dover 1937) In addition, labels such as "mixed breed," "half blood," "mulatto," and "octoroon" were commonly used and indicative of the prevailing belief that mixed race people of any heritage were fractured and incomplete.[4] The post-Revolutionary War years saw America defining itself as an independent, new nation that was separate from Europe and also from the indigenous occupants of the continent and the slaves being forcibly brought here. Racial identity was formed around the Other and it became necessary to define who was white and who was not, especially when rape and exploitation of black and Native women by white men were rampant.

Originating in the early 1900s, Stonequist's (1935) theory of the Marginal Man was popular among social scientists trying to explain the identity development of mixed race individuals. With a focus on black-white biracials, this approach argues that biracial identity is essentially problematic and the subject will inevitably be a social misfit. In the Marginal Man theory, the multiracial subject's position is socially unstable until such time as s/he is fully assimilated in one or other population, with the desirable outcome being assimilation into the dominant culture. The unlikelihood of this happening dooms the biracial subject to a liminal existence (Ifekwunigwe 2004). In literature we see this theory manifest in the figure of the tragic mulatta, the mixed race orphan, and mentally unstable biracial characters. Indeed, these traits are present in children's books published in the last decade, suggesting a cultural reluctance to move away from outdated, racist views. Many of the children's books in the Multiracial In/Visibility chapter include characters who uncritically exhibit internalized perceptions of unworthiness.

The scientific notion of the unstable black-white biracial extended to other racial mixes but was applied differently in practice. The era of colonial expansion meant opportunities for miscegenation wherever white colonists came into contact with nonwhite people, and the offspring were the topic of keen sociological scrutiny. Cedric Dover's (1937) *Half-Caste* explicates in considerable detail his views on racial changes in early 20th century America with descriptions of all manner of "hybrids," "half Indians," "Mongoloids," and "Afroamericans," (59) with repeated reference to virility, fertility and assimilability over time. Dover asserts that the decrease in the Native population was due to assimilation into white populations, not extermination, and he references John Rolfe's marriage to Pocahontas as an example. White concern about the fertility and virility of people of color was at the core of eugenics efforts that resulted in the forced sterilization of women of color—especially Native American women—and the removal of Native children to missionary boarding schools. Children were separated from their families and forced to shed all vestiges of tribal identity in order to 'assimilate' them into white society and eventually 'breed out' any trace of indigeneity. During colonial times, mixed bloods were considered useful as liaisons and sometimes gained favor with white missionaries and government officials, functioning as translators, negotiators and "wedges" between tribal communities and white officials' land acquisition efforts. Where it was in the interests of whites to increase the number of black slaves by including black-white multiracials, it was also in their interest to decrease the number of Indians with whom land and resources would need to be shared. Thus racial ideologies were closely tied to economic interests (Morning and DeBose 2003)

Underpinning scientific theories of pathology was that notion that blood purity was a determining factor in racial identification. Principles of Mendelian genetics that were applied to plants and insects were applied to people, as if people could be 50% or 25% one race and 50% or 75% another, and assuming the parents were racially "pure" and that quantities of blood could be used to determine racial membership. The social and political implications were that hierarchies were created that placed white people at the top and black and Indian people at the bottom, resulting in the so called "one-drop rule." According to the one-drop rule, people with any known nonwhite ancestry were to be classified according to their nonwhite heritage. Thus mixed race people were made to identify singularly as nonwhite. Kenneth Prewitt's (2005) essay "Racial Classification in America: Where do we go From Here?" details the ways in which whiteness (and therefore nonwhiteness) was legally determined so as to preserve the discreteness of the categories and restrict access to civil and political privileges. This demonstrates how carefully race was conceptually constructed according to the political and historical needs of the time. Years after the Civil War, such policies were enacted when needed, such as in the removal of Japanese Americans to internment camps at the end of World War II. The other population effected by institutionalized race politics was Native Americans. The practice of tribal affiliation through blood quantum was a colonial imposition designed to restrict numbers of people when it came to allocation of land for reservations. Tribes had to be federally recognized by the U.S. government with cultural, ancestral and blood lineage determined by set parameters. Bound by this legacy, currently, some tribes use blood quantum (in combination with other factors) as a way of establishing tribal membership, while others use family lineage, marriage, long-term commitment, adoption and other factors when considering membership (Baird-Olson 2003). Over time, these practices and language have become intricately woven into the fabric of U.S ideology.

A significant event in the national discourse about multiracial identity is the 1967 case of Loving v. Virginia in which the Supreme Court overturned the ban on interracial marriage. Interracial unions, legal or not, have existed since the earliest times of colonial contact, so there is some debate about how the sudden legalizing of interracial marriage impacted the growth in population of mixed race children. Nevertheless, the event served to de-stigmatize interracial couples and their biracial children to some degree and gave rise to what is known as the "biracial baby boom" (Root 1996, xv). Racial pride advocacy that accompanied the civil rights struggles meant that children of interracial unions were raised to feel aligned with their non-white heritage in an active reclaiming of hypodescent laws which meant an even greater acceptance among communities of people of color. Studies by Rockquemore, Brunsma and Delgado (2009) highlight the importance placed on developing a positive black identity that the era encouraged for people with a range of black racial and/or cultural affiliations.

A few decades later, theories about mixed race identity development moved toward the "equivalent approach" (Thornton 1996, 109). In these studies, comparisons were made between mixed and monoracial people to determine the extent to which racial background plays a role in identity development (Gibbs and Hines 1992; Luke and Luke 1998; Pollock 2004). According to the theory, cultural factors leading to assimilation of the mixed race individual into his or her immediate environment take precedence over racial factors. It was established that given the right environment and tools with which to assimilate, mixed race individuals are as likely or unlikely to be impacted by their racial identity as their monoracial peers. Thornton (1996) found that this approach pertained to Asian-white and Latino-white biracials as well and black-white biracials. This is a significant departure from the belief that multiracial identity is irretrievably conflicted. The equivalent approach shows biracial and monoracial identity development to be no different from each other, and dependent on context. By the same token, multiracials who do experience feelings of marginalization or difference may do so because of internalized racism, and reluctance to assimilate culturally.

In the early 1990s, the Office of Management and Budget (OMB) faced pressure from the legislative front as well as from nationwide activist organizations such as the Association for MultiEthnic Americans (AMEA), A

Place for Us (APFU) and Project RACE (Reclassify All Children Equally) as well as many college-based organizations to change the Census and other race-defining instruments. At the root of the activism was a tangible discomfort among parents of school-aged children who were forced to choose only one racial identity on school paperwork. Kim Williams (2005) found in her fieldwork that the most vocal activists in this multiracial movement were white middle-class women married to African American men. Critics of these efforts argue that the motivation was the concern that the children of these unions would have to identify as black, according to the existing paradigm, and that the activist mothers sought a new category to distance their children from claiming a black identity. Indeed, this sentiment is echoed in the few children's books in which whiteness is only mentioned as a racial identity by white mothers who urge their children to consider identifying as multiracial when they begin to show an interest in their nonwhite heritage. This concern with multiracial identity propelled *by* adults *for* children is eerily parallel to the sentiments in the world of children's literature that is so carefully managed *by* adults *for* children. Nevertheless, these efforts are largely responsible for the change in the U.S. Census that, since the year 2000, permits participants to "mark one or more" boxes from the racial categories provided.

The activism that was instrumental in the change in the U.S. Census began the second phase in the arc of multiracial discourse. Ifekwunigwe (2004) calls it the "age of celebration," (8) with self-identification being of primary importance. This wave of multiracial identity articulation saw individuals and families negotiating the color line for themselves. Studies by Lee and Bean (2010, 2012) showed that Asian and white, and Latino and white parents tended to identify their children as white at a much higher rate than black and white parents. The children of those marriages also tended to self-identify as white or embraced cultural elements such as food and celebrations when doing so made them more "interesting" than being "just white." (427) The lived realities of contemporary Americans vary widely in their connection to the country's racial past. Immigration, migration, an increased acceptance of interracial, interfaith, intercultural unions, and numerous other factors of globalization means that people's perspectives and life experiences may be only fleetingly shaped by historical racial practices and more so by current attitudes. Realistic fiction for children allows us to examine the ways multiracial lives are being reflected in literature and engage in important conversations.

The focus on choice and self-expression has become a point of concern among some critical mixed race scholars (Spencer 2011, 2014; McKibbin 2014) who argue that this preoccupation detracts from important social and political issues of equity and gains fought for by the civil rights movement. The need for self-identification and public affirmation was documented in a series of articles called "Race Remixed" written by Susan Saulny (2011b) and published in the *New York Times*. Here, testimonies of young multiracial Americans highlighted the importance of being free to choose and determine when and how to "be" whichever racial (or other) identity they wanted. Cast in the rhetoric of individualism and freedom of choice, this selection of voices was completely disconnected from the ways that race is connected to racism and injustice and contributes to ideas about color-blindness. Children's literature typically tends to follow rather than interrupt paradigmatic notions that favor individualism over collectivism, and in this regard books depicting multiracial experiences are no different. However, in the realm of multicultural children's literature, and the real-life experiences of children of color, the opportunity to identify, relate, be affirmed and validated happens all too infrequently. Stories that tell young readers that their lives are worth reading about in books are a starting point in the development of confident young people who can then become active members of society and advocates for social change.

An unfortunate consequence of the discussion of multiracial identity is that it has been used by some to put forth the argument that we are now in a post-racial society and that race does not (or should not matter). Specifically, anti-affirmative action spokespeople such as Newt Gingrich, Dinesh D'Souza and Ward Connerly have used the movement's rhetoric to advance their own "post-race" agendas. The term "postracial" emerged as the numbers of Americans intermarrying increased and the success of a few celebrities of color gained public attention. The term declares an irrelevance of race and racial categories citing the election of President Obama, the success of athletes (Tiger Woods, Derek Jeter, Apolo Ohno) and icons of popular culture (Lenny Kravtiz, Trevor Noah, Cameron Diaz, Keanu Reeves) as evidence that race is no longer a barrier to success. Advocates of a postracial ideology are interested in sweeping aside the effects of centuries of institutionalized racist policies that exclude people of color from having equal access to opportunities for successful lives (education, housing, healthcare, fair pay, legal recourse etc.) in favor of a false narrative of racial equality. The concept of "colorblindness" is akin to "postracial" in practice, if not in sentiment. People who claim they "do not see race" deny the fact that by the sheer fact of being sentient and immersed in U.S. culture means that our perceptions are ingrained with deep, subtle, and not-so-subtle assumptions and judgements that inform the way we move in the world. Discourse around mixed-race issues has been used by advocates of a postracial and colorblind America to bolster their arguments that race no longer matters. Needless to say, race will continue to matter as long as inequality exists.

By the mid 1980s and through the 1990s, researchers (many of whom were mixed race themselves, e.g., Hall 1992; Kich 1992; Nakashima 1996) began to disseminate a third way of understanding mixed race identity development. Thornton (1996) called this the "variant" approach. This approach challenged the problem and equivalent approaches by asserting cases of biracial identity that maintained positive, healthy integration into multiple racial and cultural contexts. Breaking from the dominance of hypodescent laws, the variant approach shows how a distinctly biracial or mixed race identity can develop. People who experience conflict or difficulty do so as part of the process of developing a self-concept, rather than as a result of being biracial. Nor is over-identification with one group/parent regarded as the only option for a stable identity. Of course, amount of contact with each group is an important factor in developing this balanced biracial sense of self, as is cultural context. Perhaps most importantly, the variant approach accepts complex and nuanced aspects of mixed race identity, and finds there is tremendous variety in the range of racial self-perceptions even among biologically similar individuals. Diversity and complexity of experiences are key factors in the Multiracial Awareness group of children's books.

An aspect of multiracial diversity that is explored much more in scholarship than in children's literature is that of nonwhite mixed race identity. In my research for this project I was able to identify eleven titles (see Appendix E) that include multiracial characters from nonwhite backgrounds. It is likely that there are more books but that they are folded into the larger realm of multicultural literature, identified by a single racial label, or not at all. The protagonist of *Secret Saturdays* (Maldonado 2010) is Puerto Rican and black, and the book's Library of Congress subject keywords include "racially mixed people" and "African Americans," which is why the book appears in searches for mixed race fiction. Conversely, the protagonist of *Going Going* (Nye 2005) is Lebanese and Mexican but the publication data does not include any racial, cultural or ethnic keyword label. According to a report by the Pew Research Center in 2010, 70% of new marriages were between white and nonwhite couples leaving approximately 30% between nonwhite couples. The number of nonwhite multiracials in fiction is negligible compared to these data.

Scholarship in mixed race studies that looks at nonwhite multiracial identity includes additional ways in which people are, and have always been pushing at paradigmatic racial boundaries. In California, in the 1920s, the ambiguity around classification of people of Mexican descent meant that antimiscegenation laws were typically ignored when Punjabi men married Mexican-origin women. These unions did not disturb the color line that separated whites from nonwhites (DaCosta 2007). The children of the Punjabi-Mexican unions in the Imperial Valley had strong affiliations with India due to the patriarchal structure of their contexts. These children were identified by the Census as "Hindu", even though that is a religious descriptor and inaccurate as an ethnic or racial marker (Spickard 2001). Similarly, racial rules did not apply in Hawaii where Chinese and Native Hawaiian communities formed "third cultures" (15) that blended cultural customs to form a distinctly different identity. These historical scenarios show how the identities of mixed race Asians in America developed within very diverse circumstances with varying levels of confusion, oppression and privilege based on context and time (Spickard 2001). Along those lines, Michael Omi (2001) reminds us that today it means something very different to be Asian and white than Asian and black. The character of Mai Kim, in Sharon Flake's (2001) novel *Money Hungry*, is Korean and black, and her identity struggle is shaped by a dual anxiety associated with being perceived as a foreigner (a constant reality for Asian Americans) and the one-drop legacy of slavery.

For certain, the discursive trajectory around multiracial identity has moved out of the hands of white scientists and social scientists invested in maintaining racist hierarchies, and into the hands of multiracial scholars, activists, artists, writers and thinkers (Rockquemore, Brunsma, Delgado, Kina, Fojas, Spencer, Root, Williams-León, Spickard, Price, Zack). Their work testifies to the tremendous range of perspectives and experiences among multiracial Americans, all of which negotiate, challenge, interrupt, redefine, and transform ways of thinking about racial identity.

Data about multiracial Americans indicate that this is a demographic to be taken seriously for the way in which it is changing the racial and cultural composition of the country. According to a Pew report (2012), intermarriage is on the rise and in 2012, counted for 15% of all new marriages, double what it was in 1980 (6.7%). Multiracials report that they are proud of their mixed race heritage and that being mixed has made them "more open to other cultures." (1) At the same time, more than half the multiracial population surveyed reported having experienced racial slurs or jokes. Social perceptions still hold that people with black heritage are identified and mostly self-identify as black, while those with Native, Asian, and Latino/a (and white) ancestry have some choice to identify as white, or biracial or bicultural when doing so adds an "extra" cultural dimension (Lee and Bean 2012). Multiracial children under the age of eighteen are the fastest growing demographic in the country (Lee and Bean 2012). The postracial myth is challenged by the fact that more than half of multiracial adults have experienced racial discrimination. Teachers who claim to be colorblind, curricula that omits multiracial topics, bullies who target their peers with racist 'jokes' and taunts, and multiracial children who never see themselves in stories: these are part of today's reality. *Multiracial Identity in Children's Literature* is guided by two essential ideas. First, that texts function as tools in the construction of meaning, identity and power; what Botelho and Rudman (2009) call the "sociopolitical function of texts." (108) And second, that knowledge of the ways current publications for children perpetuate or resist perceptions of mixed race identity can help teachers in their selection and use of books with multiracial content.

Notes

1 Tess and Gaby, the teen protagonists of Nancy Bo Flood's (2016) novel, *Soldier Sister, Fly Home* identify as Navajo and white.
2 In *Son Who Returns* (2014), Mark Centeno identifies himself as "four kinds of brown" (8) using two tribal labels and two national labels as adjectives. The author, Gary Robinson describes himself as being of Cherokee and Choctaw Indian descent, choosing specific tribal names over the more general term "Native American."

3 Maria P.P. Root (2003) uses an ecological framework to describe multiple factors that influence an individual's decision to identify as multiracial. These include: generation, immigration, connection to language, customs and culture, geography, position in the racial paradigm, and personality.
4 Karren Baird-Olson (2003) includes a list of 36 language labels used to describe people descended from indigenous peoples and colonizers (196).

References

Baird-Olson, Karren. 2003. "Colonization, Cultural Imperialism, and the Social Construction of American Indian Mixed-Blood Identity." In *New Faces in a Changing America: Multiracial Identity in the 21st Century*, edited by Loretta I. Winters and Herman L. DeBose, 194–221. Thousand Oaks, CA: Sage Publications.
Botelho, Maria José, and Masha Kabakow Rudman. 2009. *Critical Multicultural Analysis of Children's Literature: Mirrors, Windows, and Doors*. New York: Routledge.
Clemetson, Lynette. 2000. "Color My World: The Promise and Perils of Life in the New Multiracial Mainstream." *Newsweek*, May 8, 70.
DaCosta, Kimberly McClain. 2007. *Making Multiracials: State, Family, and Market in the Redrawing of the Color Line*. Stanford, CA: Stanford University Press.
Darwin, Charles. 2004 [1871]. "On the Races of Men: . . . The Effects of Crossing." In *"Mixed Race" Studies: A Reader*, edited by Jayne O. Ifekwunigwe, 47–51. New York: Routledge.
Delany, Martin. 2004 [1879]. "Comparative Elements of Civilization." In *"Mixed Race" Studies: A Reader*, edited by Jayne O. Ifekwunigwe, 52–53. New York: Routledge.
Dover, Cedric. 2004 [1937]. "God's Own Chillun." In *"Mixed Race" Studies: A Reader*, edited by Jayne O. Ifekwunigwe, 59–64. New York: Routledge.
Flake, Sharon. 2001. *Money Hungry*. New York: Jump at the Sun/Hyperion Books for Children.
Flood, Nancy Bo. 2016. *Soldier Sister, Fly Home*. Watertown: Charlesbridge.
Gibbs, Jewelle Taylor, and Alice M. Hines. 1992. "Negotiating Ethnic Identity: Issues for Black-White Biracial Adolescents." In *Racially Mixed People in America*, edited by Maria P. P. Root, 223–38. Newbury Park: Sage.
Gobineau, Joseph Arthur De Count. 2004 [1853]. "Recapitulation: The Respective Characteristics of the Three Great Races; the Superiority of the White Type, and, within This Type, of the Aryan Family." In *"Mixed Race" Studies: A Reader*, edited by Jayne O. Ifekwunigwe, 39–41. New York: Routledge.
Hall, Christine C. Iijima. 1992. "Please Choose One: Ethnic Identity Choices for Biracial Individuals." In *Racially Mixed People in America*, edited by Maria P. P. Root, 250–64. Newbury Park: Sage.
Ifekwunigwe, Jayne O. 2004. *"Mixed Race" Studies: A Reader*. London: Routledge.
Kich, George Kitahara. 1992. "The Developmental Process of Asserting a Biracial, Bicultural Identity." In *Racially Mixed People in America*, edited by Maria P. P. Root, 304–17. Newbury Park: Sage.
Knox, Robert. 2004 [1850]. "Do Races Ever Amalgamate?" In *"Mixed Race" Studies: A Reader*, edited by Jayne O. Ifekwunigwe, 37–38. New York: Routledge.
Lee, Jennifer, and Frank D. Bean. 2010. *The Diversity Paradox: Immigration and the Color Line in Twenty-First Century America*. New York: Russell Sage Foundation.
———. 2012. "A Postracial Society or a Diversity Paradox?" *Du Bois Review* 9, no. 2: 419–37.
Leland, John, and Gregory Beals. 1997. "In Living Colors." *Newsweek*, May 5, 58.

Luke, Carmen, and Allan Luke. 1998. "Interracial Families: Difference within Difference." *Ethnic and Racial Studies* 21, no. 4: 728–54.
Maldonado, Torrey. 2010. *Secret Saturdays*. New York: G.P. Putnam's Sons.
McKibbin, Molly Littlewood. 2014. "The Current State of Multiracial Discourse." *Journal of Critical Mixed Race Studies* 1, no. 1. http://escholarship.org/uc/item/2x28p06t.
Morning, Ann, and Herman L. DeBose. 2003. "New Faces, Old Faces: Counting the Multiracial Population Past and Present." In *New Faces in a Changing America: Multiracial Identity in the 21st Century*, edited by Loretta I. Winters, 41–67. Thousand Oaks: Sage Publications.
Nakashima, Cynthia L. 1996. "Voices from the Movement." In *The Multiracial Experience: Racial Borders as the New Frontier*, edited by Maria P. P. Root, 79–97. Thousand Oaks: Sage Publications.
Nye, Naomi Shihab. 2005. *Going Going*. New York: Greenwillow Books.
Omi, Michael. 2001. "Foreword." In *The Sum of Our Parts: Mixed Heritage Asian Americans*, edited by Teresa Williams-León and Cynthia L. Nakashima, ix–xiii. Philadelphia: Temple University.
Pollock, Mica. 2004. "Race Bending: 'Mixed' Youth Practicing Strategic Racialization in California." *Anthropology & Education Quarterly* 35, no. 1: 30–52.
Prewitt, Kenneth. 2005. "Racial Classification in America: Where Do We Go from Here?" *Daedalus*, Winter, 5–17.
The Rise of Intermarriage: Rates, Characteristics Vary by Race and Gender. 2012. Report. Washington, DC: PewResearchCenter.
Robinson, Gary. 2014. *Son Who Returns*. Tennessee: 7th Generation.
Rockquemore, Kerry Ann, David L. Brunsma, and Daniel J. Delgado. 2009. "Racing to Theory or Retheorizing Race? Understanding the Struggle to Build a Multiracial Society." *Journal of Social Issues* 65, no. 1: 13–34.
Root, Maria P. P. 1996. *The Multiracial Experience: Racial Borders as the New Frontier*. London: Sage.
———. 2003. "Five Mixed-Race Identities: From Relic to Revolution." In *New Faces in a Changing America: Multiracial Identity in the 21st Century*, edited by Loretta I. Winters and Herman L. DeBose, 3–20. Thousand Oaks: Sage Publications.
Saulny, Susan. 2011a. "Black? White? Asian? More Americans Choose All of the Above." *The New York Times*, January 30, A1, A20-A21.
———. 2011b. "Race Remixed: In a Multiracial Nation, Many Ways to Tally." *The New York Times*, February 11, A1, A17.
Spencer, Rainier. 2011. *Reproducing Race: The Paradox of Generation Mix*. Boulder, CO: Lynne Rienner Publishers.
———. 2014. "Only the News They Want to Print: Mainstream Media and Critical Mixed-Race Studies." *Journal of Critical Mixed Race Studies* 1, no. 1. http://escholarship.org/uc/item/3b34q0rf.
Spickard, Paul. 2001. "Who Is an Asian? Who Is a Pacific Islander? Monoracialism, Multiracial People, and Asian American Communities." In *The Sum of Our Parts: Mixed Heritage Asian Americans*, edited by Teresa Williams-León and Cynthia L. Nakashima, 13–24. Philadelphia: Temple University.
Stonequist, Everett V. 1935. "The Problem of the Marginal Man." *American Journal of Sociology* 41, no. 1: 1–12.
Thornton, Michael C. 1996. "Hidden Agendas, Identity Theories, and Multiracial People." In *The Multiracial Experience: Racial Borders as the New Frontier*, edited by Maria P. P. Root, 101–20. Thousand Oaks: Sage Publications.
White, Jack E. 1997. "I'm Just Who I Am." *Time*, May 5, 32.
Williams, Kim M. 2005. "Multiracialism and the Civil Rights Future." *Deadalus*, Winter, 53–60.

3 Multiracial Stories in Picturebooks

We read the world through our senses, assimilating its colors, sounds, shapes, and textures into existing cognitive schema, constructing knowledge as we do so. Very young children with access to books start "reading" by looking at pictures, absorbing cues even before they have language. When adults read to young non-readers, they supplement the visual information with language, allowing for knowledge to be constructed at a deeper level. The importance of visual literacy has typically been secondary to textual literacy in education, despite research about the critical role of pictures in reading (Nodelman 1988; Sipe 1998) and emotional literacy (Nikolajeva 2013). The effectiveness of multimodal literacy requires adults to show children how to read illustrations and discuss the information they communicate independently from and in relation to the accompanying text. According to Frank Serafini (2015) "by its very nature and forms of publication, the contemporary picturebook is a multimodal text" (413) that offers readers (or listeners) the experience of making meaning through the two modes of image and language. Lawrence Sipe (1998) describes the relationship between pictures and text as "synergisitic . . . in which the total effect depends not only on the union of the text and illustrations but also on the perceived interactions or transactions between these two parts" (98–99). Today scholars of children's literature accept the combining of the words "picture" and "book" into "picturebook" to signify the inextricable interplay between text and image (Nikolajeva and Scott 2001; Haynes and Murris 2012; Hintz and Tribunella 2013). Thus, readers create meaning based on the text, the images and their pre-existing assumptions about how to read both together. Readers of picturebooks with text and images about biracial people may, at a very subliminal level, be accommodating information into new schemas of learning, or assimilating it into existing schemas depending on their own experiences.

Like text, pictures are not neutral and they contribute to the ideological discourse of the time in which they are created and consumed. Today's children are more exposed to racial diversity in their contexts than ever before, yet their reading material does not reflect their realities. A recent study by Melanie Koss (2015) revealed that a majority of the picturebooks published in 2012 featured white primary characters and cultures. Where racial diversity was represented, it was devoid of cultural specificity. These findings suggest that the cultural information accessible to the youngest readers through picturebooks still reflects hegemonic perspectives of U.S. society. In his Newbery Award acceptance speech, Matt de la Peña (2016) began by quoting a line from Denis Johnson's *Jesus' Son* that captured his feelings at that moment: "I had never known, never even imagined for a heartbeat, that there might be a place for people like me." de la Peña had just won the Newbery Award for *The Last Stop on Market Street* (2015), a simple, powerful and beautiful story about a brown-skinned boy's day in town with his grandmother. de la Peña, who identifies as Mexican and white, knows full well the place of writers and books of color in the world of children's literature, which explains his amazement at being awarded the Newbery. He adds that he and the book's illustrator, Christian Robinson, wanted to make sure their book featured diverse characters in an urban setting, but not one in which diversity was the focus of the story—in other words, a mirror, but with universal appeal. In this respect, *Last Stop on Market Street* follows in the footsteps of *The Boy Who Didn't Believe in Spring* (Clifton and Turkle 1973), *The Snowy Day* (Keats 1976), *A Chair for My Mother* (Williams 1982), and other picturebooks that are not "about" being a child of color. Picturebooks depicting multiracial characters, although few in number, span the spectrum from being didactically overt in tackling mixed race experiences, to integrating that element with other issues, to making no mention at all in the text, but leaving it to the reader to notice, or not, the visual depictions of people. Currently, the body of multiracial picturebooks is small but growing. Arnold Adoff's *Black is Brown is Tan*, published in 1973 is the first picturebook about an interracial family, and Karen Katz' *The Colors of Us*, in 1999, illuminated myriad skin tones that a child might notice. Yokota and Frost (2003) surveyed the field and called attention to the lack of options. Unfortunately, a shortage persists, adding to the evidence that publications for today's children are not keeping up with the demographics. The titles provided Appendix A build on their list with publications since the year 2000.

Richard Delgado (1995) reminds us that "ideology—the received wisdom—that makes current social arrangements seem fair and natural" (65) tends to be invisible. Using this element of critical race theory, we can read many current multiracial picturebooks as doing the work of pushing back at ideologies that disapprove of interracial families or the possibility of stability for biracial children. The cover of Alma Flor Ada and Elivia Savadier's (2002) *I Love Saturdays y domingos* depicts a happy family comprised of two white-skinned and two brown-skinned adults smiling down on their slightly lighter brown-skinned child. They are framed by an open window, a blooming flowerbox and a palette of warm pink, yellow and orange tones. The effect is immediately welcoming, and it is sustained throughout this bilingual celebration of an interracial family. *I Love Saturdays y domingos* follows Andrea Cheng and Ange Zhang's (2000) *Grandfather Counts* as a story of a child who happily bridges cultures and languages with her grandparents, providing affirming mirrors and welcoming windows for young readers.

Picturebooks are typically intended for the youngest readers who often rely on images to make sense of text that they cannot yet decode. Thus they incorporate both visual and textual information. In the context of depicting racially diverse groups of people, and mixed race individuals, illustrators use skin tone and facial features to make the distinctions they need. All the books I found for this study feature white and nonwhite biracials, and none included Native children. Keeping their young audiences in mind, authors and illustrators who include explicit content about multiraciality use different strategies to express it. Generally speaking, white-black biracial experiences include information about variations in skin color, and books with Asians and Latinos have an immigration and/or bilingual approach. Bishop (1982) notes that when writers and illustrators of African American characters use language and colors that describe a range of skin tones, they are ascribing to an awareness of the "naturalness of such descriptions among Afro-Americans and perhaps indicative of an effort to create and promote positive associations with the darkness that carries so many negative connotations in the English language." (70–71) Karen Katz's (1999) *The Colors of Us* certainly makes use of this strategy, associating skin colors and their respective people with beloved foods such as cinnamon, French toast, peanut butter, chocolate cupcakes, honey, and so on. The same pattern can be seen in *I'm Your Peanut Butter Big Brother* (Alko 2009), *Mixed Me: a Tale of a Girl Who is Both Black and White* (Catledge and Rivie`re 2012), *Mixed Blessing* (Cosman and Kendall 2012), and many other books that intentionally affirm brown-skinned bodies. *Fussy Freya* (Quarmby and Grobler 2008), *Bringing Asha Home* (Krishnaswami and Akib 2015), *I am Flippish* (Ryan and Soliz 2011) and *Grandfather Counts* include words in Hindi and Chinese as subtle communicators of Asian heritage. *I Love Saturdays y domingos* and *Marisol McDonald Doesn't Match* (Brown and Palacios 2011) are both bilingual, integrating Spanish and English in different ways.

Building Empathy

In "Picturebooks and Emotional Literacy," Maria Nikolajeva (2013) discusses the pedagogical use of picturebooks to foster the skill of empathy with young children. She defines empathy as "the ability to understand other people's emotions . . . arguably the most important capacity that distinguishes human beings from other living organisms." (249) Readers connect with the emotions of fictional characters through text and images, building empathy as they make meaning. Multiracial picturebooks provide ample opportunity for young readers to begin to understand racial differences at an accessible level and make sense of difference as a positive rather than a negative element of life.

Mixed Me Books: Counterstories and Celebrations

A predominant social and literary narrative about mixed-race identity is the idea of the inherently troubled subject who is always struggling to belong because of feeling different. Mixed Me books highlight the element of difference (ambiguous racial appearance) and reclaim it as special and unique. All the books in this corpus interrupt the "problem" of mixed race identity being inherent to biracial experiences. They depict biracial children and their interracial parents (and sometimes grandparents), and address the ways the children are questioned by peers and adults seeking to racially categorize them. All of these books are written by authors who themselves are biracial, or are in interracial relationships and have biracial children. Tiffany Catledge and Anissa Rivere, author and illustrator of *Mixed Me: A Tale of a Girl who is both Black and White*, share in the back matter that they created the book in response to a gap in the literature that reflects their biracial heritage. Similarly, Marsha Cosman, author of *Mixed Blessing: A Children's Book About a Multiracial Family* includes a note in which she describes her own interracial family. Several Mixed Me books are self-published, hinting perhaps at the dearth of representative picturebooks that leads people to write and publish their own. Literary elements such as plot and character development are minimal, thus the books can be described as being narrative non-fiction. Teachers might include Mixed Me books in their classroom libraries and use them in read alouds, guiding young children to talk generally about difference, specifically about racial identity, and directly about the impact of teasing.

Mixed Me books are unsubtle in their affirmation of biracial children's identity, which is consistently described in terms of skin color. All the books in this category feature black and white biracials. Skin color provides no information about a person's identity, yet in reality, it is the first and often only factor from which assumptions are made. Children in interracial families are questioned not only about their own appearance, but also about their phenotypical difference from their parents. Skin color is the primary reason the characters in these books are marked as different, so it is through skin color that readers are invited to understand difference and participate in its affirmation. Both the text and the images are explicit in their descriptions of interracial families and biracial children. They include positive images of the white parent and the black parent and their child between them, countering social attitudes about incompatibility in interracial unions. *I Am Your Peanut Butter Big Brother* (Alko 2009) features a boy wondering what his new sibling will look like. The narrator imagines a series of possibilities, starting with himself, "I blend from semisweet dark Daddy chocolate bar and strawberry cream Mama's milk." The image depicts an African American man and a white women holding hands and smiling. They are positioned facing the reader, filling most of the page. Their stance is firm and their faces are happy. Dad stands in front of a bar of chocolate and Mom is in front of a glass of strawberry milk–the sweet "ingredients" of the narrator. He wonders what the baby's eyes will look like, "hot cocoa footballs set wide apart or a perfect pair of pennies? My eyes blend from Daddy's charcoal tires and Mama's honey-roasted almonds." He imagines his new sibling building sandcastles and playing in puddles. Images always include a variety of children and adults, and the parents appear together several times. The overall effect is of a tightly knit, racially integrated community. *I Am Your Peanut Butter Big Brother* celebrates racial diversity by calling attention to it in terms that the young intended audience can appreciate. Research in mixed race studies posits that where context and family structures support the possibility, multiracial subjects draw on multiple identities to form a distinctly different one (Rockquemore, Brunsma and Delgado 2009). *I Am Your Peanut Butter Big Brother* describes a racially-unnamed identity shaped by people and experiences rather than labels. On her website, the author, Selina Alko talks about her own experience growing up with a Turkish father and being in an interracial relationship. Her other publications also foreground diversity, social justice, and human rights, specifically her nonfiction account of Loving v. Virginia, *A Case For Loving: the Fight for Interracial Marriage* (2015), illustrated by Alko's partner, Sean Qualls. In the synergy between text and images, the information being conveyed about mixed race identity is positive and affirming.

I Am Mixed, by Beauvais, Jones and Webster (2012) features twin brother and sister, Jay and Nia, who are phenotypically quite different. Their differences are described to highlight the fact that biracial twins can look different from each other, as well as from their biological parents. Nia is dark skinned and has dark hair, while Jay is lighter. Both children are depicted with bright smiles and shining eyes: happy siblings who play outdoors and enjoy being together. It is when they are in school that their bubble is punctured. People ask them "funny things" such as why Nia's hair is neither straight nor curly, but "bendy." At home her mother embraces her and affirms her beauty with love "Your skin is the night and your eyes are the stars, your smile is the moon that kisses my heart." Jay's parallel narrative shows him affirming himself though identification with music "I am all things piano bass and djembe drum." The accompanying image shows Jay dressed as a classical pianist, a rock musician and a djembe drummer, suggesting the array of possibilities ahead of him. From there the narrative blends to combine both Nia and Jay's affiliations with dance, art, labor and history: "I am an Irish jig to an African beat. I am a Cuban painter with brush in hand, I am a Haitian farmer healing the land." On the walls hang portraits of Maria Callas, Ludwig Van Beethoven, Sonny Boy Williamson and Nina Simone—visual connections to white and black musical traditions. The juxtaposition of both children in all the subsequent images simultaneously highlights and erases their phenotypical differences. In the context of dancer, artist and farmer, the children's appearance is secondary to their actions. Ultimately, Jay and Nia are adored by their parents and connected to place and culture, secure in their mixed race identity. *I Am Mixed* gently but firmly confronts readers, young and old, who might look at children like Jay and Nia and wonder how they can be related, rewriting the narrative of phenotypical similarity among twins and listing, for those who are curious, all the ways in which being black and white can be fun and empowering.

Taye Diggs and Shane Evans' (2015) *Mixed Me!* takes a distinctly bolder approach and is the only book in the corpus of this study that mentions the word "race." The book begins with a direct comment on how Mike feels others are defining him: "they call me Mixed-up Mike . . ." Mike has plenty to say in response, starting with a pronouncement of how "super-crazy-fresh-cool" his bouncy ginger Afro is. Illustrations depict an energetic boy who loves running and jumping and feeling his mass of curly hair dance in the wind. Messages about the ubiquity of all things mixed are strategically included in the illustrations. The dog is named Mixamillion and eats "Various Vittles," Dad looks dapper in a tie, shirt and vest, and bedroom slippers, while Mom's outfit is a colorful mix of geometric shapes and textures. Even the soap is labeled "Multi Use Soap." Mike is secure in his parents' love so that when the public is confused about the phenotypical dissonance they perceive, he has a response ready: "My mom and dad say I'm a blend of dark and light. 'We mixed you perfectly and got you JUST RIGHT.'" The matter of peer pressure is introduced when Mike's friends ask him to choose whom to be friends with. His response is confident and defiant: "Why pick only one color or face? Why pick one race?" Furthermore, Diggs and Evans dedicate a double-page spread to Mike's hair and the public attention it attracts. Mike's wide-eyed gaze is directed at the reader, and tells readers unequivocally that touching his hair is not allowed. *Mixed Me!* locates the "problem" of being multiracial squarely in the narrow views of society that questions Mike's interracial parents, his choice of friends, his hair, and his skin. In no uncertain terms, readers are invited to align themselves with Mike and reject such perspectives, "I'm doing my thing, so don't forget it. If you don't get, then you don't get it." Thus, a complicated concept of racial identity is made accessible to very young readers, planting important seeds about diversity and recognition, rather than erasure of difference.

What Mixed Me books lack in literary nuance, they make up for in heart. There is no subtlety in the experience of being asked, told or accused of being different, and Mixed Me books claim that unsubtlety and reframe it. Biracial children who see themselves in Nia, Jay, or Mike's shoes will be left in no doubt that their identities are valued. The bright colors, energetic movements and happy faces parallel the text and bolster the message. At the same time, there are no monstrous antagonists making these characters feel bad—rather a general audience being nudged to rethink assumptions and behavior. Mixed Me books offer "vicarious emotional experiences" for readers with limited life experiences to think about difference and develop empathy through connecting with the characters. (Nikolajeva 2013)

Culturally-Connected Books

Another set of books includes culturally-specific details in addition to universal themes and typical literary elements. Their narratives include the typical literary elements of fiction such as plot, characters, conflict, and resolution. They also include content about history, culture, geography, and traditions, that depicts the biracial experience as being more than a matter of skin color and phenotypical dissonance. The bilingual books discussed here contribute to the construction of integrated biracial, bicultural and bilingual identities. *Marisol McDonald Doesn't Match* and *I Love Saturdays y domingos* are in Spanish and English, *Cooper's Lesson* (Shin, Cogan and Paek 2004) provides English and Korean text, and the protagonist in *Take Me Out to the Yakyu* (Meshon 2013) can describe his experiences in both English and Japanese. Culturally-Connected books include Asian-white, Latino-white, and black-white biracial characters for whom cultural and historical practices supersede issues of phenotype.

Biculturalism is evident in the ways that adult characters impart information to the biracial protagonists. In *My Two Grandads* (Benjamin and Chamberlain 2011), we learn that Aston understands his heritage through music. Aston and his grandads love music. Grandad Roy (black) is from Trinidad and plays the steel drums; Grandad Harry (white) is from Lancashire and plays trumpet in a brass band. The images of all three characters explicitly convey their racial differences. The cover and first pages depict the three characters, one dark brown, one pinkish, and light brown Aston standing between them, holding hands and smiling. The closeness of the family members is established right away and sustained with images of several of them (including parents and grandmothers) integrated throughout the story. This way, when Aston has a dilemma about choosing one grandfather to perform at his school summer fair, the possibility of any cultural or racial differences being obstacles has been precluded. Subsequently, we see Aston with each grandfather, learning about their skills and cultural heritage. The images in *My Two Grandads* supplement the textual information. In Grandpa Roy's practice room are images of steel drum bands, various musical instruments and a dark-skinned woman on a poster of Trinidad (3–4). There is also a musical score sheet for the popular song, "Brown Girl in the Ring," and pictures of a brown-skinned girl dancing in the background. Aston is shown playing a steel drum. Similarly, the illustration of Grandpa Harry's home depicts Aston and Harry practicing a Yorkshire folk song from the score sheet for "On Illky Moor Bah T'at." (7–8) The juxtaposition of these images serves a dual purpose. It sets up Aston's dilemma about having to choose which grandfather to invite to school, and establishes his close connection to both, equally. We might also read this matter of having to choose as a thinly-veiled reference to the ways in which mixed race individuals are often called to feel they must choose one affiliation over another. Ultimately, Aston does not have to choose: both his grandfathers perform at the fair and Aston gets to be proud of both of them. Like the Mixed Me books described earlier, Culturally-Connected books highlight the unique possibilities of racial and cultural interactions when context, support and appreciation allow for them. Benjamin's earlier book, *My Two Grannies* (2007) explores a similar idea with a female protagonist and grandmothers as sources of cultural and historical knowledge.

The role of social environment on racial and cultural identity development is apparent in *Marisol McDonald Doesn't Match/Marisol McDonald no combina*. This story is rich in cultural and linguistic visual and textual details, and the storyline highlights the many ways in which children are called upon to make decisions about their identity in small but significant ways. There are a number of ways in which Marisol "doesn't match" and being biracial is just one. Technically, the term "match" is misleading and it really means that she isn't fitting expectations. Speaking directly to the reader, this red-haired, brown-skinned girl announces, "My name is Marisol McDonald and I don't match. At least that's what everyone tells me." (2) She makes this matter-of-fact statement while hanging upside down from a tree branch, wearing striped leggings and a flowered shirt. At this point she is simply repeating what "everyone" says without being invested, but gradually, their observations wear her down. Readers are guided to notice the cumulative effect of seemingly innocuous comments, not by mean bullies, but by friends, family and trusted adults. Cousin Tato tells her that her brown skin and red hair don't match, her brother tells her that her green polka dot and purple striped clothes don't match, and her teacher tells her that her signature, part print and part cursive, doesn't match. The pressure from this constant criticism builds and draws the reader to empathize with Marisol. Eventually, her sense of self is so eroded, she decides to conform.

Marisol and her family are bilingual and dialog includes consistent code-switching that gives equal prominence to both English and Spanish. Text is provided in each language separately, and when characters speak, the same words are translated. For example, the English version reads, "'Can I have a puppy? A furry, sweet *perrito?*' I ask my parents. '¿*Por favor?*'" (8), and on the next page the Spanish text reads, "'¿Puedo tener un perrito? ¿Un *puppy* dulce y peludito?–le pido a mis padres–*Please?*'" (9)

Although images of Marisol and her friends dominate the book, one double-page spread depicting this multiracial family provides many cultural and racial details. Mami has dark skin and long black wavy hair, while Dad has fair skin and red hair. The brother has light brown skin and dark hair, and Marisol has her father's red hair. They are seated around a table laden with salad, burritos, and wraps, all assembling their own meals. On the fridge are notes in Spanish, a picture of a llama, and the word "Peru" on the salad bowl and picture add a specific geographic connection. There is no doubt that this is a safe and happy environment. In her attempt to "match" Marisol dresses in an outfit that is all the same color, tidies her hair, and colors boring pictures neatly within the lines. On these pages she is a small figure with a sad expression, physically and emotionally removed from the things that make her happy. The pain of having to be someone she is not just to meet the expectations of her peers is evident. In *Marisol McDonald Doesn't Match* it is clear that being different makes other people uncomfortable, and Marisol's attempt to accommodate them is unjustifiable. Marisol's teacher notices the change and writes her a letter about all the ways in which she loves Marisol for being unique. Marisol's identity is affirmed and the book ends on an even happier note, with her getting a "mismatched and simply marvelous" puppy who she names Kitty. Like *Mixed Me!* this narrative affirms a racially unique appearance, and demonstrates how a child in a loving home with strong ties to her heritage can flourish despite pressure to conform. The role of the teacher is worth noting since she too participated in the series of criticisms by pointing out Marisol's unconventional signature. We might read this as a sign that teachers have power, even in seemingly insignificant ways, to do harm, and then to fix it. Ultimately, it is the teacher's note that undermines all the other criticisms and assures Marisol that she is wonderful the way she is. Therein, also, lies the power of the teacher to make amends.

Sometimes, however, even people from within one's cultural group can be the source of pain. *Cooper's Lesson* reveals layers of complexity. *Cooper's Lesson* is one of the few books in the corpus of this study about Asian biracials, and the only one with explicit cultural information depicting a biracial experience complicated by more than ambiguous physical appearance. Cooper is Korean and white. He feels very deeply deficient because he cannot speak Korean, and we get the immediate impression that he has internalized as his problem the concept of not belonging to either group. The text is bilingual, with separate English and Korean sections and occasional Korean words dotting the English narrative. Cooper's mother sends him to Mr. Lee's store on an errand. This fills Cooper with anxiety as Mr. Lee has scolded him for not being able to speak Korean. On the way Cooper recalls his grandmothers teasing him about being "half and half" (4) and is ashamed of his brown hair and freckles that mark him as "less Korean." A series of events results in Cooper and Mr. Lee sharing their experiences about feeling that they did not fit in, and ultimately all signs point to Cooper accepting his biracial, bicultural self.

In addition to being stories that affirm multiracial heritage through language, culture, and history, the books described above also point to the role of context in the construction of biracial identity. The protagonists are surrounded by grandparents and communities of people who encourage the active incorporation of multiple elements of their heritage. Culturally-Connected books are more enjoyable than Mixed Me books because they are free of the pedantic tone, and include sophisticated language and complex characters and plots. They lend themselves well to being read aloud and teachers might share them simply for their virtue of being good literature.

Additionally, they can be read to prompt discussions about culture and identity on many levels.

Biracial Blended Picturebooks

Biracial Blended books contain no textual information at all about race or culture, yet the images explicitly depict interracial families and biracial protagonists. The way racial identity has little or no bearing on the experience of the protagonist suggests that they blend in to their contexts without the adverse effects of feeling different. The books in which biracial identity is visually depicted in explicit or implicit ways span a range of appealing topics. For example, *One Word From Sophia* (Averbeck and Ismail 2015) is about a little girl who needs to learn to use the magic word, "please," *Sonya's Chickens* (Wahl 2015) is about the interconnectedness of life and death as she experiences it with the chickens she raises, and *Blackberry Stew* (Monk and Porter 2005) is about recalling memories of a loved one who has passed away. For the most part, these books are coded as having biracial content based on the phenotype of characters, i.e.: on skin color. It is important to note that in the absence of any textual information to confirm a racial affiliation, reading these images racially relies on identifying "typical" markers of the color, texture, and shape of physical features.

In *One Word From Sophia* we see the family, consisting of Mother, Father, Uncle Conrad, Grand-Mamá, and Sophia seated around the table as Sophia announces that she wants a giraffe for her birthday. The text provides the information that Mother is a judge, Father is a businessman, Uncle Conrad is a politician, and Grand-Mamá is "very strict." The images depict Mother and Grand-Mamá with dark brown skin, and the men with pinkish skin. Sophia, seated between them, has slightly lighter brown skin than her mother. Subsequent images show her presenting her argument to each family member, and in the juxtapositions of their differently-colored bodies her biraciality is simultaneously highlighted and irrelevant. Sophia is endearing and intelligent. She appeals to each adult's professional sensibility, making a legal argument to her mother, an economic one to her father, and a political one to her uncle, complete with pie charts and data. They all deny her request based on their views that her presentations were too "verbose," "loquacious" and "effusive." The reader learns these sophisticated terms along with Sophia, but ultimately the word "please" wins the day. Yasmin Ismail's whimsical watercolor illustrations complement the text with energy and movement that match Sophia's determination. Like *The Last Stop on Market Street*, *One Word From Sophia* includes racial diversity without focusing on it. The images of pink and brown bodies never let us forget that Sophia is biracial, and readers will connect with this child's persistence for the thing she wants.

Sonya's Chickens complicates a racial reading as images of the characters are sometimes very small, and sometimes partial. The cover depicts a brown-skinned girl holding a chicken, and on the first page, the darker brown hands of an adult are handing her some chicks to care for. A scene depicting Sonya, a toddler, and Mother, includes contrast that allows for a reading of the family as interracial—Mama's skin is discernibly paler than her children's. This detail is reiterated in a subsequent scene depicting the family around the dinner table. This time we see Papa, who has much darker brown skin and hair than the children and the phenotypical difference between parents and children is explicit. The setting—a farmhouse—includes items such as quilted furnishings, and colorful wall decorations that are not recognizably connected to any specific culture or artistic tradition. These details are visually descriptive, but not operational in the story of Sonya's recognition of the circle of life. *One Word From Sophia* and *Sonia's Chickens* tell engaging stories set in racially diverse family environments. Similarly, in Atinuke's (2013) *Splash, Anna Hibiscus,* people, context and specific Nigerian references provide cultural information both textually and visually without identity being part of the plot or conflict. With or without an adult scaffolding a racial analysis, young readers are likely to notice the phenotypical differences among characters. As such Biracial Blended books "normalize" interracial families by not calling attention to race. This approach is in stark contrast to Mixed Me books and serve an aesthetic rather than an efferent purpose.

My search for multiracial picturebooks revealed several that are identified by Library of Congress keywords or published reviews as containing multiracial content. Their narratives make no mention of racial or cultural identity, and visual information is implicit, leaving it to the reader to "read" the faces of characters and notice (or not) that they are biracial. The cover of *Maxwell's Mountain* (Becker and Wong 2006) depicts a happy boy with vaguely East Asian features. On the second page, his mother, with ginger hair and paler skin than his makes this identification slightly obvious by contrast. Next we see both parents with him, and the father's features are more clearly Asian. The fact that the author's last name is Wong might nudge the reader to presume an Asian connection. *Maxwell's Mountain* is about a little boy who is determined to climb the "mountain" in a nearby park by himself. His desire for independence and meticulous planning skills will appeal to all children—Max just happens to be biracial. Similarly, the little boy in *Buzz* (Wong and Chodos-Irvine 2000) can only timorously be read as biracial because the stylized images do not contain "typical" racial characteristics. The boy in the cover has black hair and blue eyes, the father has brown hair and blue eyes, and the mother has black hair and eyes. Reading the boy as biracial rests on assuming that this is an interracial marriage and that the boy has his father's eyes and mother's hair. In *Olu's Dream* (Evans 2009), Olu and his father have different shades of brown skin and hair. One scene includes a female figure, presumably his mother, whose skin tone and hair could lead her to be read as white or East Asian. *Olu's Dream* is about bedtime routines, delights and fears, and provides a mirror for children and parents of color for whom bedtime stories are few and far between. Casting Olu as biracial depends on scrutiny and imagination. Books like *You Were the First* (MacLachlan and Graegin 2013), *Fussy Freya*, and *Blackout* (Rocco 2011) also rely on the reader's lens to read visual cues about racial identity. Biracial Blending books posit the naturalness of interracial families precisely because they do not call attention to racial or cultural identity.

Toward a More Multiracial World of Picturebooks

The number of multiracial children is growing. According to a report by the Pew Research Center (2015) in 1970, only 1% of babies lived with two interracial parents. That number rose to 10% by 2013 and currently, 46% of all multiracial Americans are younger than eighteen. It is surprising that the book publishing industry has not captured this population as a potential market. Maybe it is just a matter of time. Currently the scarcity of quality literature for young readers means that they are not seeing themselves in reflected in the books that are part of their formative years. Furthermore, the limited range of racial mixes does not even come close to reflecting contemporary society.

It is encouraging that the existing corpus of books though limited in scope and number, tells a hopeful story of mixed race experiences for young readers. Ranging from the overly insistent approach in the Mixed Me books, to the subtle manner in the Biracial Blending books, the mixed race experience is one that is grounded in loving families and myriad opportunities for characters to learn about life. As mirrors for biracial readers, these picturebooks are positive and affirming, and as mirrors for young readers who may be prompted to question their biracial friends, books like *Marisol McDonald*, *Cooper's Lesson* and others point out the potential impact of their words and give pause to reconsider. While none of the antagonists are held accountable for hurting anyone's feelings, readers are moved to see that their words and behavior are undesirable. This concept can have important pedagogical implications if teachers choose to highlight the impact words and assumptions can have. Within the safety of loving families, multiracial characters are cherished for being unique, and with the support of parents and grandparents, they learn about their histories and traditions. Characters who encounter questions and doubt are taught how to respond with confidence and not feel like they must choose to affiliate with one racial group over another. Books like these can be used in creative ways in classroom discussions about difference and kindness. A critical examination of this corpus of books reveals that the current trend in multiracial picturebooks is one of cultural and racial pluralism that celebrates diversity and promotes ideas about a common humanity (Ching 2005). Depictions of negative responses to difference posit bullies and racists in a general, unnamed public, rather than embodied in real human beings. *Marisol McDonald* is one exception to this trend as the antagonists are her brother, cousin, friends and teacher. Readers are able to see themselves in these figures and, perhaps, recognize the effect of their words.

Race itself is absent from the language of difference in these picturebooks. Adults tend to be uncomfortable talking about race and racism, and especially with children. Where parents may make some efforts, teachers are bound by their own discomfort and lack of analysis and language and couch their reluctance in expressions about protecting the innocence of children. Picturebooks such as these allow for discussions of difference from which deeper discussions can grow. The way that many picturebooks present race as solely a matter of skin color and hair texture may be, on one level, accepted as age-appropriate. On the other hand, the celebratory tone and essentializing of mixed race identity as nothing more than a dark color blending with a light one to create a very special medium one, glosses over issues of power. Ultimately, it is incumbent on the adults who mediate books with the youngest readers to articulate the deeper issues at play in multicultural literature so that perceptions are challenged before they become rooted too deeply.

Finally, quality literature about biracial children must simply be included in libraries and read alouds and literature lessons because they tell good stories. When children see themselves and their friends' lives reflected in stories, they learn that they are valued. The books examined here range from pedantic to subtle in terms of their biracial content, and from poorly written to award-winning. Mixed race and bicultural lives are very much a part of American society, and it is time they are part of the literary experiences of young children. Parents and teachers play an important role in making these experiences accessible by the decisions they make about the books they use in curricula and story time. They must not be reduced to being instruments of teaching about special topics, but incorporated in such a way that their content becomes inherent to learning about life.

References

Ada, Alma Flor, and Elivia Savadier. 2002. *I Love Saturdays y Domingos*. New York: Atheneum Books for Young Readers.
Adoff, Arnold, and Emily Arnold McCully. 1973. *Black Is Brown Is Tan*. New York: Harper & Row.
Alko, Selina. 2009. *I'm Your Peanut Butter Big Brother*. New York: Alfred A. Knopf.
Alko, Selina, and Sean Qualls. 2015. *The Case for Loving: The Fight for Interracial Marriage*. New York: Arthur A. Levine.
Atinuke, and Lauren Tobia. 2013. *Splash, Anna Hibiscus!* Tulsa, OK: Kane Miller.
Averbeck, Jim, and Yasmeen Ismail. 2015. *One Word from Sophia*. New York: Atheneum Books for Young Readers.
Beauvais, Garcelle, Sebastian A. Jones, and James C. Webster. 2012. *I Am Mixed*. Los Angeles: Stranger Comics.
Becker, Shari, and Nicole Wong. 2006. *Maxwell's Mountain*. Watertown, MA: Charlesbridge.

Benjamin, Floella, and Margaret Chamberlain. 2007. *My Two Grannies*. London: Frances Lincoln Children's.
———. 2011. *My Two Grandads*. London: Frances Lincoln Children's Books.
Bishop, Rudine Sims. 1982. *Shadow and Substance: Afro-American Experience in Contemporary Children's Fiction*. Urbana, IL: National Council of Teachers of English.
Brown, Monica, and Sara Palacios. 2011. *Marisol McDonald Doesn't Match/Marisol McDonald No Combina*. San Francisco: Children's Book Press.
Catledge, Tiffany, and Anissa Rivie`re. 2012. *Mixed Me: A Tale of a Girl Who Is Both Black and White*. North Charleston: CreateSpace Independent Publishing Platform.
Cheng, Andrea, and Ange Zhang. 2000. *Grandfather Counts*. New York: Lee & Low Books.
Ching, Stuart H. D. 2005. "Multicultural Children's Literature as an Instrument of Power." *Language Arts* 83, no. 2: 128–36.
Clifton, Lucille, and Brinton Turkle. 1973. *The Boy Who Didn't Believe in Spring*. New York: Dutton.
Cosman, Marsha, and Kyra Kendall. 2012. *Mixed Blessing: A Children's Book about a Multiracial Family*. CreateSpace.
de la Peña, Matt. 2016. "Newbery Medal Acceptance Speech." *The Horn Book Magazine*, July, 56–64.
de la Peña, Matt, and Christian Robinson. 2015. *Last Stop on Market Street*. New York: G.P. Putnam's Sons.
Delgado, Richard. 1995. "Legal Storytelling: Storytelling for Oppositionists and Others: A Plea for Narrative." In *Critical Race Theory: The Cutting Edge*, edited by Richard Delgado, 64–74. Philadelphia: Temple University.
Diggs, Taye, and Shane Evans. 2015. *Mixed Me!* New York: Feiwel and Friends.
Evans, Shane. 2009. *Olu's Dream*. New York: Katherine Tegen Books.
Haynes, Joanna, and Karin Murris. 2012. *Picturebooks, Pedagogy, and Philosophy*. New York: Routledge.
Hintz, Carrie, and Eric L. Tribunella. 2013. *Reading Children's Literature: A Critical Introduction*. Boston: Bedford/St. Martin's.
Katz, Karen. 1999. *The Colors of Us*. New York: Henry Holt.
Keats, Ezra Jack. 1976. *The Snowy Day*. New York: Puffin.
Koss, Melanie D. 2015. "Diversity in Contemporary Picturebooks." *Journal of Children's Literature* 41, no. 1: 32–42.
Krishnaswami, Uma, and Jamel Akib. 2015. *Bringing Asha Home*. New York: Lee & Low Books.
MacLachlan, Patricia, and Stephanie Graegin. 2013. *You Were the First*. New York: Little, Brown.
Meshon, Aaron. 2013. *Take Me Out to the Yakyu*. New York: Atheneum Books for Young Readers.
Monk, Isabell, and Janice Lee Porter. 2005. *Blackberry Stew*. Minneapolis, MN: Carolrhoda Books.
Multiracial in America: Proud, Diverse and Growing in Numbers. 2015. Report. Washington, DC: Pew Research Center.Retrieved from http://www.pewsocialtrends.org/2015/06/11/multiracial-in-america/#the-size-of-the-multiracial-population.
Nikolajeva, Maria. 2013. "Picturebooks and Emotional Literacy." *The Reading Teacher* 67, no. 4: 249–54.
Nikolajeva, Maria, and Carole Scott. 2001. *How Picturebooks Work*. New York: Garland Pub.
Nodelman, Perry. 1988. *Words about Pictures: The Narrative Art of Children's Picture Books*. Athens: University of Georgia Press.
Quarmby, Katherine, and Piet Grobler. 2008. *Fussy Freya*. London: Frances Lincoln Children's Books.

Rocco, John. 2011. *Blackout*. New York: Disney/Hyperion Books.
Rockquemore, Kerry Ann, David L. Brunsma, and Daniel J. Delgado. 2009. "Racing to Theory or Retheorizing Race? Understanding the Struggle to Build a Multiracial Society." *Journal of Social Issues* 65, no. 1: 13–34.
Ryan, Leslie V., and Adolph Soliz. 2011. *I Am Flippish*. Los Angles: CreateSpace.
Serafini, Frank. 2015. "Miltimodal Literacy: From Theories to Practices." *Language Arts* 92, no. 6: 412–23.
Shin, Sun Yung, Kim Cogan, and Min Paek. 2004. *Cooper's Lesson*. San Francisco, CA: Children's Book Press.
Sipe, Lawrence R. 1998. "How Picture Books Work: A Semiotically Framed Theory of Text-Picture Relationships." *Children's Literature in Education* 29, no. 2: 97–108.
Wahl, Phoebe. 2015. *Sonya's Chickens*. Canada: Penguin Random House.
Williams, Vera B. 1982. *A Chair for My Mother*. New York: Greenwillow Books.
Wong, Janet S., and Margaret Chodos-Irvine. 2000. *Buzz*. San Diego: Harcourt.
Yokota, Junko, and Shari J. Frost. 2003. "Multiracial Characters in Children's Literature." *Book Links*, December, 51–57.

4 Multiracial In/Visibility
The Legacy of Pathology in Contemporary Fiction

Sociologists and scientists in the late 19th and early 20th century viewed race as a matter of biology, discernible by the identification of physical features and blood quantum. Scientists spoke of race in terms of purity and impurity and created taxonomies of populations from around the globe. The belief was that the more "pure" the lineage, the stronger the constitution, and that mixing "weakened" the species. Martin Delany (1879) asserted that "pure European and pure African races, the most distinct and unlike each other in general external physical characteristics, are of equal vitality and equally enduring." (54) He proceeded to argue that the continued "crossing" of one race with another did not produce a new race, but an "abnormal" one. The ideological legacy of such notions persists today in the experiences of contemporary mixed race people for whom the question "what are you?" (and other renditions of it) reflect the public's discomfort with people who do not match assumptions. In addition to there being too few children's novels reflecting mixed race experiences, of those, too many present a bleak picture that is eerily reminiscent of early scientific and sociological accounts of maladjusted, isolated, emotionally disturbed biracial existences purported to be genetically doomed. Multiracial characters in a significant number of novels are filled with self-loathing. They are both highly visible because their racial identity renders them different, and marginalized, made invisible because of it. Books in this corpus feature protagonists whose life experiences revolve around loneliness and isolation due to the fact that they do not belong in any racial group. Although the source of their unhappiness is external, these multiracial characters internalize negative responses that belittle and undermine them, and in doing so, fulfil the expectation of being socially isolated subjects. Many of the characters in these books are in a state of identity crisis with race being the predominant focus. As mirrors, In/Visibility books might offer solace to readers with similar experiences. By reading against the subject position and asking questions about how and why texts construct biracial identity this way, critical readers can develop empathy and an understanding of how identity is shaped by internal and external forces. A shared trait among In/Visibility books is that they locate the 'problem' of being mixed within the character rather than in society.

Another feature of In/Visibility books is an abundance of stereotypes. A common argument by the opponents of interracial marriages is that racial and cultural differences inevitably lead to incompatibility, thus further damaging biracial offspring from such unions. We see this trope reflected in In/Visibility books: none of the protagonists come from intact or stable homes. Divorce, death, and physical and/or emotional absence render the protagonists solitary figures without family or friends as support structures. Children often blame themselves for rifts between their parents, and protagonists make that connection in racial terms. Danny Lopez, in *Mexican WhiteBoy* (de la Peña 2008) blames himself for this father's departure to the extent that he tries to be "more Mexican" (28) in order to reconnect.[1] In *Letters to my Mother* (Cárdenas and Unger 2006), the unnamed, Afro-Cuban narrator lives with relatives who abuse and deride her because of her dark skin, making her feel unwanted and unloved. Hers is a story of survival and strength that might have resonate with readers. It reflects the disapproval that still exists towards interracial sexual unions, and posits biracial identity as one that is fraught with trauma.

Reynolds (2009) describes another stereotype in multiracial fiction for young adults—one she calls "Missing Half" (21) stories. As the name implies, these stories feature protagonists who feel incomplete because of estrangement from one parent, and by extension, an entire racial and cultural side of the family. The Missing Half theme occurs frequently in contemporary fiction about black-white biracials. Without exception, the protagonists are constructed so that the reader has no choice but to view their identity crisis as inherent to their biracial identity, not as a function of a racist society. The repetition of the absence of one parent ascribes to the notion of incompatible interracial unions. Broken families occur frequently in contemporary fiction for children and young adults, but in those, presumably monoracial situations, race is not tied to family rift as it is in multiracial fiction.

The Missing Half theme also occurs frequently in in fiction with Native American and white protagonists. Another theme is that Native-white biracials must act as liaisons between Native and white groups.[2] Yet another is that they must endure a solitary journey in the wilderness, battling the forces of nature.[3] Sometimes the three patterns are combined. The majority of books marked as containing multiracial Native-white content are historical fiction, set during colonial times. Family units are dysfunctional, featuring alcoholic fathers and dead or absent mothers.[4] One way to understand these authorial choices is that creating a biracial character released the author from the responsibility of cultural authenticity required to credibly represent a Native character. Furthermore, by removing the protagonists from their contexts, and placing them alone in nature, characterization and descriptions can focus on the individual rather than in relation to others, which would necessarily be more involved. With few exceptions, multiracial fiction about Native-white experiences were problematic in their portrayal of Native peoples, relying on recognizable stereotypes of generic Indians rather than tribally-specific information. These and other patterns are discussed in Chapters 7 and 8 through deconstructions of multiracial identity in *Adaline Falling Star* (Osborne 2000) and *Hidden Roots* (Bruchac 2004).

The literary quality of some In/Visibility books is worth noting, especially for pedagogical purposes. Jaime Adoff's three novels in verse, *Jimi & Me* (2005), *Names Will Never Hurt Me* (2004), and *The Death of Jayson Porter* (2008) use rich, descriptive blank verse, tightly-structured plots, and empathetic characters to tell deeply poignant stories. In his blog, Adoff writes about his recovery from drug addiction and subsequent motivation to use literature to reach teens (2016). His books describe biracial experiences as being lonely and painful, even tragic. On the other hand, we can read them critically, asking questions about the social forces that cause people to internalize self-destructive perceptions.

Isolation

A number of theoretical models for delineating racial identity development provide a framework for understanding broader social perceptions of biracial identity. Everett Stonequist's (1937) Marginal Man theory was popular and influential among sociologists and has been challenged by contemporary scholars in many fields (Rockquemore, Brunsma and Delgado 2009) for its limitations. At the core of this theory is the notion that isolation and social and emotional estrangement are inherent in biracial lives. The historical context from which this theory emerged was one of deep and extreme racial prejudice, and its persistence, decades later, in contemporary children's literature is troubling. According to Stonequist's "deficit model" biracial people cannot fit in either of the worlds to which they are connected (Stonequist focused on black and white races). As a result, adolescent identity development is fraught with trauma and the possibility of a stable, well-integrated sense of self is precluded from the start. The Marginal Man theory locates problems with dysfunctional identity development within the subject, not in prejudiced society.

In several contemporary fiction novels, biracial protagonists are depicted as isolated, unhappy figures for whom assimilation or adjustment within a larger group is impossible. A significant number of books include biracial characters without parents. One, if not both parents are dead or absent, and if a parent is physically present, she/he is emotionally unavailable. In *Jimi & Me* (Adoff 2005), thirteen year-old Keith's father has been shot, and mother is depressed. He has no friends and his daily life is marked by people's responses to his conspicuous appearance. In addition to being one of the only brown-skinned students at his school, he dresses in 60s style psychedelic outfits inspired by his love of Jimi Hendrix. He is picked on by other students and spends most of his time alone and lost in thought. He wonders if when people yell out "Hey, freak, what are you supposed to be?" (108) they are referring to his clothes or his skin. Keith suspects it is both.

He has no desire to associate with his peers and holds himself aloof, watching them with amusement and cynicism: "sometimes it's cool being in the middle like me. I get to see both sides." (167)

Ultimately being biracial is significant only in that it adds to Keith's in/visibility. When he falls for a white girl in his class who reciprocates with friendship but not romance, he thinks it is because he is biracial. *Jimi & Me* is about dealing with loss and grief but being biracial seems to preclude the possibility of finding community that could be supportive during this process. Keith's situation is deeply sad, and Adoff's lyrical language effectively evokes empathy for Keith and parallels many of the troubling aspects of adolescence in which teens find themselves. Keith's isolation seems not only to be inevitable and inescapable, but due partly to his own creation and intricately tied to his biracial heritage. Events in Keith's life have to get even worse before they can get better. In the end he has worked through some complex emotions connected to his father and family secrets and lies. We can read Keith's withdrawal as a natural response to trauma. He has nowhere to turn because the adults in his life are unavailable and many of his peers are racist–the only way to understand himself is through difference.

Isolation and loneliness mark the lives of the Danny Lopez, the protagonist of *Mexican WhiteBoy* (de la Peña 2008), and two secondary characters, Uno and Liberty. All three teenagers yearn for connection with their absent fathers, believing (in different ways) that their fathers left them because of real or perceived difficulties in raising biracial children (Chaudhri 2013). Danny's father is Mexican, Uno's is African American, and Liberty's is white, and together this trio compound the notion of unstable interracial unions across cultures. Danny's in/visibility is reflected in his decision to leave his mother's suburban life—where he feels like a misfit because of his Mexican heritage—and his simultaneous, tentative desire to fit in with his Mexican American family. In his mind, he belongs with neither group and cannot connect on an emotionally fulfilling level with anyone. The girls in the *barrio* think he is cute, and the boys are appropriately welcoming of Danny. But in Danny's mind the only way for him to belong anywhere is if he belongs with his father—making *Mexican WhiteBoy* a classic Missing Half story.

Uno is Mexican and African American, and like Danny, yearns for a relationship with his father who lives with a new family in another town. Uno's is a parallel Missing Half story that seems to underscore the concept that identity is still guided by the law of hypodescent that determines an individual's racial identity according to the darker-skinned ancestry. Uno's absent father is African American, and though his community, his mother, stepfather and step-brother in the *barrio* are Mexican, Uno's appearance marks him as black and he is set apart because of it. His stepfather is abusive and cruel, and his mother's hatred of her ex-husband is loaded with racial slurs. Like Danny, Uno locates his loneliness in his mixed race identity and wishes he could distance himself from his mother and live with his father. This similarity is one factor that enables Danny and Uno to become friends.

A more minor character is Danny's love interest: Liberty. Like Danny, she is a newcomer to National City, and light-skinned. She doesn't speak English, having recently arrived from Mexico. Danny learns that her father is white, lives in the U.S., and that Liberty managed to persuade him to send for her. She does not live with him though, as he has another family somewhere else. Danny compares their situations and notes with wonder "Liberty's come to National City to be more American. And he's come to be more Mexican." (187) We learn little else about Liberty: her only function seems to be to be symbolic. She represents a different kind of mixed race person.

In their separate ways these three characters are seeking acceptance in places and with people with whom they currently have unreliable connections. Danny, Uno and Liberty feel alone and incomplete: their wholeness rests on uniting with their missing racial and cultural heritage. For most of the novel, mixed race identity is the source of unhappiness and in this way *Mexican Whiteboy* perpetuates elements of the Marginal Man theory of inevitable dysfunction inherent in biracial experience.

Multiracial identity is not the focus of *Black Mirror* (Werlin 2001) but our attention is drawn to it repeatedly in connection with the protagonist's understanding of herself in the midst of trauma. The novel opens with nine-year-old Frances, newly motherless, being told by her paternal grandmother that no matter what her appearance indicates, she will not grow up into a "dainty Japanese woman" (3) like her mother, but a "voluptuous Leventhal" (3) taking after the Jewish side of the family. This pronouncement precedes Frances' unhappy reflection on the unending comments and questions about her racially ambiguous appearance, most significantly the question "Where are you *from?*" (4) that marks her as a perpetual outsider. A series of other comments including "dwarf, freak, mix, some kind of Asian" (4) lead Frances to want to hide away from anyone's attention, hate her face and body, and avoid mirrors. Within the first two pages, the reader understands that it is an unlucky stroke of fate that a person is born biracial and there is nothing to be done about it. As if to compound the misfortune of appearing racially ambiguous, we learn that her brother, Daniel, "escaped" looking mixed or Asian and was wildly popular at school. By the end of the first chapter we know that Frances is sad, angry and introverted because she is mixed. Daniel's unexpected death due to a drug overdose is the other reason for Frances' unhappiness. Like Keith, Uno, and Danny, Frances' tragic experiences are compounded by the fact of being biracial—the element of difference that precludes friendships with peers. Here again, we see the trope of the social misfit being perpetuated through these depictions of multiracial experience.

The self-hatred instilled by her grandmother when she was young is manifest in her confusion about the issues surrounding Daniel's death and her role in preventing it. Having grown up unloved, she assumes that people who talk to her or offer her friendship are being condescending and she pushes them away. In this way she is depicted as creating her own isolation.

When she does allow herself to connect to other people, she aligns herself with other marginalized characters. Her occasional companions are Andy, the school landscaper who is believed to be slightly cognitively challenged, and Ms. Wiles, an unconventional art teacher. Having established Frances as conflicted, bitter and alone, the author drops the mixed race theme and focuses the novel on unraveling the mystery of Daniel's death and a complicated drug-ring on campus.

With the exception of Andy and Ms. Wiles, Frances has very little interaction with other people. Her mother left the family to live in a monastery in Osaka, her father is withdrawn and unavailable, and her grandmother belittles her all the time. For the most part she is alone with her thoughts. Following the Jewish tradition after a death, Frances covers all mirrors in her house to remind her of her "failure" (28) to prevent Daniel's death and to avoid seeing herself. No mention is made of racial identity until half way through the novel, when Frances decides to uncover a mirror and see if, like the ugly duckling, she has changed in to a swan. Readers are provided a three-page self-critique of her hair and facial features. She decides that her ears are like those of an "alien," her nose is "haughty," her eyes are "ordinary Asian eyes," and concludes that she is, at best, "interesting-looking" (155). More significantly, Frances decides that she feels no connection at all with the reflection in the mirror and she covers it up again with the refrain "Frances the mongrel. Frances the dwarf." (154) *Black Mirror* is told in the first person so readers only get Frances' perspective. Her situation is undeniably tragic, but Frances is so hardened, and her self-deprecation so complete, that readers will struggle to empathize.

After the mysteries are solved, Frances' transformation is evident in a brief resolution that she had been unable to see herself for who she really is "Intriguing. Attractive. Unique." (248) Ultimately it is troubling that the author felt that Frances needed to be a biracial character especially when her racial identity is presented as the source of her self-deprecation and social withdrawal and something that she needs to overcome. Furthermore, racial identity is depicted as purely phenotypical. Before she falls asleep at the very end of the novel, Frances thinks she might "dare" (249) to paint a self-portrait. We are meant to believe that her metamorphosis from "freak" to "unique" is spurred by internal motivation, while people around her remain unchanged. This representation is very directly aligned with the Marginal Man theory.

Mental Illness

In *Border Crossing* (Anderson 2009), multiracial identity is depicted as one of many sources of instability for the protagonist, Isaiah, nicknamed, Manz. He is the son of Delores (white) who gave birth to him when she was sixteen years old, and Andres "Loco" Martinez (Mexican). Delores' father disowned her "not when he found out she was pregnant, but when he found out she was pregnant by a Mexican," (4) so she ran away with Loco to try and start a life of their own. Manz is born into this poor and rootless family and isolation turns to trauma as Delores becomes an alcoholic, Loco's mental illness surfaces and he is killed, either in a car accident or suicide. Delores gives birth to another child, stillborn because of severe fetal alcohol syndrome. When the novel begins, sixteen year-old Manz is tormented by the death of his stillborn brother, the inexplicable death of his father, the possibility of a relationship with Vanessa Ortiz, and mysterious voices in his head that turn out to be early signs of schizophrenia.

Manz identifies as Mexican but others remind him that he is "only half Mexican," (28) and his maternal grandmother calls him "the half-breed." (28) The story is set in a small town in Texas where racial tensions run high. Manz's best friend, Jed, is white, as is Delores' boyfriend, Tom. Both are fond of making sexist, racist and homophobic jokes, which irritate Manz who reminds them that he is part Mexican. Other than in self-defense, Manz has no way to express his racial identity. When he meets Vanessa Ortiz, he is attracted not only to her beauty but also to her secure sense of her Mexican heritage. She symbolizes a connection with his father and a part of himself that he lacks. As their friendship develops, *Border Crossing* takes on the trope of the Missing Half narrative in a most disturbing way. During a party at Vanessa's house, Manz is surrounded by Mexican art, food, a bustling bilingual family—all of which are conspicuously absent from his own life—and he feels distinctly uncomfortable even while he yearns for it. A lecture by Vanessa's father about Operation Wetback and the repatriation of his family, even those who were citizens, triggers the paranoia and voices in Manz's head more insistently than they have ever been before. From that point his schizophrenic fears are around being identified as Mexican and deported. He is terrified of being 'discovered' and thinks the solution lies in running away to Mexico where he can live in anonymity.

Manz's paranoia escalates and his life spirals into chaos even while it seems no one around him notices any change in him. A series of dramatic and near fatal events unfold, including one in which Manz drives his car into the river in an ominous echo of his father's accident. As a result Delores seems to recognize that Manz is suffering from paranoid schizophrenia like his father. At the end Manz receives treatment in a mental institution and there are signs of recovery although he is still plagued by the voices. When his mother comes to visit him, she too seems to be more stable and it is hard not to associate her improvement with Manz's being out of the house. Manz's racial identity crisis, at first so explicitly depicted in association with his mental illness, is never mentioned again. *Border Crossing* is a contemporary novel that raises the issue of mental illness (an important and valid reality) but it is problematic that schizophrenia had to be so closely linked with biracial identity. It almost serves as a testament to the racist scientific theories that promoted connections between mental illness and degeneracy and interracial breeding. If the author's intention had been to shed light on the trauma of schizophrenia, she could have done so without conflating it with mixed race identity. If her intention was to write about people who live in fear of border patrol round ups, she could have done so without a mentally ill protagonist. Nancy Reynolds reminds us that white authors seem inclined to create biracial characters because they don't want to create white ones, and the responsibility of authenticity in a character of color is too precarious (24). This certainly seems to be the unfortunate case in *Border Crossing*.

The Death of Jayson Porter (Adoff 2008) is by far the most grim of Adoff's books. The narrator/protagonist, Jayson, is the son of a black drug-addict father and a white abusive, alcoholic mother. Jayson lives in the projects in Florida, but attends a private school in the suburbs paid for by his mother's friend Trina. Jayson, one of two black students at the school, is isolated and miserable. He identifies as biracial and has a keen awareness of the fact that most of the world doesn't understand that and reads him as black. This awareness makes him project how he thinks other black youth perceive him:

> Probably thinks I'm a little *too* light. He's got that skeptical look. I see that look on the bus all the time. Out here, in the 'hood, they don't know biracial exists. All they know is that I'm a little too light to be black. . . and I don't speak Spanish neither. So they check off that "other" box in their head. 'Other' means you *ain't* a brutha. So you ain't down.
>
> (21)

Jayson's experiences with both blacks and whites in having to explain his racial identity over and over again frustrate him to the point that he gives up, "And they always think whatever I am, it's not as good as what *they* are. I know I'll never belong, so now I don't even try." (83) Since neither people nor environment offer an alternative way of thinking about his racial identity, Jayson's isolation is at once imposed and self-inflicted.

Jayson's self-hatred is rooted in the knowledge that he was conceived by accident during a one-night stand. Contempt for his promiscuous mother who "loves the bruthas" (13) is evident and explicitly value-laden throughout the book. A series of traumatic events shape Jayson's downward spiral that leads to a suicide attempt. His mother is physically and emotionally abusive, and his father, who lives elsewhere, is unavailable because of his own drug addiction. Then Jayson learns that these people are not his biological parents after all. Trina is his biological mother and no one knows who his father was. Stunned and disgusted, Jayson is on the brink of jumping off his building, but a text message from his girlfriend saves his life. He spends the next few days in a deep depression, barely cognizant of anything but a plan in his head to run away. A few days later he returns home to learn that his only friend was killed in a meth lab explosion. In the days that follow it dawns on Jayson that running away is not enough, only death can save him and he jumps from the seventh floor "knowing that in seconds the pain will be gone forever and I'll be free." (168) He doesn't die, but is badly injured physically, and of course mentally. The rest of the book shows Jayson in various stages of treatment and counseling. This tragedy brings Trina back into the picture and at the end we see Jayson going to live with her; alive, but still very much damaged. *The Death of Jayson Porter* reifies the image of the abject biracial, and resurrects the tragic mulatto figure with only the slimmest chance of leading a happy life.

Abandonment

Racial identity is the least of America's concerns in E. R. Frank's (2002) eponymous novel, yet it appears to be the reason for his traumatic life. Born to a crack addict mother, America was placed in foster care with a wealthy white family as an infant. When he starts "turning his color," (15) the family rejects him and their nanny, Mrs. Harper, takes him in. She genuinely cares for him, but is unaware that her half-brother, Browning, is sexually abusing America. America sets fire to Browning's blanket, kills him and runs away. The instability in his life only increases as he is shuttled between mental health facilities and homes. Depression, isolation, PTSD, and suicide shape his young life. In each new place, other people identify America racially. They tell him that he isn't black, or white, that he's Cambodian, Chinese, Hispanic, Arab and Indian. America never responds but it is clear that his mixed heritage and indefinable appearance set him apart from people around him who regard him with suspicion. Thus although shared experience with trauma could be a reason for America to connect with other boys in foster settings, this possibility is prevented by his being mixed race. In one particularly poignant scene his own brothers find it difficult to relate to him racially:

> 'You white,' Lyle says.
> 'No, I'm not,' I say.
> 'He white,' Lyle says to Brooklyn.
> 'He not black,' Brooklyn says.
> 'He mixed,' Brooklyn says.
> 'He not our brother,' Lyle says.
> 'I like his eyes,' Brooklyn says, and then he knocks me on the floor.
> (36)

If there was any chance of a connection forming, it is precluded by this exchange. For America, being racially mixed equals being rejected.

When he gets older America reflects on what he imagines is written about him in his file:

> *America's mother was a real easy woman. Plus, America's mother was proud she had sex with so many different kinds of people. By the time*

> America's mother gave birth to America, she knew his father could be just about any man in the entire country. She knew America might look like just about any kind of man she ever met. That's how America's mother thought up the name America.
>
> (131)

Thus, his mother's promiscuity is associated with his undetermined racial heritage, adding to his self-hatred. Unfortunately, this is a familiar trope in the body of titles found in this study. Its disproportionate recurrence perpetuates the idea that mixed race subjects are born because of rape or accidental conception by irresponsible adults.

America is a painful story that probably rings true for too many children who suffer at the hands of troubled adults and an overburdened, inadequate social services system. The name "America" is cryptically symbolic of an imagined 'Everychild' for whom racial identity is one part of many other aspects that make one American. Though mixed race identity is of secondary importance to the protagonist himself, it serves to underscore his troubles, and compounds his unhappiness.

In the end, America's life begins to improve and for the first time he thinks of himself without hatred:

> Sometimes from somewhere over my bed at night, I look down and I see me. I'm not that little kid anymore, I'm not all lazy and warm and bad. I'm this bigger kid, this almost-man type, and I've got big hands and a big face, and my feet hang off the end of the little bed, and I'm not white and I'm not black, and I'm not anything, but I'm a little bit of everything, and it's just like that. I look down and it's just me.
>
> (204)

When it comes to a racial identity, America is unable to determine one for himself–not surprisingly, given the lack of information in his life. He rejects a racial identity (and the associated experiences), and embraces a racial 'invisibility'.

Up From the Sea (Lowitz 2016) is an example of a recent publication that includes a biracial Japanese-white protagonist whose biracial identity plays a small role in the story. Kai lives in fictional town near Tokyo that was devastated by the March 2011 earthquake and tsunami. The aftermath of the tragedy and lives of the survivors are central to this novel in verse. Kai was living with his mother and grandparents at the time, and all three of them are lost. His father, an American, we learn, left without apparent warning one evening six years earlier. This has left Kai with an inevitable feeling of abandonment, and romanticized notions of his parents being like John Lennon and Yoko Ono. The only role racial identity plays in *Up From the Sea* is to establish Kai's sense of abandonment. The earthquake left him completely alone, and in his sadness, he recalls other sad times all of which are associated with his being mixed. Prior to the earthquake, Kai tried to play soccer like his father used to. He was not very good and other boys teased him, calling him *hafu* (94), which is a diminishing Japanese word for someone who is half Japanese. Kai's grandfather countered the insult by telling him that he is "Double . . . had the best of both worlds" (94) and told Kai to ignore the taunt. With practice, Kai's soccer skills improve and he is given the role of midfielder. The metaphor is unsubtle, and he connects the position to his racial identity: ". . . in the middle" (97) between parents and countries. At his lowest point he cannot even bear the parts of himself that remind him of his father. In a poem titled "It Hurts Too Much to Hope" (105) we see Kai burying his pain and anything associated with his father, such as speaking English, playing soccer, and his light-brown hair that he hides with a cap. The only other mention of racial identity comes when Kai and a rival soccer player fight and the boy calls Kai a "stupid foreigner." (114) The events in the story: national tragedy, loss, friendship, athletic rivalry, and yearning for a change, are developed with depth and empathy and readers from any background will be able to relate. Other characters—"fully" Japanese ones—are convincingly drawn, so the function of Kai's being biracial serves only to highlight his loneliness, and perhaps, to remind readers that multiraciality is part of other national/cultural identities too.

Lives of "Incomplete Amalgamation"

Multiracial In/Visibility books depict characters damaged because of their biracial heritage. They come from dysfunctional families in which one or both parents are dead, physically absent or emotionally unavailable due to addiction or mental illness. There is a strong suggestion that if they were monoracial, their lives would have been better. The concept of "amalgamation" (fusion) was of immense interest to scientists and sociologists who treated racial groups as discretely separate and debated whether miscegenation created blended species or completely new ones. Darwin (1871) cited trusted scholarship about the "inferior vitality of mulattoes" (47) that upheld beliefs about the "weakening" of the human race. Stonequist agreed that "there is something universal in the problem of racial hybrids." (65) This "problem" he explained was not only due to the fact that children of interracial parents look different, but one of "incomplete amalgamation" (65) that made multiracial children overly concerned about social status and constantly in a state of finding affiliation with one or other group. This analysis is evident in the ways In/Visibility books construct biracial identity.

Critical race theorist, Richard Delgado (1995) describes the deep psychological harm caused by "words that wound" (163). Over time, negative stereotypes, taunts, jokes, and other racist practices do irreparable emotional damage and internalize the negativity. America, Keith, Frances, Danny, and other characters in these stories are subjected to racial slurs targeting their mixed identity. From the start characters had already internalized racism and exhibited the effects in the form of low self-esteem and self-hatred. We might read In/Visibility books as exposing the racism felt by biracials even though the national discourse invites us to believe that we are in a post-racial era. Such an analysis requires reading against the text because the narratives themselves do not present these grim biracial experiences as critical of society. The process leading up to the point where we meet the characters is not shown and as a result, being biracial seems to be the *reason* characters are isolated and unhappy. Depictions of racism are filtered through characters' memories, dreams, diary entries, even as imagined moments. In all three of Jaime Adoff's books, protagonists are deeply emotionally wounded, lack supportive peers or adults, and are withdrawn from society. Their plight invokes our sympathy, but isolation comes across as a choice. In *The Road to Paris* (Grimes 2006) and *America*, protagonists are introduced believing that their biological parents abandoned them because they are biracial—there is nothing else to explain the adults' absence. In *The Likes of Me* (Platt 2000), Cordy, yearns to shed her skin like a snake, believing that if she emerged differently, people would like her. Similarly, the nameless narrator in *Letters to My Mother* (Cárdenas and Unger 2006) dislikes her dark skin because of the negative attention it brings. In historical fiction, Native American characters are completely removed from their contexts so that they have no contact with potentially stabilizing forces, and their lost or misunderstood sense of self is presented as a matter of internal, biracial conflict. The singular focus on already-internalized feelings upholds the "problem" of multiracial identity as inherent. The external causes of those feelings are vague at best, and often completely absent.

In these books, characters' responses to racism are valid: they withdraw because they have nowhere to turn. What is problematic is the presentation in which readers see only lonely, wounded characters figuring out how to survive on their own. Such stories are silent on the matter of systemic racism. Some authors seem loath to write directly about racism, even while they choose to include it as part of their characters' realities. Readers may well come away from books like these believing that it is indeed an unfortunate twist of fate to be born biracial and that isolation is a natural consequence—just as Everett Stonequist asserted in 1937. It is important that readers be guided to read multiracial fiction critically and with support that enables them to question the depiction of the inevitability of mixed race dysfunction by linking contemporary literature with century-old science. The longevity of the ideas says something about how much still needs to be done to change them.

Ultimately, books in the Multiracial In/Visibility category bring attention to the fact that the long arm of racism extends even to people who are part white. They show us that prejudice operates in subtle ways, like neglect, isolation and invisibility. Many stories depict dark and traumatic experiences that nevertheless have optimistic endings. Jayson is reunited with his biological mother, America finds stability in a group home, Matt is able to love his adoptive family while he clings to memories of his biological one. Even Adaline and Cordy learn that when family members disappoint, allies can be found in unexpected places (stray dogs and circus comrades). Gritty endings about learning to cope with life's struggles replace the happily-ever-after myth. They reinforce the notion that an individual can overcome all obstacles no matter how precarious one's situation may be. They provide mirrors for readers who may understand this kind of rejection, affirming their life experiences within a larger context.

On the other hand, social critique is completely lacking. Biracials are cast as the unfortunate result of adult folly, rejected by everyone. Even readers who can relate to these stories of despair will come away feeling that only drastic events, total emotional independence, and sheer force of will can effect change. If anything, the appeal to teenage angst goes too far in these books. Kim Williams (2005) points out that protecting children's self-esteem was key for the advocates of the multiracial movement. (59) The damage to self-esteem is evident and critically important, but to describe it as inherent to the biracial experience is dangerous.

Notes

1 See "Growing Mixed/Up" in *Diversity in Youth Literature* for an analysis of how Danny Lopez negotiates his white and Mexican identity.
2 Fiction that includes the liaisons theme: *Crossing the Panther's Path* by Elizabeth Alder (2002 *Trouble at Fort La Pointe*, by Kathleen Ernst (2000), *Where the Great Hawk Flies, Escape to the Everglades, Battle Cry*, by Jan Neubert Schultz (2006).
3 Fiction that includes the solitary journey/survival in nature theme: *Crossing the Panther's Path, Call Me the Canyon, The Last Snake Runner, Adaline Falling Star.*
4 Fiction that includes alcoholic and/or absent parents: *Zane's Trace, Call Me the Canyon, Adaline Falling Star.*

References

Adoff, Jaime. 2004. *Names Will Never Hurt Me*. New York: Dutton Children's Books.
———. 2005. *Jimi & Me*. New York: Jump at the Sun/Hyperion.
———. 2008. *The Death of Jayson Porter*. New York: Jump at the Sun/Hyperion Books for Children.
———. *The Life Experience*. Accessed August 1, 2016. http://www.jaimeadoff.com/about-me/.
Alder, Elizabeth. 2002. *Crossing the Panther's Path*. New York: Farr Straus Giroux.
Anderson, Jessica Lee. 2009. *Border Crossing*. Minneapolis, MN: Milkweed Editions.
Bruchac, Joseph. 2004. *Hidden Roots*. New York: Scholastic.
Cárdenas, Teresa, and David Unger. 2006. *Letters to My Mother*. Toronto: Groundwood Books.
Chaudhri, Amina. 2013. "Growing Mixed/Up." In *Diversity in Youth Literature: Opening Doors Through Reading*, edited by Jaime Campbell Naidoo and Sarah Park Dahlen, 95–104. Chicago: American Library Association.

Darwin, Charles. 1871. "On the Races of Men: . . . the Effects of Crossing." In *"Mixed Race" Studies: A Reader*, edited by Jayne O. Ikekwunigwe, 47–51. New York: Routledge, 2004.

Delany, Martin R. 1879. "Comparative Elements of Civilization." In *"Mixed Race" Studies: A Reader*, edited by Jayne O. Ifekwunigwe, 52–53. New York: Routledge, 2004.

de la Peña, Matt. 2008. *Mexican White Boy*. New York: Delacorte Press.

Delgado, Richard. 1995. "Words That Wound: A Tort Action for Racial Insults, Epithets, and Name-Calling." In *Critical Race Theory: The Cutting Edge*, edited by Richard Delgado, 159–68. Philadelphia: Temple University.

Ernst, Kathleen. 2000. *Trouble at Fort La Pointe*. Middleton: Pleasant Company Publications.

Frank, E. R. 2002. *America*. New York: Atheneum Books for Young Readers.

Grimes, Nikki. 2006. *The Road to Paris*. New York: G.P. Putnam's Sons.

Lowitz, Leza. 2016. *Up From the Sea*. New York: Random House.

Osborne, Mary Pope. 2000. *Adaline Falling Star*. New York: Scholastic Press.

Platt, Randall. 2000. *The Likes of Me*. New York: Delacorte Books for Young Readers.

Reynolds, Nancy Thalia. 2009. *Mixed Heritage in Young Adult Literature*. Lanham, MD: Scarecrow Press.

Rockquemore, Kerry Ann, David L. Brunsma, and Daniel J. Delgado. 2009. "Racing to Theory or Retheorizing Race? Understanding the Struggle to Build a Multiracial Society." *Journal of Social Issues* 65, no. 1: 13–34.

Schultz, Neubert Jan. 2006. *Battle Cry*. Minneapolis: Carolrhoda Books

Stonequist, Everett V. 1935. "The Problem of the Marginal Man." *American Journal of Sociology* 41, no. 1: 1–12.

Stonequist, Everett V. 1937. "The Racial Hybrid." In *"Mixed Race" Studies: A Reader*, edited by Jayne O. Ifekwunigwe, 65–68. New York: Routledge, 2004.

Werlin, Nancy. 2001. *Black Mirror: A Novel*. New York: Dial Books for Young Readers.

Williams, Kim M. 2005. "Multiracialism and the Civil Rights Future." *Deadalus*, Winter, 53–60.

5 Multiracial Blending
The Post-Racial Myth in Contemporary Fiction

In *Shadow & Substance,* Bishop (1982) described a corpus of books she called "melting pot books." They included African American characters who were black only insofar as they were given dark skin—information that was shared with the reader through an illustration, or a passing textual description. Any cultural or historical markers were completely absent. Similarly, a number of publications of contemporary fiction that include multiracial characters do so in ways that call attention to their biracial identity as a matter of description alone, omitting any differences that necessarily accompany racial identity. In these books, having been physically described, multiracial characters blend into their contexts with other, supposedly monoracial characters. Blending books span a range of universal topics such as family relationships, school, friendships, and genre. They are also more varied in terms of diversity, and include white and Latino, black, Asian and nonwhite biracial fictional experiences. Multiracial characters in Blending books do not struggle with their racial identity as do the characters in In/Visibility books, although they are aware that they are perceived as different and are often asked the inevitable "what are you?" type of question. Readers will find that for these characters, biracial racial identity is a small part of who they are and insignificant to plot development. Ella in *Camo Girl* (Magoon 2011), D Foster in *After Tupac and D Foster* (Woodson 2008) and Jewel in *Bird* (Chan 2014), for example, are set apart from their peers because of their personalities, interests, and dispositions, and just a little bit more by the fact of being biracial. Authors, Chan and Magoon identify as mixed-race and biracial respectively in biographical material on their blogs. Their subtle treatment of racial identity as one of several identity factors in their characters' lives is worth noting. In other books, having a multiracial detail makes the protagonists slightly more interesting to other characters, and perhaps increases the marketing potential if the books can be promoted as multicultural. Other than the words that describe them, characters in *Ollie and the Science of Treasure Hunting* (Dionne 2014), *Chasing Vermeer* (Balliett and Helquist 2004), *Absolutely Almost* (Graff 2014), and *A Clear Spring* Wilson (2002), are no different from the white characters in their immediate contexts. Conversely, the protagonists in *Stringz* (Wenberg

2010), *Cashay* (McMullan 2009), *We Were Here* (de la Peña 2009), and *Miracle's Boys* (Woodson 2000) align themselves with the black and Latino communities in which they live. The range of these fictional experiences analyzed in this chapter sheds light on the variety of ways racial identity functions in different contexts.

Race as a Descriptive Detail

Some Blending books include multiraciality as little more than a library keyword tag. In my correspondence with a subject cataloging policy specialist at the Library of Congress I asked about the criteria for a book to be given the subject keyword "racially-mixed people." I was told that the "heading was established in 1991 and has been in use since then. There are no specific criteria for its use. It may be assigned to any book that deals with people of mixed race." This general application of a racial label that determines, in a way, the future of a book, highlights the constructedness of literary multiculturalism. Subject keywords flag books so they appear in searches, catalogs, and lists used by teachers, librarians, parents, and even young readers themselves who might be searching for books with particular content.

In one set of Blending books, race is so insignificant a part of the character's identity it may go unnoticed. So it is in Lisa Graff's (2014) *Absolutely Almost*, in which Albie describes himself as "half Korean, half Swiss" (16) by way of explaining his connection to his best friend, Erlan, who is Kazakh. Albie points out that people think they are related because they're both Asian, ". . . we're not even from the same sort of place. But sometimes people have trouble figuring that stuff out." (16) Albie's matter-of-fact acceptance of such ignorance is important because it sets him apart as more knowledgeable than others. Albie has trouble with spelling and math and his academic struggles are a source of worry for his parents and make him a target for the class bully. But he is very observant, "good at noticing" (27) and what he notices are the nuances in spoken and unspoken interactions among the people around him. He is kind, compassionate, creative, and appreciated for his quirkiness by the people who know him. Albie is also sad inside because he knows he has not lived up to his parents' expectations. There is nothing about his being half Swiss or half Korean that plays into his story, which suggests that Albie's life is unaffected by his biracial identity. As a mirror, *Absolutely Almost* is likely to appeal to readers who struggle in school and whose unconventional or creative talents go unrecognized. If some of those readers happen to be part Korean, or biracial in another way, the racial mirror might provide additional affirmation. We might even go so far as to imagine that the character of Albie interrupts the stereotype of the Asian model minority student who excels at school—a detail that is especially pertinent to teachers. Ollie's racial identity, in *Ollie and the Science of Treasure Hunting*, is relevant only in that he corrects someone's assumption about his

Asian background: "'I'm part Vietnamese, not Japanese,' I explained. 'My mom is white, and my parents don't know how to do origami. I watched a video online.'" (96) Michael Omi (2001) argues that from an assimilationist perspective the "increased racial hybridity of the Asian American" (xi) is often read as the narrowing of boundaries between social groups and hence, a decrease in levels of prejudice. He argues further that any articulation of multiracial identity should pay attention to the issue of power inherent in the discursive and social racial practices. Authors who blithely imagine biracial experiences without considering the role of power might be inadvertently ascribing to the assimilationist paradigm.

Biracial identity is only a tangential part of *Celia's Robot* (Chang 2009), but not because it is irrelevant or problematic to Celia, rather, because it is a fully integrated part of who she is. Celia Chow's mother is white and father is Taiwanese, and Celia is "the only Asian-looking kid" (5) at school. Where Graff and Dionne avoid including the inevitable attention that a biracial child's appearance attracts in *Absolutely Almost* and *Ollie*, Chang addresses it directly in *Celia's Robot*. Readers learn that when Celia and her mother are out in public, people think she is adopted: "One guy in a museum asked, 'Where did you get her?' Mom just smiled and answered, 'In the usual way.'" (5) This interaction is effectively framed to demonstrate the impunity with which observers objectify multiracial people. Celia also has to deal with a racist bully at school. The problems are believable parts of her everyday reality; as much a part as other school and family-related issues. Both white and Chinese family members weave in and out of the household goings-on, and references to food, customs, manners and values, and even a smattering of Chinese words are seamlessly integrated into the narrative without being the focus. The real focus is the robot and its role in helping Celia become better organized. As a novel about biracial identity, *Celia's Robot* effectively balances a variety of themes and offers a perspective that while people of color are seldom allowed to forget about race, but this fact is not necessarily all-consuming.

Jacqueline Woodson's (2002) *Miracle's Boys* is a deeply moving, sad story of three boys who find themselves suddenly orphaned in New York City. Their mother, Milagro, was Puerto Rican, and their father was African American. Apart from their Spanish middle names, the boys are not depicted as being connected to their Puerto Rican heritage, which is somewhat surprising given where they live. Their appearance marks them as black, and as per the rules of hypodescent, they are received in the community as black boys. The story follows the boys, Lafayette (age 12), Charlie (age 15) and Ty'ree (age 22) as they struggle to survive alone and grief-stricken. After his mother's death, Lafayette figures that practicing his meager Spanish will enable him to hold on to his mother's memory, but this is tenuous detail that is not sustained in the novel. Woodson's body of children's books capture a diversity of identities, racial and otherwise, in subtle but significant ways. Staggerlee Canan, in *The House You Pass on the Way* (Woodson 1997) considers her place in the world as biracial, and as a bisexual or lesbian teen. So does Carlton, a secondary character in *Behind You* (Woodson 2004) and *If You Come Softly* (Woodson 1998) who struggles with the death of his best friend and the recognition of his own sexual orientation. D Foster, the enigmatic focal character in *After Tupac and D Foster* is rendered all the more mysterious by the sudden appearance of her white mother after living in foster care for years. Woodson captures the joy and pain of adolescence in ways that readers from any racial groups can relate to, with an added layer that speaks directly to the experiences of urban, African American, multiracial, and LGBTQ youth whose realities are undeniably shaped by a knowledge of racism and homophobia. Thus, while multiracial identity is not the sole source of personal conflict, it is one of many important elements of identity with which teens grapple.

These books, as well as others included in this chapter, reflect an element of the racial reality in the U.S. In their study, "A Post Racial Society or a Diversity Paradox," Lee and Bean (2012) discuss how the one-drop rule of hypodescent and immigration inform the self-identification tendencies among interracial families. They found differences among racial combinations. Nearly 72% of Asians and 52% of Latinos intermarried with whites, compared with 17% of blacks. This is in direct contrast with the publications of multiracial children's books which predominantly feature black-white biracials, with the other groups falling significantly behind (Chaudhri and Teale 2013). Another interesting finding was that parents of children under the age of eighteen racially identified their children as multiracial at correspondingly proportionate rates: 15% of Asians, 12% of Latinos and 7% of blacks. Interviews with the families revealed that Latinos and Asians married to whites also chose to identify their children as white, and adults of the same combinations frequently did the same, or chose a racial identity depending on the context. This was not an option for black interracial families and their children whose experiences document too much social scrutiny to permit choice or flexibility. Most self-identified as black when questioned and were aware of other people's discomfort. This discrepancy in how multiracial identity operates within the current racial paradigm has been documented in studies across disciplines (Brunsma and Rockquemore 2001; Bost 2003; Winters and DeBose 2003; daCosta 2007), suggesting that while attitudes towards interracial unions are becoming more positive in general, the ways in which race operates varies between racial groups. Patterns in children's fiction mirror this dynamic to a certain extent. Readers may find credible mirrors in Blending books that feature multiracials who identify consistently as black, or "raceless" which is code for white.[1]

A number of other books that include multiracial identity as an element of description include Blue Balliett's acclaimed trilogy, *Chasing Vermeer* (2004), *The Wright 3* (2006), and *The Calder Game* (2008). The protagonists of this mystery series are Calder Pillay and Petra Andalee—slightly unconventional children whose eye for detail and sophisticated intellect are enhanced by their interesting families. Readers are provided these descriptions early in the novel:

> Like many kids in Hyde Park, Petra was a club sandwich of cultures. Her father, Frank Andalee, had relatives from North Africa and northern Europe. And her mother, Norma Andalee, was from the Middle East. Petra didn't think much about what racial category she belonged to—her family had let go of that way of looking at things a long time ago.
>
> (20)

Perhaps the context—an affluent Chicago neighborhood surrounding the University of Chicago, and a progressive private school—allows for the "letting go" of racial identity. Or perhaps it is the function of a white author's imagination. In today's world it is hard to imagine any American child with Middle Eastern heritage being allowed to forget such a fact. The absence of a racial identity is part of the privilege of being white that most American biracials cannot claim. In a study among white college students, Martin et al. (1996) found that racial identity was not something white people had to think about, labels were irrelevant, and even those who adopted the white label could not explain what it meant. This sentiment is echoed in Balliett's articulation of her character's identity but says more about the author than about the character. A second description, closely following this one explains that Petra is one in a line of first daughters in the family named Petra, also the name of the ancient Jordanian city. Other than this her racial and cultural background are not part of the story. Similarly, this description of Calder's heritage provides the context for why he is able to think in imaginative, mathematical ways:

> Calder, like Petra, was a hybrid kid. His dad was from India, and he had a calm way of speaking that made everything sound important. His job had to do with planning gardens for cities . . . Calder's mom, Yvette Pillay had short hair the color of an apricot and a jingly laugh that made other people laugh even when thy didn't know why. She was Canadian and taught math at the university.
>
> (23–24)

Balliett's books are about adventure and creativity, art, science, and math, not about identity, so readers can appreciate that Calder and Petra are unconcerned with who they are, and more interested in solving mysteries. That they happen to be biracial is a pleasing detail and a reminder that in the still very white world of children's literature, children of immigrants, connected to other cultures, can have adventures too. At the same time, the nonchalance with which Graff, Balliett, Dionne incorporate biracial characters suggests a multicultural 'flavoring' that feels unreal.

Acclaimed author of *Going, Going*, Naomi Shihab Nye (2005) draws on her own bicultural heritage in her subtle portrayal of Florrie, who identifies as Mexican and Lebanese. Elements of her heritage are integrated throughout the novel via a sprinkling of Spanish and Arabic, and easy cultural references that feel natural. Nye wants readers to know that Florrie is an outgoing, compassionate, socially-aware teenager who isn't afraid to defy convention or mobilize people to change their ways. On her sixteenth birthday, Florrie vows to stop shopping at franchises and support local businesses instead. She rallies friends and family to do the same. It is not until we know her as an activist that we learn that her grandfather immigrated from Lebanon, married a Mexican woman, and started a Mexican restaurant. Hani Hamza is Florrie's inspiration as a supporter of independent businesses. She writes an essay about him for school and clearly admires him a great deal. Florrie is a confident, self-aware young woman surrounded by friends and family in a boisterous, caring environment. Her identity is informed by their responses to her activism which everyone supports to varying degrees. We can read Florrie's multiracial identity as something that "just is"—not a problem to be negotiated, or a cause to be championed. Nye never lets us forget that we are reading about a racially diverse set of people in the distinctly urban San Antonio context.

Multiracial Identity as a Matter of Phenotype

The term "phenotype" refers to that which is physically observable in a living organism. In other words: physical traits such as facial features, body shape, skin color, etc. Some authors of multiracial fictional characters go to considerable length to include descriptions that not only provide the reader with a visual, but also establish the protagonists as different from other people—first phenotypically, then in other ways. Sometimes, the difference begins and ends with phenotype, simply providing the reader with visual information, as it does in *A Clear Spring*. Here multiracial identity does not play a part in the story. For Willa and Tammy, characters in *A Clear Spring*, racial self-identification is connected to how others view them:

> Sometimes people asked her why her name was Lopez since she didn't look Latina. Willa's hair was brown and straight, and her eyes were blue like her mother's. Tabby didn't look Latina either. She looked African American. But the two of them were partly Latina. Half!
>
> (102)

A Clear Spring is a well-intentioned novel with lots of young-reader appeal that tries to encompass all manner of diversity in the most quotidian way. Eleven-year-old Willa Cather Lopez goes to spend the summer in Seattle with her lesbian aunts. Along with her cousins Tabby and Phyllis, she embarks on a mission to expose a nearby industry that is dumping chemicals in a stream.

Meanwhile she is supposed to be dealing with her parents' recent divorce and the reason she is sent to Seattle in the first place is to connect with family. These connections are formed immediately and without effort because this is a family that is accepting of everyone and everything. The aunts are lesbians, Aunt Carmen is Panamanian, cousin Tabby is biracial with black and white parents, and wayward fathers (like Willa's) are an accepted entity.

The purpose of the book seems to be to depict an all-American family composed of blacks, whites, Latinos, straights, gays, carnivores and vegetarians, corporate employees and environmentalists, all living happily together. In blending so much diversity, *A Clear Spring* fulfils Bishop's concern that such melting pot books ignore important and specific differences, and cast a somewhat generic tone to the characters. Beyond Willa and Tabby's delight that they are both half Latina, there are no culturally specific references. Aunt Carmen says only one word in Spanish and nobody knows anything about Panama other than that there is a canal there. At one point, in an effort to teach the girls about their Panamanian heritage, Aunt Ceci pulls out a family photo album and shares stories too complicated and irrelevant for either characters or readers to follow. Willa appears amused at her lack of connection to her Panamanian heritage:

> She'd never heard these stories of the aunts before, or of little Fernando in his fancy suit or of the romantic meeting between Fernando and Josie. Willa hardly spoke a word of Spanish. When she was little her father used to teach her phrases, but he didn't really speak it either, just like Aunt Ceci and Aunt Carmen didn't. It was funny, Willa thought, the way languages could be forgotten by a whole family.
>
> (102)

The upshot is that the entire family is now completely assimilated and happy and immigrant relatives are distant memories; dead or dissociated.

Phenotypical ambiguity, that is to say, ambiguity in the sense that a person's appearance is not immediately racially classifiable by an observer, is often a pivotal part of multiracial people's identity. The experience of having to explain one's racial identity or answer repeated questions about it reifies the feeling of being Other, no matter how one feels about oneself. Personal narratives that document the experience of being multiracial are at the heart of edited collections such as Fuyo-Gaskins' (1999), *What Are You?* and *Half and Half* (O'Hearn 1998). Kip Fulbeck's, The Hapa Project, combines photography and personal narratives of 1200 volunteers who self-identify as multiracial and is a testament to the extraordinary variety of ways multiracials perceive themselves and negotiate how the world perceives them. In every photograph the individuals gaze directly at the viewer, daring us to stare and let our assumptions be disturbed. Thus, phenotype is the starting point, the experience of having to explain one's identity based on a viewer's inability to locate it, and an inevitable part of a child's experience in the classroom. Readers of multiracial Blending books are invited to participate in this experience via characters who respond with varying levels of nonchalance, resentment, pride, and every feeling in between.

The books described here depict a few ways in which multiracial characters perceive of their phenotypical identity. *Somewhere Among*, (Donwerth-Chikamatsu 2016), is set in Japan, and the protagonist is Ema Satoh who is white and Japanese. Ema is preoccupied with her appearance for the first twenty-eight pages of this 439 page novel in verse, suggesting that she is acutely aware of being different. The way other people stare at her or comment makes her sad. While riding in a taxi she notices the driver looking at her in his rear-view mirror as if he is trying to make sense of her face. A child she encounters in an elevator calls her a "foreigner." (3) Initially, Ema equates her loneliness with being biracial. However, this is not a sustained theme in the story and is dropped quite early when more pressing family matters take precedence. *Somewhere Among* bears the Library of Congress keyword tag, "racially-mixed people," and the back of the book jacket displays the poem titled "Multitudes" in which Ema describes an inner tension about her bicultural, bilingual, biracial heritage. This highlights the multiracial element of her story, when in fact there are many more and dominant matters in *Somewhere Among*. As the story progresses, Ema's concern about her appearance dissipates and we see that her life integrates both American and Japanese traditions, points of reference, and beloved family members that have a deeper influence on who she is than her appearance does.

For other protagonists, racial identity is closely connected to context and phenotype is merely descriptive. Cashay, the protagonist in *Cashay* (McMullan 2009) comments on the possibility of her father being white or light-skinned as a way of explaining her own light brown complexion: "I'm not black and I'm not white either. I'm some share of colored my mama calls *café au lait*. . . . I saw my daddy once. He was a light brown man with a little head who laughed a lot and then went to Memphis for good." (4) Later on in the novel, she makes other references to her skin color, but for the most part, Cashay identifies as black and lives in an African American community where her racial identity is not questioned.

Place and Belonging

Research in sociology has established that context plays a key role in how multiracial identity is formed. The work of David Brunsma and Kerry Ann Rockquemore (2001, 2005, 2009) provides a useful lens through which to read the experiences of some of the multiracial characters in children's fiction. Within the long-standing paradigm of racial hierarchies, the laws of hypodescent have determined that multiracial people be assigned the racial category of their nonwhite heritage. Even among minority multiracials, the assignment is to the racial group with the lowest social ranking. In a longitudinal study of the ways in which parents of kindergarten-age children racially identify their children, Brunsma (2005) found that with very few exceptions, white-nonwhite children were identified with their nonwhite parentage, following the norms of hypodescent (1148). This was particularly true of black-white families. The same pattern is evident in contemporary fiction with black-white biracial protagonists who live in predominantly black contexts. The protagonists of *Cashay, Stringz, Secret Saturdays* (Maldonado 2010), and *Camo Girl* share the element of having one African American parent; the other being white or Latino. Another commonality is that the characters live with their African American mothers, the fathers having left or died. Information about their larger contexts suggests that they live in African American communities, so it is not surprising that the protagonists identify as black. Most contemporary fiction with multiracial character adheres to this paradigm, as the novels analyzed here demonstrate. However, the degree to which it is easier for biracials to identify the way most people in their contexts do varies. *Stringz* and *Cashay* depict black-white biracials who identify as black, *Somewhere Among, Up From the Sea* (Lowitz 2016), and *The Turn of the Tide* (Parry 2016) include Japanese-white biracials who live in Japan and identify as Japanese until they are reminded that they are biracial by occasional antagonism towards their mixed heritage. On the other hand, Sharon Flake's novels complicate the notion that context can be a primary determining factor in biracial self-identification with Mai and Ming who relate differently to their black and Korean heritage. Together these novels provide a variety of ways of reading literary constructions of multiracial identity.[2]

Fourteen year-old Jace Adams, the protagonist of *Stringz*, is a talented cello player adjusting to a new life in Seattle. He identifies as black and the world around him reads him as such and makes sure he doesn't forget it. His music teacher does not believe Jace's cello recording is genuine and makes an essentializing comment about "you people" (37) understanding basketball. White passengers on the bus move away from him, and even his aunt expresses opinions that indicate she sees him as a potentially-troublemaking black youth. Jace interrupts everyone's stereotypes about him when he makes known his sports and music preferences: surfing over basketball, Coldplay over rap music, and an interest in jazz, blues and classical music, declaring "I couldn't care less what people thought I was supposed to like—I was into all kinds of music, and I guess that made me even more of a freak." (73) These interests, not the matter of his having an Irish father make Jace feel different. He lives with his aunt in an African American neighborhood that provides him racial anonymity until he leaves it for school and music pursuits. Jace never knew his father and does not feel a connection to him. There is nothing in the text to suggest that phenotype marks him as biracial, so it is believable that he identifies as black. Perhaps one way to understand this aspect of the book is that it is an example of how sometimes mixed race people identify monoracially, especially when appearance is a strong marker and the absence of family of the other racial group make it simpler or more logical to identify with those who are present than those who are not. *Stringz* is entertaining and well-crafted with a credible plot and interesting cast of characters. Jace is lonely, but also resourceful, witty, talented and compassionate. Should readers choose to understand Jace as multiracial, they will appreciate that his experience is shaped by many factors—friendship, family, music, introspection, etc.—with race being just one of them.

Set in the Cabrini Green housing project in Chicago, *Cashay* (McMullan 2009) is also marked as being about a multiracial character, but the protagonist identifies quite singularly as African American. At the start of the novel, readers learn that Cashay's sister is killed by a stray bullet and their mother resumes a drug habit to alleviate her grief. Cashay is essentially alone until a volunteer at an afterschool program enters her life. The story is told from Cashay's perspective, and readers see how she understands the role of race in both their lives. Allison is white. She has access to knowledge and information that Cashay is eager to learn. In their time together, Cashay develops an interest in economics and in the process, understands the intersection of race and economics and how they operate in her reality. Cashay reflects:

> I look at this lady, this Allison with her legs and her nails and her smile and her cell phone. If I were white, all white, really white with blue eyes and hair the color they call corn silk, then maybe I could make something of myself. Maybe I'd be pretty, get a good job answering phones, wear skirts, and drink coffee from a white cup with a saucer after lunches in sit-down, tablecloth restaurants with the rest of my white girlfriends. We'd laugh and talk about our biggest problems—lipstick colors, boys, where to eat next—and we wouldn't ever worry about money, bullets, drugs, or our mamas.
>
> (62)

In this moment Cashay believes that being part black has kept her from a life of affluence and ease. This realization motivates her to study harder, Cashay absorbs everything Allison has to teach her and begins to think of life in the rhetoric of economics. She feels the power of this growing knowledge and the possibilities inherent in using it to move on. In the end she goes to live with her aunt, finds a job, gets accepted into a good high school and all signs point towards a hopeful future. Identifying as biracial is not an option for Cashay whose early life is shaped by the forces of danger and poverty in a homogeneously African American urban housing project.

In these and other Blending books, the matter of characters being biracial is mentioned only in passing and may easily go unnoticed by readers. That these books are labeled as books about biracial characters seems to be a marketing decision. All have the Library of Congress keyword, and come up in searches for mixed race fiction. Jacket flap blurbs and reviews make note of biracial identity, even when characters do not. On the other hand, readers are reminded that sometimes biracial people identify—out of choice or necessity—with the people in their immediate surroundings. These Blending books reflect the persistence of the hypodescent law, and a general acceptance of multiraciality among African Americans.

The role of context on identity construction is evident in books with Asian and white biracial characters as well. Ema, in *Somewhere Among* has lived in Japan all her life and thus is immersed in the customs, traditions, and history. She keeps in close contact with her white American maternal grandparents and spends the summers with them regularly. She moves easily between English and Japanese languages, codeswitching with the expertise of a fluent bilingual. While she develops an understanding of the "multitudes" she is supposed to contain, the people, places and historical events in both countries increase in significance for her so that she appreciates the cultural importance of events such as July 4th in the U.S. and Tanabata on July 7th in Japan. Given that she lives in Japan, it is only natural that her perspective originates there, and it is the American perspective that she has to make an effort to incorporate. This is particularly evident around the anniversary of the U.S. bombing of Hiroshima and Nagasaki which evokes dialectically opposed emotional responses from her family members. In this moment, if Ema had to choose allegiances, it is hard to image she would not side with her beloved Jiichan whose family was killed in Nagasaki. Similarly, the Japanese-white protagonists (both named Kai), in *The Turn of the Tide* and *Up From the Sea* grew up in Japan and essentially think of themselves as Japanese. By contrast, Skye, the protagonist of *Flying the Dragon* (Lorenzi 2012) grew up in Washing D.C. and identifies as American until Japanese relatives move nearby and her parents send her to Japanese school to learn more about her heritage. Hers is a story of connecting with people and being open to new ways of thinking about her family and herself. Skye and her cousin Hiroshi are engaging characters whose experiences adjusting to each other will resonate with readers. By reading critically against the narrative, readers can consider how Skye's sense of herself changed when her context changed, demonstrating the role of external forces in the construction of identity.

Context and phenotype are not as easily resolved in two novels by Sharon Flake. *Money Hungry* (2001) and its sequel, *Begging for Change* (2004) give significant space to two biracial secondary characters. Mai and Ming Kim are brother and sister with differing attitudes towards their black and Korean heritage. Flake is the winner of the John Steptoe New Talent Award and has been nominated for the Coretta Scott King award, both of which recognize authors whose work contributes to literature about African American experiences. In *Money Hungry* and *Begging for Change,* Flake invites readers into the complex, loving, striving lives of several teen and adult characters. Mai and Ming's stories reflect how an element of difference within a racially homogenous community can be perceived. Mai is deeply troubled by her Korean heritage and she is vocal about it with her friends and to her parents. She is embarrassed by her Korean father's accent and mocks his mannerisms, wishing her mother had married "a nice black man" (34) like her friend Zora's mother. Mai's friends are unsympathetic, telling her she is lucky to have two parents who love each other and look after their children. Mai identifies as black and will fight anyone who says otherwise. Meanwhile, her brother identifies as biracial, black, African American or Korean depending on his mood. Their friends are accepting of both siblings' choices, but the antagonist, Kevin, uses the Kims' Korean father as the focus of his cruel jokes. This infuriates Mai and she defends herself by denying her Korean heritage and arguing that she is black. Ming, on the other hand, embraces his biracial identity, primarily because his attractive looks win him favor with the girls, but also because he genuinely appreciates being unique in this way. It is through Ming that readers are invited to view a rare, fictional, Korean and black experience. Ming speaks Korean and works at his parents' food truck serving their own blended cuisine: *bibimbap, chajang* and collard greens. Granted this is not a particularly deep cultural connection, but it is one that most kids in the community appreciate and Mai resents. At one point the protagonist looks around the Kim's home and notes that the décor is a perfect balance of cultures, "There's some of everything in here. African masks, watercolor paintings of Korea, and a painting of Mai and Ming when they were babies." (103) She comments on how similar Mai and her father look, but Mai denies it vehemently. The other side to this biracial experience is the prejudice. In *Money Hungry*, apart from Kevin's taunts, Mai is the only character who expresses antagonism about being biracial, making her anger seem internalized and without basis. Mai's identity crisis is not the focus of these novels but it plays a significant role in Flake's depiction of this close-knit group of friends. All the girls are dealing with different family-related matters such as divorce, separation, or drug-addiction. Some have loving mothers, others do not. Whatever their situation, the girls are intimately involved in each other's lives on a daily basis, providing love, companionship, reality-checks and beauty advice as close friends do.

Matters with Mai escalate in the second novel, *Begging for Change* when she gets a tattoo on her arm that reads "100% black." (22) Her parents are devastated but her friends offer a plethora of reactions. Zora says tattoos are unsanitary and Ja'nae disputes Mai's claim and the "truth" of the tattoo. Mai reminds her friends that they all do things to their bodies that are not "true", pointing out their colored contact lenses, hair extensions, and acrylic nails. In this scene, Flake efficiently aligns the performance of racial identity with other ways of performing identity, and Mai wins the argument. Mai keeps angering her parents and eventually, readers are given a reason that explains her bitterness and self-hatred. At the start of the school year, some older girls cut off her hair, stuffed it in plastic bags and taped it to the restroom mirror. In addition, Mai endured insults focusing on her multiracial appearance, undermining her black heritage "asking about [your] skin color and hair before they even ask your name." (46)

Readers are provided this information late in the narrative, but in time to elicit empathy for her. Mai's experience is in complete contrast to Cashay and Jace's as her desire to identify as black and blend in with her context is constantly thwarted from within the community. Things get worse before they get better. Her Korean cousins come to stay and their physical presence serves as a reminder that Mai cannot escape this part of who she is. Ling and Su-bok are welcomed by Mai's friends who like them immediately. The girls' conversations about race and identity reveal a variety of perspectives, a range of experiences with racial stereotypes, and their understanding of the fluidity of racial identity. Ultimately, Mai hits rock bottom, and in her vulnerability, allows her father to reach out to her. His words are warm and loving, "'You look in the mirror and all you see is a little black girl,' he says, pushing curls out her eyes. 'I see my sister and my mother. People I love, just like you.'" (206) Mai tells him about how much pressure she feels from people who demand that she choose one side or another and are never happy with her choice. Her father tells her that she does not owe anyone anything, and that when confronted, she should hold her head high and tell them whose daughter she is "sweet as honey and brown as fresh baked bread." (207) The matter ends here and readers can assume that the love and protection of her father will help Mai feel better about who she is, whoever she chooses to be.

Blended Together

Perhaps one of the most successful fictional renditions of a culturally integrated identity can be found in Paula Freedman's (2013) *My Basmati Bat Mitzvah*. Some heavy-handed stereotypes aside, this novel depicts a biracial, bicultural protagonist, Tara Feinstein, who is equally connected to both her Indian and her Jewish cultural backgrounds. Tara is twelve years old and approaching the time for her bat mitzvah. Her main internal conflict is that she does not know if she believes in God or not and that if she is unsure, then having a bat mitzvah would be insincere. Connected to that is her concern that having a bat mitzvah will make her "more Jewish" and therefore "less Indian." (10) The latter worry is aggravated by a judgmental peer at Hebrew school who declares that Tara cannot really be Jewish because her mother is Indian. This matter seems to be included for the benefit of an outsider audience and is quickly resolved by Tara's rebuttal that her mother converted to Judaism, and the fact that a person cannot be "half Jewish." Tara is happy to be different and openly shares aspects of her Indian and Jewish cultures with friends. At Hebrew school she loves learning about history and traditions and has a strong connection with Rabbi Aron in whom she often confides. When he was alive, her maternal grandfather, Nanaji, was the source of wisdom, history and spirituality from an Indian perspective. As Tara confers with Rabbi Aron, and reflects on what Nanaji taught her, she recognizes that their messages are similarly grounded in a love for all living things, the need for deep thought, and the acceptance of complexity in times when one wants simplicity. *My Basmati Bat Mitzvah* is told in the first person. Tara's vivacious, assertive, and vulnerable personality is hard to resist and readers will immediately be drawn into her colorful life full of friends, family, and teenage drama.

Where other blended books such as *A Clear Spring* and *Absolutely Almost* seem to suggest the postracial idea of racial identity being absent from multiracial life experiences, *My Basmati Bat Mitzvah* is thick with multiple levels of cultural integration. In Tara's life, Hindi and Yiddish occupy equal space in reference to everyday material items, cultural concepts, and terms of endearment. Her Jewish Gran and Indian Meena Auntie teach her about the devastating impact of the Holocaust and Partition; she is equally interested in the history she learns at Hebrew school and in the latest Bollywood movie trends; she celebrates Hannukah and Diwali; and describes herself as a "normal Jewish kid-with a healthy sprinkling of *masala* on top." (85) With no prompting from anyone else, Tara puts forth the idea of infusing Indian elements into her bat mitzvah, including wearing a sari and serving Indian food. She is quick to explain to those who ask questions, and corrects peers who make assumptions about her identity, and she is not shy about confronting the ignorant classmate who conflates being Indian with being Muslim, and Pakistan with Palestine. Ultimately, when Tara's conundrum about the existence of God is settled, it is not hard to imagine that she will continue to explore all parts of her racial, cultural and spiritual self.

Yumi Ruiz-Hirsch is Cuban, Japanese, Jewish and Russian, which, her mother declares, makes her a "poster child for the twenty-first century." (2) Information on the jacket-flap highlights Yumi's heritage, calling it "complicated," and indeed, occasionally, Yumi reflects on her anomalous mixed identity. For the most, part, however, *I Wanna Be Your Shoebox* (Garcia 2008) is crammed with multiple plots, a host of charismatic characters, and tight humor that are far more prominent than Yumi's fleeting mixed-race identity crisis. Yumi's life is replete with all things multicultural and readers are invited into her life where cultures and histories blend and criss-cross. Yumi's mother was born in Cuba and raised in Brooklyn. Her sister, Tia Paloma, and parents, Abuela and Gramps are significant secondary characters. Yumi's father is a composer who plays in a punk-rock band. His parents, Saul and Hiroko, are the focus of Yumi's life when we meet her. Saul is 92, and recently diagnosed with cancer. Yumi is devastated and insists that in their remaining time Saul tell her everything about his whole life, adding that she knows who he is, but wants to know who he *was*. She understands that identity is rooted in history and over the course of the novel she learns about his family's immigration from Russia, their struggle through the Depression, and the fifteen best years of his life when he was stationed in Japan and met and married Hiroko. Saul's narratives provide calm and respite between a host of other matters facing Yumi at school and at home.

She is organizing a concert, her mother's job might mean they have to leave Los Angeles, and friendships and crushes are becoming confusing. On top of that, her mother takes her to Guatemala where Tia Paloma is in the process of adopting a baby.

Garcia's depiction of this thirteen year-old's evolving sense of self feels believable: it is entirely realistic that while she deals with the impending loss of her grandfather and all the other disruptions to her life, she also thinks about her multiracial self occasionally, wondering where she fits in. Yumi reflects on ways her parents have encouraged her to think about race. Her mother and her Nigerian friend joke sardonically about how their presence is in higher demand than usual during Hispanic Heritage and Black History months—like "seasonal items" (37)—calling attention to this tokenizing multicultural practice. Yumi wonders why there isn't a month for multiracial people like herself. She also recalls that she and her father participated in the Hapa Project where they responded in writing to the question "what are you?" Yumi identified herself as a writer, and her father commented on the fluidity of identity depending on context. These moments of concerned self-awareness are few and far between. Meanwhile between Saul's lengthy descriptions of his life experiences and the arrival of her Cuban grandparents, meals at the Jewish deli, bargain shopping in the Latino wholesale market, *Santería*, and Johnny Cash all occupy equal importance in this family. Ultimately, Saul dies holding Yumi's hand, having told her his history, which is now hers. Yumi's connections to her family members and their histories was already strong, but it is solidified when she takes it on herself to continue the collecting and passing on of histories. She holds her baby cousin, Isabel, in her arms and imagines telling her their stories–"maybe one day I'll get to tell Isabel about this early time together. I want to share with her the story of my life, the way Saul is doing with me." (82) In *I Wanna Be Your Shoebox*, identity and belonging are about valuing the experiences, past, present and future, of people.

The Post-Racial Problem

Multiracial Blending books include a wide range of topics, characters and ways of 'being' biracial. Books like *Absolutely Almost* appear to subscribe to the color-blind paradigm that maintains that it is possible to look past race. It may well be that some young multiracial readers can connect to this depiction, and have never been made to feel different in a hurtful way. For them these books will be affirming mirrors. They also interrupt the notion that literature about people of color must always include the "problem of race." Certainly, Blending books depict a range of positive experiences, have interesting plots, engaging characters, and are relatively free from harmful stereotypes. Their universal appeal is attractive, but as Bishop points out, the problem with such books is that they "not only make a point of recognizing our universality, but that they also make a point of ignoring our differences." (33) They subscribe to the notion that we are now in a "post-race" era in which race is no longer noticed. As mirrors and windows, Blending books suggest the possibility of culture-free biracial identity that is no different from any other kind of American identity. In other words, multiracial characters are part of an assimilated population assumed to be culturally and historically neutral. Critical readers would do well to question the credibility of these fictional representations and contrast them with the current reality in which people who do not phenotypically fit expectations, or whose names or accents or parents signal difference, are called upon to explain themselves regularly.

Stories in which characters choose their nonwhite identity over a biracial one are also reflective of a social reality. Rockquemore, Brunsma, and Delgado (2009) describe research on mixed race issues in the 1960s and 70s which the "development of a black identity was considered the healthy ideal for mixed race individuals." (17) Since a large number of African Americans believe themselves to have multiracial heritage, it was not considered necessary to think of people with one black and one white parent any differently. Like the Black Power movement in the 1960s, La Raza and the American Indian Movement encouraged members of the community to assert racial identity and claim group membership. (DaCosta 2007). Racial pride, knowledge of history, culture and languages, and group loyalty in order to increase visibility and power created an environment that made the inclusion of mixed people desirable and necessary. The insight that Blending books offer is that sometimes context shapes mixed race experiences so they are no different than mono-racial ones. The danger is that they will be received as evidence of our having become a post-racial society in which race does not exist or matter. A few recent publications of biracial experiences that do not negate the reality of racism add to this small corpus of contemporary and historical fiction and are discussed in Chapter 6,. Multiracial Awareness. When the realm of books with mixed race content has expanded to include much more diversity than currently exists, Blending books will represent a few of the more subtle constructions of biracial identity.

Notes

1 See Chapter 8, Hidden Identities: Whiteness and Passing for a discussion of white racial identity construction in children's fiction.
2 Other novels in which multiracial protagonists' identity is significantly linked to context (people and place) to connect with their nonwhite heritage include: *Sister Soldier, Fly Home, Son Who Returns, Aleutian Sparrow, Lion Island, Mexican-Whiteboy, Becoming Naomi León, Going Going, After Tupac and D Foster, My Basmati Bat Mitzvah, Begging For Change, Money Hungry, The Other Half of My Heart, What the Moon Saw, Gray Baby, Angelfish*. Picturebooks that provide significant textual and visual information about context include: *I Love Saturdays y domingos, I'm Your Peanut Butter Big Brother, That's My Mum, I Am Mixed, My Two Grandads, My Two Grannies, Marisol McDonald Doesn't Match, Gem, Family, Blackberry Stew,* and *Cooper's Lesson.*

References

Balliett, Blue, and Brett Helquist. 2004. *Chasing Vermeer.* New York: Scholastic Press.
———. 2006. *The Wright 3.* New York: Scholastic Press.
———. 2008. *The Calder Game.* New York: Scholastic Press.
Bishop, Rudine Sims. 1982. *Shadow and Substance: Afro-American Experience in Contemporary Children's Fiction.* Urbana, IL: National Council of Teachers of English.
Bost, Suzanne. 2003. *Mulattas and Mestizas: Representing Mixed Identities in the Americas, 1850–2000.* Athens: University of Georgia Press.
Brunsma, David L. 2005. "Interracial Families and the Racial Identification of Mixed-Race Children: Evidence from the Early Childhood Longitudinal Study." *Social Forces* 84, no. 2: 1131–57.
Brunsma, David L., and Kerry Ann Rockquemore. 2001. "The New Color Complex." *Identity: An International Journal of Theory and Practice* 3, no. 1: 29–52.
Chan, Crystal. 2014. *Bird.* New York: Atheneum Books for Young Readers.
Chang, Margaret Scrogin. 2009. *Celia's Robot.* New York: Holiday House.
Chaudhri, Amina, and William H. Teale. 2013. "Stories of Multiracial Experiences in Literature for Children Ages 9–14." *Children's Literature in Education* 44, no. 4: 359–76.
DaCosta, Kimberly McClain. 2007. *Making Multiracials: State, Family, and Market in the Redrawing of the Color Line.* Stanford, CA: Stanford University Press.
de la Peña, Matt. 2009. *We Were Here.* New York: Delacorte Press.
Dionne, Erin. 2014. *Ollie and the Science of Treasure Hunting: A 14 Day Mystery.* New York: Dial Books for Young Readers.
Donwerth-Chikamatsu, Annie. 2016. *Somewhere among.* New York: Atheneum Books for Young Readers.
Flake, Sharon. 2001. *Money Hungry.* New York: Hyperion Books for Children.
———. 2004. *Begging for Change.* New York: Jump at the Sun.
Freedman, Paula J. 2013. *My Basmati Bat Mitzvah.* New York: Amulet Books.
Fulbeck, Kip. *The Hapa Project.* http://www.thehapaproject.com/.
Fuyo-Gaskins, Pearl. 1999. *What Are You? Voices of Mixed-Race Young People.* New York: Henry Holt.
Garcia, Christina. 2008. *I Wanna Be Your Shoebox.* New York: Simon and Schuster Books.
Graff, Lisa. 2014. *Absolutely Almost.* New York: Philomel Books.
Lee, Jennifer, and Frank D. Bean. 2012. "A Postracial Society or a Diversity Paradox? Race, Immigration, and Multiraciallity in the Twenty-First Century." *Du Bois Review* 9, no. 2: 419–37.
Lorenzi, Natalie Dias. 2012. *Flying the Dragon.* Watertown, MA: Charlesbridge.
Lowitz, Leza. 2016. *Up From the Sea.* New York: Random House.
Magoon, Kekla. 2011. *Camo Girl.* New York: Aladdin.
Maldonado, Torrey. 2010. *Secret Saturdays.* New York: G.P. Putnam's Sons.
Martin, Judith N., Krizek, Robert L., Nakayama, Thomas K., and Bradford, Lisa. Spring 1996. Exploring whiteness: A study of self labels for white Americans. *Communication Quarterly* (44)2.
McMullan, Margaret. 2009. *Cashay.* Boston: Houghton Mifflin.
Nye, Naomi Shihab. 2005. *Going Going.* New York: Greenwillow Books.
O'Hearn, Claudine C. 1998. *Half and Half: Writers on Growing Up Biracial and Bicultural.* New York: Pantheon Books.
Omi, Michael. 2001. "Foreword." In *The Sum of Our Parts: Mixed-Heritage Asian Americans,* edited by Teresa Williams-León and Cynthia Nakashima, ix–xiii. Philadelphia: Temple University Press.
Parry, Rosanne. 2016. *The Turn of the Tide.* New York: Random House.
Rockquemore, Kerry Ann, David L. Brunsma, and Daniel J. Delgado. 2009. "Racing to Theory or Retheorizing Race? Understanding the Struggle to Build a Multiracial Identity Theory." *Journal of Social Issues* 65, no. 1: 13–34.

Wenberg, Michael. 2010. *Stringz*. Lodi, NJ: WestSide Books.
Williams-León, Teresa, and Cynthia Nakashima. 2001. "Reconfiguring Race, Rearticulating Ethnicity." In *The Sum of Our Parts: Mixed-Heritage Asian Americans*, edited by Teresa Williams-León and Cynthia Nakashima, 3–10. Philadelphia: Temple University Press
Wilson, Barbara. 2002. *A Clear Spring*. New York: Feminist Press at the City University of New York.
Winters, Loretta I., and Herman L. DeBose. 2003. *New Faces in a Changing America: Multiracial Identity in the 21st Century*. Thousand Oaks, CA: Sage Publications.
Woodson, Jacqueline. 1997. *The House You Pass on the Way*. New York: Delacorte Press.
———. 1998. *If You Come Softly*. New York: Putnam's.
———. 2000. *Miracle's Boys*. New York: G.P. Putnam's Sons.
———. 2004. *Behind You*. New York: G.P. Putnam's Sons.
———. 2008. *After Tupac & D Foster*. New York: G.P. Putnam's Sons.

6 Multiracial Awareness
Power and Visibility in Contemporary Fiction

The persistence of racial labels has always been accompanied by questions about what it means to be labeled. There is, of course, the matter of labels being necessary for the equitable allocation of resources intended to equalize the playing field and make up for historical injustices. Here labels are associated with power and continue the practice of grouping people for the purpose of determining access to power. Racial labels also serve as descriptors that give us phenotypical information. Sometimes that information is also cultural, associated with traditions and customs shared broadly among group members. Beyond that, racial labels mean little more than what the bearer/subject of that label makes of it. If the spectrum of what it means to be white or black, or Asian or Latino/a is varied, the spectrum of what it means to be multiracial is exponentially more varied. In an extensive study in the UK, sociologists Peter Aspinall and Miri Song (2013) found that multiracial participants sometimes moved between choosing a single racial heritage or multiple ones depending on context, history, experience with racism, age, and other factors, demonstrating clearly that assigned racial categories may be discrete entities when it comes to institutional practices, but are quite permeable when it comes to personal and social practices. Perhaps more than other demographic groups, multiracial people are poised to dismantle hegemonic notions about race. The multiracial movement began with and continues to be about visibility and the freedom to self-identify. This was the issue at the heart of the activism in the 1990s that was partly responsible for the change in the Census standards. The data from the 2000 and 2010 Census reports (Jones and Bullock 2012) are evidence that contemporary Americans welcome the opportunity to self-identify racially: 6.8 and 9 million people respectively. Recognition, both public and private, as Maria P.P. Root (1992) reminds us, begins with naming oneself: "in essence, to name oneself is to validate one's existence and declare visibility." (7) The focus on visibility raises important questions. Does the push for self-identification move beyond affirmation? Do multiracials play a role in confronting racism? According to a recent report by the Pew Research Center (2015), 60% of multiracial adults "are proud of their mixed-race backgrounds and feel that their racial heritage has made them more open to other cultures." This positive feeling comes despite reports by the same participants of having experienced racial discrimination at some level. Currently, 6.9% of Americans self-identified as multiracial—a small but significant population that is growing. So what does it mean to self-identify as mixed race or multiracial? If contemporary children have an awareness of their multiracial heritage, how may they see themselves reflected in the literature?

Bishop (1982) identified "culturally conscious" (49) books that appreciate and celebrate uniquely African American experiences while maintaining universal elements that make them accessible to all children. Similarly, Multiracial Awareness books depict protagonists with an understanding of their mixed heritage: they are conscious of belonging to more than one racial group and, due to stable forces in their environments, less likely to choose a particular heritage over another. This awareness of heritage can be in the form of cultural, racial, linguistic, or a mixture of all of those identities. Characters are not conflicted about or surprised by their multiracial heritage and they respond to external curiosity or negativity with refreshing self-confidence. Another shared trait in Awareness books is that they reveal the dynamic process of identity development. Readers come to understand the nuances of biracial identity through cultural, historical, linguistic connections alongside the protagonists. Usually this means that there are adult characters and/or contexts that contribute to the mixed race character's positive awareness about his or her racial heritage. Awareness books are different from Blending books in that they include biracial identity as a significant component of the texts, shaping character development, plot, and tone, but overwhelming literary elements or themes. Not surprisingly, the authors of the books in this category are themselves biracial or bicultural[1] and understand the complexity of negotiating American racial perspectives.

The books analyzed in this section depict protagonists who, to some extent, negotiate the power granted by their "whiter" appearance and the associated privileges and guilt. They also feel the cultural pride and social oppression of people of color. The general theme of Awareness books is along the lines of the "I am who I am" trope frequently found in middle grade children's fiction, and these characters are who they are *because of*, not *despite*, their mixed race heritage. Another significant theme is that characters like Robin, Rain, Brendan and Cesi are depicted in proactive roles, challenging the limited ideas about racial identity that they encounter in other characters. They transform these individuals as they transform themselves. Furthermore, they emerge from conflict intact and more secure, rather than broken or unaffected. The representative texts analyzed here focus on the ways in which protagonists with a keen awareness of their multiracial identity use their positions on the margins of conventional society to challenge assumptions about race and expose it for the construct that it is.

Confronting Prejudice

Part of the lived reality of multiracial people, both real and fictional, is that they are made to feel inadequate by others from both sides of their heritage—"only half"—which implies a deficiency of some sort. The assumption is that there is a "whole" way of being (culturally or racially) that a multiracial person cannot inhabit. In *Angelfish*, by Lawrence Yep (2001), a turning point in Robin's life comes when Mr. Tsow insults her by calling her a "spoiled white girl." (9) Her response is believably complicated: she is confused, hurt, defensive, but never without the agency to define and defend herself. Tsow's comment sparks a desire in her to want to know more about her Chinese heritage, perhaps in an effort to fortify herself with a fuller sense of who she is. Learning about her white heritage is not part of this process. In fact, in keeping with the prevailing literary paradigm whiteness in children's literature tends to be unnamed, devoid of culture, heritage, or history.[2]

Robin Lee, the protagonist of *Angelfish*, is Chinese and white and an avid ballet dancer. An accident results in her working in Mr. Tsow's fish and aquarium shop to repay the cost of the damage she caused. Tsow is a curmudgeon who judges her immediately, amending his earlier insult ("spoiled white girl") to a different one when she assures him that she is part Chinese, calling her a "spoiled half person" (11) instead. His arrogance is cruel and reflective of the way in which racial purist immigrants look down on second and third generation and racially mixed Asians. Tsow's comment seems to trigger a dissonance that Robin has not felt before and from this point forward she pays close attention to and seeks out information about her Chinese heritage. Robin's connection to her racial heritage is grounded in culture and history and adults who provide information. Robin's grandmother, who we understand has always been a strong figure in her life, takes on a larger cultural role, initially as a foil to Mr. Tsow and begins to play an instrumental role in Robin's sense of self.

As in many of the books in this study, parents play a minimal role in their child's racial identity development. In *Angelfish* we only know that Robin's mother is second generation Chinese and a busy bookkeeper, and her father is "American" (white) and makes documentary films. Since her parents are busy, Robin and her siblings and cousins are left in Grandmother's care. It is here that she learns about her Chinese heritage. Robin reflects:

> Before Grandmother had joined us in America, I didn't pay much attention to Chinese things. Back in those days, China had been the Great Wall and nothing else. Since she has been with us, though, I had begun to realize just how little I knew. There were so many small, everyday things that made up her Chinese world that I didn't know anything about. Her apartment was like a window into another universe—one that I was just beginning to explore with her help.
>
> (61)

Robin and Grandmother share a close relationship and Robin tells her how Mr. Tsow hurt her feelings. Grandmother is incensed and wants to set him straight. Robin is moved to ask if other Chinese people think of her that way too. We get the sense that this is the first time she has been made to question her racial identity. Grandmother's frank response—that some ignorant people might, but most do not—satisfies Robin for the moment. Grandmother reflects briefly that hurtful people have often experienced cruelty themselves and she and Robin even speculate on a way to get Tsow to feel better about himself. With Grandmother's wisdom and support Robin is able to turn feelings of self-doubt into empathy and compassion.

Triggered by Mr. Tsow's refusal to accept her as Chinese, Robin becomes self-conscious and a little defensive. She also seems to be newly awakened to the details of her Chinese heritage. She notices the variety of Asian neighborhoods in the city and makes more of an effort to speak in Chinese, especially with older people. She comes to learn that Mr. Tsow, a northerner, might feel superior to southern Chinese and she takes his criticism of her mixed heritage less personally. Through interactions with people and being around Grandmother, Robin feels like she is part of a community, to the extent that she is less uncomfortable when people question her identity, "Auntie Ruby studied me curiously. By now I was used to that because of my American looks, so I greeted her politely in Chinese. Auntie Ruby nodded approvingly." (110) She is even secure enough to make a feeble attempt to assert her American (i.e.: white) heritage. Feeling protective of her white, spaghetti-eating father, she pipes up a defense that is not just of diverse types of noodles, "Since my father wasn't Chinese, I felt I ought to defend not only other cuisines, but other relationships. 'Well, at least it's noodles,' I said." (114)

Robin works hard at Tsow's store and earns his grudging respect. She does not suffer his mean comments passively and eventually he stops. Their companionship is solidified towards the end of the novel when Tsow's brother, an even more bitter and angry man, meets Robin in the store. He attacks her verbally, saying she is "no more Chinese than a fire hydrant." (183) Tsow comes to her defense, comparing her to his prized fish, the angelfish "'Would you call those fish mongrels? No, they have the best features and that's what makes them beautiful and unique.'" (183) Perhaps having a mirror held up this way enables Tsow to recognize his own prejudice in his brother.

In most children's fiction, including multiracial fiction, it is the protagonist who has to experience transformation. In *Angelfish*, Robin is made aware of her ignorance of her Chinese heritage and makes an effort to be more connected, but her transformation is secondary to Tsow's. His hateful attitude towards her at the start was based on nothing more than her appearance. Rather than shy away, she forced him to engage with her as she worked off her debt, telling him about her friends, family, and love of ballet. When he was disparaging, she defended herself. Through getting to know her, Tsow could no longer hold on to old prejudices. In the end we see Robin secure in the knowledge that she has an additional ally to add to her world of Russian ballerinas, Chinese aunties and myriad friends. *Angelfish* demonstrates that prejudice is part of a social system and hurtful to those who maintain it as well those who are victims of it. Furthermore, it depicts a biracial character who is accepted and appreciated by people who choose not to hold on to ideas of racial purity.

If the angelfish was the metaphor for racial transformation in old Mr. Tsow in Yep's book, rocks are the metaphor in *Brendan Buckley's Universe and Everything In It* (Frazier 2007). It is an unsubtle metaphor: rocks are a mixture of substances, minerals are pure, Grandpa Ed prefers minerals, and it is up to Brendan to get him to appreciate rocks.

The way that characters learn about their racial identity is a way that readers do too. We first learn that Brendan Buckley is biracial when his grandmother, Gladys, greets him with an affectionate "How's my milk chocolate?" (6) For the reader's benefit, Brendan explains: "Dad's the chocolate, Mom's the milk. That's how I became milk chocolate." (6) This description comes early in the book while we learn about Brendan's penchant for science, making observations and asking questions. Like Robin, Brendan's racial turning point comes when an observer's comment makes him feel bad about himself. At the mall one day, a little boy comments to his own mother that Brendan and his mother "don't match." (34) Gladys' response is to chide the boy's mother, telling her she should teach her son that "Black people come in all shades" (36), thus sweeping Brendan's mother, who is white, into the fold with herself and Brendan. This interaction causes Brendan to reflect on his racial identity and he notes that he doesn't often think about it except when people point out the difference between his and his mother's skin colors. He identifies quite securely as black, aligning himself with his father and paternal grandparents and his friend Khalfani, and admits that if ever he wished something were different about his family, it would be that his mother had darker skin so that people would not question their being together. For Brendan, the judgment of outsiders undermines his sense of security in his family. Identifying as black rather than biracial is simple, but this simplicity is complicated further as Brendan begins to ask questions about his maternal grandparents and their absence from his life.

The realm of multicultural children's fiction includes many examples of positive, affirming, authentic and historically-grounded experiences about people of color. Some authors, such as Jacqueline Woodson, Christopher Paul Curtis, Joseph Bruchac and Cynthia Kadohata (to name a few) are intentional about creating protagonists of color whose lives are touched by the racism that is so ubiquitous in our culture. Sundee Tucker Frazier is one such multiracial author whose fiction makes visible the complex ways in which identity is shaped through dynamic and multi-faceted processes. She does not sugarcoat the fact that Brendan's racial identity includes knowing about racism, and she makes sure the reader is aware of it also. When Brendan's father reminds him, "the world *is* going to see you as black," (39) readers are invited to partake of parental advice that will be familiar to some families of color, especially some black families: "Dad was always saying how I needed to learn to control my actions and most of all my anger, because people look at black boys more suspiciously than they look at others ... He also told me that black boys are stopped by police more and are questioned more roughly, and that's why he became a policeman. So he could help change the system." (40) Brendan's mother's contribution to this conversation echoes the tenor of the white mothers who fought for the creation of a multiracial category on the census: she tells him he can identify as biracial if he prefers.

Mr. Buckley's comment about systemic change is not lost on Brendan, who takes it upon himself to change one person: his estranged grandfather, Ed DeBose. Thus, in *Brendan Buckley's Universe*, it is the racist who needs to be transformed, not the multiracial protagonist. This depiction is in sharp contrast to In/Visibility books in which the reverse is true.

Brendan's awareness of his racial identity comes from his father and his paternal grandparents who have instilled in him knowledge about black history, culture and racism. In fact his racial awareness is more comprehensive than most fictional protagonists' and shapes how he moves in the world on a daily basis. Knowing about the Montgomery Bus Boycott struggles imbues the simple matter of choosing a seat on the bus with historical significance. He rejects a seat in the back with his friend because of the symbolic resonance of that position, and instead, chooses to sit in the middle. Brendan's education is quite comprehensive: Grampa Clem took the sting out of an insult aimed at Brendan's being mixed by assuring him that "Everyone's mixed with something," (56) and Gladys' comment that white people want their skin to tan only to certain point of darkness—"Give me a tan, but don't make me black!" (54)—begins to make sense as Brendan gets older. All this knowledge is constructed in the context of his mother's silence about being white, and the conspicuous absence of her parents in their lives. Brendan's accidental discovery of his maternal grandfather is the catalyst to another dimension of racial awareness.

Brendan and Ed DeBose meet unexpectedly at a mineral and gemstone exhibit. After the initial disbelief at having accidentally found his grandfather has worn off, Brendan resolves to visit Ed. Brendan identifies himself as Ed's grandson, and they begin an awkward but strong connection around their shared interest in rocks and minerals (in secret). Brendan admires rocks for their plasticity and variety, while Ed prefers the purity of minerals. Their preferences serve as a vehicle for them to talk about difference without talking about race or the family. It is important that Brendan (and the reader) gets to know Ed with all his foibles, before the fact of his racism is tackled. By that time, the connection is established, which makes the need for Ed to take responsibility even more acute. It is also necessary for Brendan to learn more about racism. His growing awareness reaches a new level the first time he experiences violent racism. A group of white boys harasses Brendan and Khalfani, throwing rocks to make them bleed because they wanted to see if black people had purple blood. In the ensuing discussion with his family, Dad and Gladys are blunt about white people transmitting racism to their children. The conversation is cut short by Mom's interruption: "some white people . . . not all kids." (77) Her desire to distance herself from a legacy of racism is evident. Brendan quickly makes the connection between this conversation and his white grandparents' absence and he wonders if racism is the reason they have never been part of his life. He cannot believe that the Ed DeBose he has come to know could be racist enough to separate from his daughter for marrying a black man. After all, he seems to like Brendan, and he has a black friend with whom he plays chess. Yet there remains the nagging possibility that this is the case, and it turns out to be true. In a series of confrontations between Brendan, his parents, and Ed, the fact is revealed that Ed did indeed try to stop the marriage. His explanation: "Well, I guess it just didn't seem right . . . at the time. Races mixing like that." (165) This trope of racism embodied in older characters who ascribe their attitudes to past norms is also evident in *Stealing Home* (Schwartz 2006) and *Gray Baby* (Sanders 2009) in which white fathers reject their daughters for marrying black men. Ed blames his prejudice on the norms of the past, but he still feels that way, despite knowing Brendan. It is up to Brendan to change the old man's mind. Events come to a dramatic head that involve Ed getting stuck in a landslide and Brendan having to drive his truck and literally save Ed's life. It is possible that this near-death experience causes Ed to reflect on his mortality in light of his ideology. In the end, Ed apologizes to his daughter, son-in-law, and Brendan for how he treated them. Brendan forgives him and we are given to believe that Ed has changed his mind about interracial marriage now that he cares about his grandson.

The subtext is about purity and mixture, metaphorically represented through Brendan's consideration of rocks and minerals. Brendan's racial identity as a black boy has been relatively uncomplicated in that he identifies with and is identified by others as black, with the accompanying reality of encountering racism. Upon finding his white grandfather, he now must consider what it means to be white also. In his Book of Big Questions, he writes: "What am I? Black? Biracial? Am I white too?" (41) His mother has been unhelpful in this regard. She has detached herself from her racist father and is uncomfortable in family discussions about white racism. Ed's absence in Brendan's life is the physical and emotional manifestation of that racism. Brendan's questions do not get answered in any substantial way. It is enough that he has been the catalyst in reuniting the family. With a white grandfather in the picture, his identity as a black boy is now complicated and the only information he (and the reader) have about being white is associated with Ed and the bullies' racism, and his mother's silence. This silence around whiteness is part of the legacy of white privilege and the lack of a comfortable resolution in *Brendan Buckley's Universe* is true to fiction as it is to life.[3]

Looking Inward

Confronting prejudice in others is one thing; confronting it in oneself is another. In *Border Crossing* (Cruz 2003) and *Rain is Not My Indian Name* (Smith 2001), multiracial protagonists are called upon to examine assumptions they have developed about their own racial identity as well as about others'. Cesi, in *Border Crossing*, learns that she has internalized some shame about her Mexican heritage, which is probably connected to her father's silence around his past. Cassidy Rain, on the other hand, is confident in her multiracial heritage, to the point that she is judgmental about other multiracial Native Americans' identity claims. Cesi and Rain's stories complicate simplistic, celebratory narratives about identity, reminding readers about the fluidity of identity construction.

In the Author's Note, Cruz (2003) explains that the impetus behind *Border Crossing* lay in desire to fill a gap in children's literature in which multiracial readers like her were not represented. Cruz directly addresses the need for mirrors and windows that affirm and expand children's understanding of racial identity when she writes:

> I knew that kids like me, with mixed heritages would probably love to read a book where the main character dealt with some of the same problems or questions they had. I also knew that kids who did not come from mixed heritages might want to read a book about someone different, just like I loved reading books about people who were different from me. I wished there was a book like that so that I could share it with my students.
>
> (120)

The protagonist of *Border Crossing*, Cecelia (Cesi) Álvarez, shares the author's Mexican/Irish/Cherokee heritage, and the questions for which she seeks answers are believably vague and pressing for a twelve-year-old. She says repeatedly that she wants to know more about her Mexican heritage but does not know what to ask. Cesi is interested in some cultural element that she knows is missing from her life. She comes from a stable, intact family, and appears to live in a diverse, financially secure community in southern California. She describes herself as having "pale, pale skin" (6) compared with her dark-skinned older brother, but at this point in her life, phenotype does not play a role in her recently-sparked curiosity about herself.

Border Crossing is told in the first person and Cesi's voice and tone add nuance to her already complex preadolescent musings. She is not sure what she's looking for, but her primary question is about who she is so that she will not spend her adult life reading self-help books and doing yoga. On a deeper level, she might be intrigued by the tension she witnesses between her father and his mother, Nana. Cesi's context for how she understands herself starts with her grandmothers: one English-speaking (Maryann), the other Spanish-speaking (Nana). Both are described in considerable detail and are established as cultural representatives. Her feelings for each grandmother are revealed in descriptions of their appearances and homes. Both their homes are filled with culturally significant artifacts, photographs of ancestors, and are painted in bold colors. But where Maryann's cowboy boots, gruff voice, unconventional manners, turquoise jewelry and Navajo art are described with admiration, Nana's Mexican *ofrenda*, flowery dresses and Catholic statues are described as dusty and ancient. Maryann has played an important role in Cesi's life, especially as a storyteller. Cesi knows the stories behind all the photographs and art, of her mother's childhood and grandmother's work on the reservation. Nana's house, on the other hand is foreign and unfamiliar. Cesi is wary of the people in the photos and the clusters of clay figurines. Nana does not speak much English and Cesi does not speak Spanish so the stories are untold. The obvious conduit between them, Cesi's father, John, becomes silent and aloof when his mother and wife suggest that he is rejecting his Mexican identity. The gap in Cesi's developing self-awareness is her scant knowledge of this aspect of her heritage. Her interest is aroused by the animosity she witnesses between her father and Nana around his reticence to share about his own life. Despite her lack of information, Cesi identifies as biracial. But it is an uneasy identification that she does not quite understand. The matter of phenotype that impacts many multiracial people clearly confounds Cesi too. One reason she does not connect with her Mexican heritage is because she has internalized social perceptions of what it means to "be" Mexican—one element being appearance: "I looked like a pale girl with features that made people ask what my nationality was" (47) and she thinks that having darker skin would enable her to identify more tangibly with her Mexican heritage:

> Sometimes I felt that if my skin were darker, my hair browner, then I would be more Mexican. Maybe if I could dance like that—twirl my skirts and spin—I would look more Mexican, be more Mexican.
> (47)

This suggests that if her appearance enabled it, she could have a stronger claim to her Mexican heritage. As it was with Brendan Buckley, Cesi's life would be simpler if her racial, cultural and phenotypical identity "matched" and did not arouse anyone's curiosity. On the other hand, when people comment that her name sounds foreign and ask where her parents are from, she is bothered that people can't think of her as "more than one thing. . . more than one color." (47) Having to encounter this kind of discomfort with difference is not uncommon in the lives of many multiracial people. Ultimately,

Cesi has to confront her own preconceptions about Mexican people and culture before she can embrace a Latina identity of her own.

Cesi runs away from home for a day, thinking that a little time in Tijuana, Mexico, will teach her something about herself. On the train she meets a boy named Tony who invites her to his aunt's house for a meal. In an uncanny coincidence, Delfina considers Cesi's last name, Álvarez, and realizes that Cesi is her cousin John's daughter. Over the course of the evening Cesi is able to ask all the questions about her father that she could not before, and Delfina remembers vivid details about John's childhood that perfectly explain his internalized shame and desire to distance himself from his Mexican heritage.

In a refreshing departure from the stereotypical tropes of cultural identification, this book avoids matters of food and festivals. In *Border Crossing*, important elements about Mexican American identity involve understanding some of the difficulties of immigration, assimilation, and making hard choices. Cesi's father, John, is vague about his experiences, saying only that his mother misunderstood his reasons for not teaching his children Spanish. When his wife challenges him on this, arguing that their children know all about her side of the family, but nothing about his, John's response reflects that of many immigrants for whom invisibility through assimilation is preferable to cultural conspicuousness: "'. . . your family stories are all about America. Most of mine are about Mexico, and we're not Mexicans, we're Americans. We didn't come here so that we could look back and wish we were there.'" (32) During her visit to Tijuana, Cesi learns from Delfina that her father had some very painful experiences with racist teachers and schoolmates. He was smacked for speaking Spanish and wrongly accused of theft by a teacher who called him a "filthy thief." (98) Delfina speaks of the shame of poverty and lack of English that kept their parents from standing up to such people, how they were just grateful that their children were being educated. Later John confirms that the urgency with which he felt the need to learn English, to erase anything that might prompt racism, trumped his parents' efforts to maintain his Mexican heritage. Language is an important cultural component in Cesi's life. She recognizes that one reason she feels disconnected from Nana is because they cannot communicate. Initially, Cesi frames this matter in terms of it being Nana's deficiency in English, not her own in Spanish. Yet she is embarrassed about her own lack of Spanish, and distances herself with some contempt from "those Mexican girls with their tight braids and cold burrito lunches . . . I was certainly not one of them." (8) In this moment, Cesi's internal tug-of-war is evident: the answers to the questions she has about who she is begin with recognizing how little she knows, and that she has made assumptions and must confront them. She has the opportunity to do this when she is on a bus in Tijuana and notices that her skin is the palest among the shades of brown of the other passengers, and while she feels different, there is no sign from anyone around her that they view her as different "no one seemed to notice me standing there . . . Maybe they knew I was one of them. *I wasn't sure if I was.*" (74) Cesi's experience of feeling different is contextual. She feels more at home in Mexico, where there is greater acceptance of phenotypical diversity than in the U.S., where skin color is a significant marker of difference.

In Tijuana, Cesi's view of Mexico, gleaned from television and the news, is confirmed. She leaves her backpack in the square while she goes to play in a fountain, and returns to find all her money has been stolen. Her immediate response is to blame herself for being foolish for trusting "these people . . . they were the Mexicans I had always been warned about on television." (82) A confirmed stereotype is hard to disrupt, and it falls on her companion, Tony, to remind her that she, and he and John are also "these people" and that she was wrong to make sweeping judgments that conflated thievery with being Mexican. In her guilt, Cesi associates her prejudice with being half white, and aligns herself with John's racist teacher. The awareness of whiteness is immediately connected to a legacy of racism. Cruz does not let Cesi or the reader linger with this association, and Delfina, like Brendan's mother quickly adds that Cesi must not think that all white people are racist, just as she must not think of all Mexicans as lazy or dishonest. The juxtaposition is blatant and Cesi accepts it.

The parallel between Delfina's story about John being the victim of racism, and Cesi's own reaction to being robbed demonstrates that she has much to learn about the complexity of racial identity construction. In another parallel, Cesi learns to change her opinion about Nana. Delfina's home is decorated much like Nana's, with photographs, bright colors and an *ofrenda*. Once Delfina explains the significance of the altar and stories of the people in the photographs, Cesi reflects on how she has misjudged her grandmother.

Before her adventure comes to an end, Cesi has more to learn about her father's life. When John comes to pick Cesi up from Delfina's house in Tijuana, he is angry, worried, and chastened. Cesi's running to Mexico is a clear signal to him that he has to face his own demons for his daughter's sake and start talking about his past so she can know him, and by extension herself, better. Before they return home he drives her to his hometown in Nogales so that she can see where he spent some of his childhood. As a result she gets to see a peaceful, scenic part of Mexico to contrast with the gritty image of Tijuana. In the end Cesi says she understands more not only about the physical place, Mexico, but about the variety of positive and negative experiences that comprise her father's Mexican American identity. She has a lot more to learn but has emerged from this experience wiser and more self-aware, "I know I have more than one home now. I always had. I just hadn't known it." (118)

In *Border Crossing*, Cruz successfully achieves her goal of depicting the possibility of a positive biracial identity; one in which the subject can claim membership in multiple groups without having to renounce one or the other. A number of factors point to the possibility of Cesi's future being one in which she can continue to learn about her Mexican heritage. Her father promises to be more proactive, Cesi plans to make an effort to communicate with Nana and stay in touch with Delfina and Tony. Her mother and Maryann are supportive of this new direction and ultimately, all signs point towards an interesting journey ahead for Cesi as she explores familiar and unfamiliar aspects of her Irish/Cherokee/Mexican heritage.

An exploration of identity as an ongoing process of learning and unlearning is one of several themes in Cynthia Leitich Smith's novel, *Rain is Not My Indian Name*. As explicit as the title of this book is, the matter of racial and cultural identity is surprisingly subtle. Fourteen year-old Cassidy Rain Berghoff identifies as "Indian," (13) "Native," (48) "mixed-race," (49) "mixed-blood," (113) and specifically, "Muscogee Creek-Cherokee, Scots-Irish, German-Ojibway," (20) and like many of the teenaged multiracial protagonists in children's literature, has a multitude of matters weighing her down. The primary one is the recent death of her best friend, Galen, and another is the loss of her friendship with Queenie. As if her life was not complicated enough, Rain must also contend with the absence of her father (posted in Guam), the impending arrival of a new niece or nephew, lingering grief over her mother's death, and local gossiping busybodies. In this context, racial identity is of little concern to Rain. The author, Cynthia Leitich Smith, who shares Rain's Native-European heritage, skillfully integrates cultural and racial awareness throughout the novel so that it is very much part of the story but without being pedantic. Michelle Pagni Stewart (2009) describes *Rain* as a "Third Generation text." (46) Within the corpus of books written by Native authors, Third Generation texts are less preoccupied with dismantling stereotypes and correcting a historical literary record (which is the motivation in Second Generation texts). Instead, like *Rain*, these texts complicate identity issues among Native protagonists so that they involve layers and nuances to provide readers with an insider perspective. Convention holds that as a multiracial figure, Rain should be at least somewhat conflicted about her identity. But she is not. She is aware that she is one of a half a dozen Native people in her small, Kansas town, and has to contend with an array of problematic stereotypes. She does so with a confidence that belies the depth of her cultural awareness, and it becomes gradually clear to the reader that Rain has some more learning to do about herself, including shedding some assumptions.

Since Galen's death, she has withdrawn from all social life, interacting only with her family members and avoiding all mention of Galen. Her Aunt Georgia initiates a summer program for the American Indian youth in town. Rain is skeptical about Indian Camp, calling it "some kind of bonding thing . . . or something to do with the way Hannesburg schools taught about Indians and because of that, the way it sometimes felt to be an Indian in Hannesburg schools." (12–13) Rain's dismissive attitude toward the idea of attending the camp suggests she has no need for such things as sharing what it feels like to be Indian. Rain knows firsthand what it feels like and recounts hiding a sci-fi magazine behind her textbook to avoid enduring "Indian" themes activities around Thanksgiving Day:

> ... cardboard cutouts of the Pilgrims and the pumpkins and the squash taped to the windows at McDonald's. And the so-called Indians always look like bogeymen on the prairie, windblown cover boys selling paperback romances, or baby-faced refugees from the world of Precious Moments.
>
> (13)

This moment also serves to bring the reader along to recognize such stereotypical tokenizing. The subject position is also the position of the reader, who is invited to view these culturally-inaccurate commercialized renditions of "Indian" culture as offensive. Another reason for Rain's reluctance to be involved with the group is that her mother, who died six years earlier, had been involved in the Native community. Painful memories associated with her mother prevent Rain from renewing those connections. The universe, however, has different plans for her, and her eventual involvement with the Indian Campers leads her along a journey of learning and letting go.

Rain begins a brief summer job as photographer for a journalist (The Flash) who is covering the Indian Camp. Anticipating the reality that her readers are likely to have preconceptions about how they imagine this cast of Native characters, Smith provides explicit visual information of a phenotypically diverse array of people to interrupt our assumptions. Aunt Georgia's striking feature is her newly-dyed tomato red, cropped hair "from a distance nobody would have guessed that she was a Muscogee Creek-Cherokee. Or, for that matter, a natural redhead." (25) Rain describes her older brother, Fynn, as "Native American Fabio," (23) whereas her own coloring is lighter. The contrast in how these physically different siblings are read by the curious public is striking: while dark-haired Fynn is asked "what are you?" (48) fairer-haired Rain is asked "How much Indian are you?" (48) Rain is cognizant of how Native people recognize her membership more respectfully than non-Natives: "they never follow up with the something like 'You don't seem Indian to me.'" (48) This critical difference clearly locates the perceived difficulty around mixed-race issues in society and removes it from the individual. The first-person narrative aligns the readers with Rain, so that the undermining effects of such questions is explicit and exposes the perception that racial identity, in this case, "Indian" identity is only a matter of appearance. Ironically, Rain needs to learn about how she has internalized this misperception too.

Rain's inchoate friendship with The Flash begins with one such encounter in which she surprises him with the information that she is one of the few Indians in Hannesburg. She waits for the inevitable expression of surprise and when he does not provide one, reflects that she may have misjudged him. Much later in the novel, The Flash has occasion to share that he is Jewish and Rain is taken aback, biting back the very comment she had expected him to voice about her: "but you don't look. . . ." (113) In this moment Rain is shaken from her position that only she and her nonwhite friends are subjected to narrow racial assumptions, to recognize that she has some of her own.

Rain and the readers are treated to another eye-opener shortly after this one. Rain's former best friend, Queenie is one of the four teens in the Indian Camp. Rain is surprised and skeptical "In the sunlight, Queenie's skin looked almost the same warm tone as Aunt Georgia's. But last time I'd checked, she wasn't Native. It was a well-known fact that Queenie was the only black girl in town." (40) Much to Rain's surprise, Queenie reveals that she has recently learned she had a Seminole great-grandfather. Again, Rain is guilty of having made an assumption based on appearance even though she knows full well how limited that perspective is. A minor character and one of the participants in Indian Camp, Spence, is also described so as to provide readers a clear visual and no doubt, to interrupt stereotypes: "The son of lawyers with an in-ground pool in their suburban backyard. A tad round for a Gap ad, though he dressed for the job. Played baseball. Into computers. He could've passed for a full-blood if it weren't for his startling green eyes." (39–40) Thus, these five characters embody varied ways of inhabiting Native identities and highlight the constructedness of identity categories. If Rain was initially somewhat smug in the awareness of her own knowledge of her Native heritage, she now has a few reasons to take notice of what she was missing. We can understand these awakening moments in Rain's experience as opportunities for us to reflect on the complexity of racial identity construction; how for some it is a matter of phenotype, for others history and lived experience, for still others, recent discovery. This fluidity is not unique to multiracial experiences, as it is relevant even to so-called monoracial identity, but through the lens of multiraciality, some subtleties become apparent.

As with other multiracial characters in children's literature, whiteness is not a racial heritage to be learned about, and Rain's journey centers on learning more about being Native American. Smith is careful not to collapse all Native cultures into a monolithic Indian or indigenous category as so often happens in children's literature about Native Americans. Rain's next lesson also involves the recognition of internalized assumptions. She accompanies the campers to the trailer park where Dmitri and Marie Headbird live. Rain knows little about these siblings other than the fact that they are Ojibway. Her response upon entering the park is to hold tightly to her money and reflect that she "wasn't the kind of girl who hung out at the trailer park." (71) She is looking to buy a gift and Dmitri offers her a dreamcatcher. Before she can look at it carefully, she expresses her doubt based on the fact that she has seen so many "tacky-looking dreamcatchers" (71) before. Dmitri points out that his mother made this one and Rain sees that it is beautiful, nothing like she imagined. In the short time she spends with Dmitri in his trailer she realizes she has been wrong about trailer-life, and learns about his art and his sister's doll collection, and suddenly her lack of knowledge becomes tangible: "I washed my hands and considered mentioning to Dmitiri something we have in common, our Ojibway heritage. But I'd grown up so far away from it. I felt ashamed by how much I didn't know." (73)

Another point of connection for Rain comes from a position of defensiveness. Galen's mother, Mrs. Owen has some power in City Council and uses it to oppose Aunt Georgia's request for funding for Indian Camp. Initially, Rain was uninterested in the Camp, but her natural response to something personal being threatened motivates her to consider the cultural significance of Indian Camp to its members and Aunt Georgia—she also comes to see that it has significance in her own life. As she spends more time with Dmitri, Maria, Spence and Queenie, Rain recognizes that she should let Galen go and pay attention to the people around her who have a lot to offer: " . . . it might not be too late for me to connect with the Ojibway side of my heritage. . . . " (130) The novel ends with this hopeful possibility.

Racial Awakening

The element of surprise features fairly frequently in the array of fictional experiences in which multiracial protagonists develop racial self-awareness where before they had none. Racial awareness is accompanied by an understanding of power (albeit quite nascent) and prejudice. This depiction is in contrast to the ways some multiracial protagonists develop a cultural awareness; knowledge about customs, language, traditions etc. without knowledge about power. White characters are rarely depicted as having to think about the power and privilege that come with being part of a dominant culture. Coming at multiracial identity from a completely different angle are the literary depictions of white protagonists who are surprised to learn they have black ancestors in *Off-Color* (McDonald 2007) and *American Ace* (Nelson 2016). Their explorations of racial identity touch on the role of power as the protagonists negotiate what it means to have a personal connection to a marginalized group.

In these contemporary novels, protagonists come to learn something about racism when it suddenly applies to them. Until this point, Cameron in *Off-Color* and Connor, in *American Ace* presumed they owed their darker features to their Italian fathers. The knowledge of black ancestry brings about some interesting changes in their lives and how they view their identity. As a mirror, these novels recognize and affirm those readers who may not "look" multiracial, and in a sense, pass for white as long as they are not upfront about their ancestry. Their stories also remind us that things may not always be as they appear, and that when we judge people based on their appearance, we may be completely wrong. *Off-Color* and *American Ace* are interesting commentaries about what it means to claim affiliation with a racial group with which one had no prior connection.

In *Off-Color* fifteen-year-old Cameron Storm accidentally discovers that her father was black, not Italian, as she had believed. In *American Ace* Connor, who identified as "half Irish, half Italian" (13) learns that his grandfather was an African American air force pilot stationed in Italy during World War II. This information means different things to each character, but the one element in common is that suddenly, Cameron and Connor become aware of and interested in African American history since it now pertains to them.

The transformations are gradual. Their initial reactions focus on themselves in believable teenage ways. The fact of having a dark-skinned ancestor explains their own appearance: Connor is "tall, dark, and handsome" (31) and Cameron has olive skin, blue eyes, and dark curly hair—facts that they quite like about themselves. Next comes a moment of realizing that now they have racial identities whereas before, they never thought of themselves in those terms. Astute readers might recognize that this realization illustrates the constructedness of race as a function of binaries—as white people, Cameron and Connor never thought of themselves as racialized because of the silence around whiteness. Having a black relative throws their whiteness into relief as they consider what it means to be part black, and have to acknowledge that they are also part white. Connor conceives of his whiteness through Irish and Italian ethnic traditions and customs, while Cameron lacked even this manifestation. Both characters connect whiteness to racism. Cameron thinks her mother might have hidden the fact of her father being black because she was ashamed and that raising her as white was a form of protection. Connor's epiphany is more complicated. As someone who strongly identified as the descendent of Irish and Italian immigrants, he felt free of the "white guilt of Indian slayers / slave owners." (35) In other words, he held himself apart from this grim part of American history. Knowing that he is, in fact, deeply connected to it is very unsettling. Both characters remember participating in, or standing by when peers made racist comments about African Americans, and now feel a sense of shame, like instant internalized racism, that brings up feelings of guilt and pain.

From here Cameron and Connor's racial awareness journeys diverge. Cameron becomes interested in biracial identity, while Connor dives into genealogy research with his father, and studies slavery, Jim Crow, Historically Black Colleges and Universities, and the Tuskegee Airmen.

Cameron asks her mother, "So, like am I black now?" (100) and Patricia explains the one-drop rule but points out that Tiger Woods is the modern-day challenger to that practice. She assures Cameron that she can identify as biracial since she's "black *too*, not black *period*." (100) Cameron then starts to research multiracial people on the Internet, and the reader is bombarded with lists of biracial celebrity names, current and historical. Cameron's desire to find others like herself parallels the activism and scholarship of mixed race studies that recognizes the importance of visibility as a starting point of validation. From this point on, the author's approach to educating Cameron and the reader about multiracial identity is heavy-handed. Despite this pedantic tone, Cameron's journey is authentically complicated, shaped by friends, teachers, and community. Her simplistic questions and need to find people like herself is another sign that as a white person she didn't need to look for mirrors: they are ubiquitous. Having found a host of notable biracials online she is comforted that she is not an anomaly or a freak, she is prepared to come out to her friends.

It is in the reactions of Cameron's peers that the complexity of how people view mixed race identity is explored. They are refreshingly free of judgment and amusingly candid, albeit without any context or critical analysis. One friend believes in discrete racial categories and dismisses biraciality altogether. Another believes that phenotype determines racial identity, and yet another that Cameron should start identifying as black because it is "cool." (105) To this another friend counters that black bodies being racially profiled by police is far from cool. Granted, Cameron is not likely to be racially profiled as black and she has never experienced racial prejudice. The girls do not arrive at a conclusion, and this discussion seems intended for the readers' benefit. For Cameron, it is a small part of a long and interesting journey.

Now that she is no longer white, Cameron has a racial lens where she did not have one before. This racial lens opens her eyes in many ways. At school she is acutely aware of awkward silences and sideways glances when the word 'black' is mentioned around her. People are guarded in their humor, bringing to light the ubiquity of racist jokes. She has more opportunities to pay attention to matters of race, specifically from adults in school. She learns that her guidance counselor is also biracial and grew up in the projects in the 60s. He explains that the racial discourse of that time did not include a mixed or biracial identity and that both whites and blacks rejected him. People read him as Puerto Rican, so he claimed that ethnicity although it left him feeling "erased and untethered." (112) With age he was able to "accept all of himself" (112) although we are not told what this means. Mr. Siciliano's empathy is encouraging, and Cameron releases all her feelings of confusion and fear about not knowing who she is anymore and knowing the things her friends say about black people. Siciliano advises patience and assures her that with time, she will figure things out, that she should be wary of getting caught up in aligning herself with biracial celebrities at the expense of learning about herself, and that she can call him to talk any time. Although her specific questions are unanswered (such as, if she dates a white boy will they be an interracial couple?) she is somewhat comforted by the knowledge that she has an ally and a mentor.

This conversation is followed by a pedantic but relevant and believable class discussion about race in America led by their cool and progressive Harvard Ph.D. teacher, Sage Brown. She introduces the concept of race being a social construct, using Malcolm X as an example. The students' comments reflect their own lives and experiences with being categorized, and span a range of views on skin color, ethnicity, religion, immigration, and humanity. In *Off-Color* a variety of authentic teenage voices share contemporary perspectives on race with equal weight. Readers will find both mirrors and windows, and come away with much to think about. Cameron is emboldened by this opportunity and speaks up about her own mixed race identity. Sage silences mocking laughter and validates Cameron's description of herself as both black and white rather than one or the other: "The way I see it, 1 and 1 is 2, not 1. So that makes me two things, not one." (118) Sage's affirmation gives Cameron strength amidst her internal flux, and ultimately Cameron is well on her way to developing a biracial identity that involves learning more about African American history and a little about white privilege.

Connor's research takes him up a steep learning curve. Having known very little about African American history before this family secret was revealed, he now knows a great deal more. His father's DNA test results reveal his mitochondrial connection to six parts of the globe, leading Connor to suddenly feel like "a citizen of the world" (75). He wants to tell everyone but is wary. Like Cameron, his new racial lens makes him more aware of the racist microaggressions that permeate his school. It is worth noting that the only change in both these characters' lives is in their personal knowledge, not in the ways the world treats them.

In order to satisfy his hunger to know about his new self, Connor writes an honors thesis about the Tuskegee Airmen, highlighting their heroism in the face of virulent institutional racism within the armed forces and in society at large. This part of the book is intended to educate the readership. Ultimately, what it means to Connor and his family is that they have a new recognition of racial injustice around them. Connor does not identify as biracial or multiracial, but feels proud of his black grandfather. His transformation is that he is "both the same, and different" (117)–different in that his perspective has changed and prompts him to ask "Hey, what about the people of color?" (117)

Off-Color ends with the promise of a happy multicultural life for Cameron in a racially diverse context and a secure sense of her biracial self. *American Ace*, on the other hand, moves Connor's gaze from the self to the larger world. As such, *American Ace* offers an unusual perspective in the current corpus of multiracial children's literature, which is that racial awareness needs to start with the self, but not end there. It must extend beyond knowing who one is and where one came from, to recognizing difference and the injustice based on difference that exists everywhere.

Learning from Elders

Another type of multiracial awareness depicted in several contemporary fiction novels involves protagonists having to learn about their culture in order to realize their complete selves. Typically, this means learning about their nonwhite heritage in terms of customs, traditions and a smattering of salient vocabulary terms. There is an element of celebratory multiculturalism to these stories; they are engaging, affirming, and the characters are well-developed in plots that will appeal to a wide range of readers. Power and prejudice are minimal if not absent altogether in the construction of these multiracial experiences. Unlike Missing Half stories, these do not tell of inherent feelings of loss or disconnection. In fact, the protagonists often don't know what they have missed until they are presented a chance to learn about it. Biracial readers will find mirrors that reflect positively the cultural elements they recognize, and perhaps, new information that fills gaps in their knowledge. As windows, these books include sufficient universal elements to enable "outsider" readers to learn about lives that are simultaneously different from and similar to their own. A recurring trope in some of the more interesting literary depictions of multiracial experiences is of protagonists connecting with grandparents who take the time to teach them about their culture in ways that their too-busy parents have not. Through the process of learning about history and traditions, the protagonists in these novels emerge confident and strong, knowledgeable about many fine attributes of their heritage.[4] Stories in which protagonists learn from their grandparents have an instructional feel to them, as if the point is to teach the readers about Mexican, Japanese, Navajo, Jewish, etc. cultures. As such they should be read critically, with an awareness that to read texts as representative can be essentializing, that authenticity must always be examined, and that these are but single, fictional renditions of fictional characters' lives. On the other hand, the importance of readers recognizing themselves or their families in affirming depictions cannot be underestimated. The novels described below are just two examples of biracial identity construction: by learning from elders.

In *What the Moon Saw* (Resau 2006), sixteen-year-old Clara's voyage of self-discovery takes her to the jungles of Oaxaca where she spends the summer with her paternal grandparents. Prior to this, Clara understood herself to be Mexican because she is fluent in Spanish, her father is Mexican, and everyone around her reads her as such. An unexpected invitation to visit from her grandparents in Oaxaca sparks curiosity about her father's family and her own heritage. All Clara knows about him is that he came to the U.S. illegally, married his (white) English tutor and started his own landscaping business in suburban Maryland. His reticence to talk about his family and his emotional reaction to the invitation indicate painful, unresolved feelings that Clara forces him to face later in the novel. At this point all he can tell her is that leaving his parents when he was a teenager was extremely hard and that thinking about them would have prevented him from working hard, learning English and taking care of his wife and children. Clara has difficulty with the fact that her father came to the U.S. illegally and prefers not to think about it even though she knows it is part of who they are as a family.

Clara is artistic, levelheaded, and insightful. She is set apart from conventional teenagers by a restlessness that she can't explain and that cannot be settled by a trip to the mall or interest in the popular boys. She is fluent in Spanish and only mildly discomfited by people's comments about her racial identity. Her family is loving, stable and supportive of her desire to take this long trip alone.

Clara and her grandparents quickly become close. She learns their stories and gets to know people in their village, absorbing histories, experiences and attitudes that deeply challenge her (and the reader's) stereotypes of rural Mexican life. Clara's story is interspersed with Abuelita's narratives about growing up working in the home of a rich doña who mistreated her, and learning that she had the powers of a *curandera*. As an *indigena* she was without agency, that is, until she tapped into her powers. This part of the novel occasionally feels contrived, as if it is the author's way of fictionalizing her anthropological knowledge of Oaxaca. Nevertheless, the stories are intended for Clara to understand her origins, and for the reader to learn about a part of Mexico that is not often depicted in children's literature. Abuelita shows Clara how to make healing potions and Clara even helps her heal a baby who was stung by a scorpion. This moment is something of an epiphany for Clara: she connects with the baby on a metaphysical level, visualizing her pain and replacing it with calm.

In some ways this is a "return-to-my-roots" story in which Clara has to come to Mexico to learn about who she is. She realizes that her father's silence about his family is because he could not reconcile homesickness with forging ahead with his new life in the U.S. She is also forced to confront her own shame about the fact that he came illegally. Like him, she had chosen to avoid thinking or talking about those difficult experiences. *What the Moon Saw* ends with Clara taking a hiking trip with her father. We can infer from their conversation that Clara's new understanding of her father's early life has broken some barriers. He resumes contact with his parents and reunion trips are planned. The issue of mixed-race identity is not a focal point of the story in the recognizable way it is in most novels, and it could be argued that Clara learns to identify more singularly as Mexican than as biracial. There are moments when plot twists are overly dramatic and filled with magic, smoke, healing poultices, animal spirits and visions; all painfully stereotypical. Clara's new identity as a healer, learned and inherited from her grandmother gives her a strong sense of pride and purpose, and validates earlier feelings of detachment from her peers in a positive way. The final paragraph shows her pulling on imaginary spiderwebs that connect her to the earth and plants in the woods in Maryland even as they connect her with the waterfall and people in the Oaxacan village. It is a connection "as real as the moon's force on the oceans," (252) and one in which identity is rooted in human connections over centuries.

The theme of identity as part of connecting with people underpins Lin O'Neil's experience in *Hiroshima Dreams* (Easton 2007). Readers get to know Lin as she changes from a shy five-year-old into a thoughtful, observant teenager. This is a gentle *bildungsroman* that does not need calamity to spur self-realization. Instead, Lin's journey from child to teen is guided by the wisdom and patience of her grandmother. Issues of race and culture are depicted as part of many elements of the family's life, neither more nor less important than school, work, or relationships. Lin's mother, Mayumi's marriage to an Irish-American man is posited as an act of rebellion and escape from her life in Japan, and the cause of friction between her and her mother, Obaachan. The novel begins with Obaachan's arrival from Japan and the adjustment for her and the rest of the family as she settles in for what we soon learn is the last chapter of her life.

At age five, Lin is small, shy and thoughtful. She feels different from her peers because she has no interest in trying to fit in or be conventional. At school she notices the other children who, like her, prefer to be alone, or children who seem to be hiding pain. Lin is not lonely or unhappy except when she is called on to speak in front of everyone. Her teacher understands and does not push her. Through Lin's observations we see that her passive behavior belies a very active mind, and she is to be admired rather than pitied. Being mixed race does not factor into her developing sense of self at this point. Perhaps this is because Mayumi seems to have made an effort to distance herself and her family from anything Japanese. Obaachan's presence changes this. Obaachan and Lin are drawn to each other through their appreciation of silence, nature and riddles. They form a special bond when it is clear that they share the gift of seeing into the future. Far from being magical or mystical, their visionary abilities are the result of cultivated meditation and mindfulness. Obaachan tells Lin that it is her strength that she is different "you will always swim in your own direction." (47) While Mayumi pushes Lin to fit in, her father and grandmother accept and appreciate her the way she is. Their patience enables her to find her voice and speak up when necessary, especially when she senses pain or injustice.

As she grows up, Lin is more aware of herself in relation to her peers. At one point Lin equates her shyness with the Japanese part of her heritage, but quickly interrogates that possibility: "I try to picture myself with curly red hair and blue eyes. If I looked like that, I would not be me. I would be a girl who talks loudly, like my dad does, whose eyes laugh, like his, who everyone likes." (53) Then she remembers that her sister's appearance is more Japanese and her personality is outgoing and bold. This juxtaposition feels like an interruption of a stereotype, and it is effective in reminding readers not to ascribe Lin's quiet personality to her racial identity.

Time passes and Obaachan is diagnosed with cancer. Lin has learned that she was in Hiroshima when the bomb was dropped, and there is a strong suggestion that the cancer was connected to radiation. Meanwhile, the years they spent together taught Lin to cultivate her qualities of mindfulness and observation. During her years with Obaachan Lin has learned about her Japanese heritage in the subtle integrations of traditions, history, language, but most of all, through the gentle spirituality of her grandmother. Biracial identity was not initially part of Lin's sense of self, but by the end she has transformed her timidity into quiet confidence rooted in the awareness of her heritage and it is hard to separate that from the affirmation she received from Obaachan.

Opening Doors to Multiple Constructions of Identity

The literature discussed here offers readers opportunities to consider the role of internal and external influences in the process of racial identity construction. The experiences of Robin, Lin, Brendan and Cesi showcase biracial lives in flux, pushing against narratives that essentialize multiracial experiences as fraught, conflicted or bereft, but ultimately stronger for having to claim their own agency. The most prominent way in which Awareness books can be read as counterstories (Delgado 1995)—stories that reverse the paradigm—is that the protagonists do the work of transforming their surroundings even while they are being transformed by them. We see prejudiced characters such as Mr. Tsow and Ed DeBose called to account for the harm they cause to themselves and others by harboring racist perspectives. Furthermore, their behavior is not excused as a product of their age or time. Robin and Brendan are living proof that times have changed and old prejudices must be replaced by acceptance.

In their discussion of the construction of whiteness in children's literature, Rogers and Christian (2007) ask critical questions about ways readers can understand the construction of whiteness in children's texts. The Multiracial Awareness books analyzed here offer slight opportunity for such consideration. While protagonists confront white racism in their lives, only one character—Ed DeBose—is a fully-drawn person with whom readers can connect. Others are cameos: mothers who play small, defensive roles, or unnamed bullies from whom the readers are removed. Thus, with the exception of Ed, whiteness remains uncomplicated, made visible only in the form of isolated acts of racism rather than in the operations of daily privilege. Rogers and Christian highlight the need for analysis that focuses on the discursive and social practices that shape whiteness as embedded in the construction of all racial identities. Although limited in scope, at the very least, the Awareness books featured here make whiteness visible rather than leave it unnamed.

Botelho and Rudman (2009) posit that reading texts critically for the ways they resist dominant discourses also enables us to think of our positions as readers (128). Rain, Clara, and Cesi are established as complex, tangible characters with whom readers can immediately connect. Thus, when they recognize their own limited views about their heritage, readers who share such views are gently guided to parallel realizations. Multiracial Awareness books affirm contemporary experiences without simplifying them, inviting readers—multiracial or monoracial—to be open to investigating their own identity constructions.

Notes

1 In his biographical entry on the Scholastic website, Lawrence Yep describes himself as an "outsider" who understands through his own lived experience what it means to be on social and cultural margins. http://www.scholastic.com/teachers/contributor/laurence-yep
2 For a discussion of the ways ethnic whiteness is named and operates in multiracial children's fiction, see Chapter 8, Hidden Identities: Whiteness and Passing.
3 Sundee Frazier (2010) provides a close look at racial identity construction in *The Other Half of My Heart* in which biracial twins experience their racial identities very differently. One sister presents phenotypically as white but has a deep connection to her African American history and culture. The other sister struggles less with racial identity because people read her as black or biracial and accept her as such.
4 Other books that include grandparents in significant identify-shaping roles are: *Celia's Robot, The Other Half of My Heart, Angelfish, Camo Girl, My Basmati Bat Mitzvah, Manuel and the Madman, The Last Snake Runner, Half and Half, The Blossoming Universe of Violet Diamond*. Among picturebooks: *I Love Saturdays y domingos, My Two Grandads, My Two Grannies, The Hello, Goodbye Window*, and *Take Me Out to the Yakyu,*

References

Aspinall, P. J., and Miri Song. 2013. *Mixed Race Identities*. London: Palgrave Macmillan.
Bishop, Rudine Sims. 1982. *Shadow and Substance: Afro-American Experience in Contemporary Children' Fiction*. Urbana, IL: National Council of Teachers of English.
Botelho, Maria José, and Masha Kabakow Rudman. 2009. *Critical Multicultural Analysis of Children's Literature: Mirrors, Windows, and Doors*. New York: Routledge.
Cruz, Maria Colleen. 2003. *Border Crossing: A Novel*. Houston, TX: Piñata Books.
Delgado, Richard. 1995. *Critical Race Theory: The Cutting Edge*. Philadelphia: Temple University Press.
Easton, Kelly. 2007. *Hiroshima Dreams*. New York: Dutton Children's Books.
Frazier, Sundee Tucker. 2007. *Brendan Buckley's Universe and Everything in It*. New York: Delacorte Press.
———. 2010. *The Other Half of My Heart*. New York: Delacorte Press.
Jones, Nicholas A., and Jungmiwha Bullock. 2012. *The Two or More Races Population: 2010*. Report. U.S. Census Bureau. Retrieved from https://www.census.gov/prod/cen2010/briefs/c2010br-13.pdf.
McDonald, Janet. 2007. *Off-Color*. New York: Farrar, Straus and Giroux.
Multiracial in America: Proud, Diverse and Growing in Numbers. 2015. Report. Washington, DC: Pew Research Center. Retrieved from http://www.pewsocialtrends.org/2015/06/11/multiracial-in-america/#the-size-of-the-multiracial-population/.
Nelson, Marilyn. 2016. *American Ace*. New York: Dial Books.
Resau, Laura. 2006. *What the Moon Saw: A Novel*. New York: Delacorte Press.
Rogers, Rebecca, and June Christian. 2007. "'What Could I Say?' A Critical Discourse Analysis of the Construction of Race in Children's Literature." *Race, Ethnicity and Education* 10, no. 1: 21–46.
Root, Maria P. P. Ed. 1992. *Racially Mixed People in America*. Newbury Park, CA: SAGE Publications.
Sanders, Scott Loring. 2009. *Gray Baby*. New York: Houghton Mifflin Harcourt.

Schwartz, Ellen. 2006. *Stealing Home*. Ontario: Tundra Books.
Smith, Cynthia Leitich. 2001. *Rain Is Not My Indian Name*. New York: Harper Collins.
Stewart, Pagni Michelle. 2009. "Alive and Well and Reclaiming Their Cultural Voice: Third Generation Native American Children's Literature." In. *Ethnic Literary Traditions in American Children's Literature*, edited by Michelle Pagni Stewart and Yvonne Atkinson, 44–62. New York: Palgrave.
Yep, Laurence. 2001. *Angelfish*. New York: Putnam's.

7 Voices of the Past
Multiracial Identity in Historical Fiction

With an emphasis on realism, realistic fiction—both contemporary and historical—functions to create believable situations and characters that readers can view in relation to their own lives. Fictional realism, according to David Russell (1997) is "governed by the laws of the natural world as we understand them, and intended to provide a believable verisimilitude to life as we experience it." (190) The task is greater for authors of historical fiction who aim to recreate with credibility and authenticity a world that is removed from the reality of contemporary readers. Characters, settings, plots, language, social mores, context, and myriad other details must be rendered seamlessly so that readers of historical fiction come away with a sense of knowing a different time and place. Done well, historical fiction can educate and entertain simultaneously. It is becoming increasingly common pedagogical practice to use historical fiction in classroom curricula to supplement teaching and learning about the past because of the way narrative writing by talented authors allows young readers to access distant times and places more immediately than text books or informational text. Consider the recent impact of Markus Zusak's (2005) *The Book Thief*, which is now taught in classrooms all over the country as part of the study of the Holocaust. The choices authors make in recreating and representing a slice of history can have a lasting impact on the readers' understanding of the world in which we live.

Historical fiction relies on research and facts, and also on the imagination of the writer to render the context and characters so that they are appealing and truthful. This necessarily involves taking creative liberties. Taxel (2003 cited in *Stories Matter*, Fox and Short 2003) suggests that authors of multicultural historical fiction must decide whether these liberties are taken for literary reasons, and whether or not such liberties distort history to mirror the dominant view of culture, events, people and other elements being portrayed.[1] An example of how this can happen is in the novel *The Likes of Me* (Platt 2000). The biracial character, fourteen year-old Cordy Lu is white, Chinese, and albino. All three of these traits are posited as the reason for her social isolation and emotional estrangement from her father and stepmother. A series of bizarre and disturbing events establish Cordy as so socially maladjusted that her only chance of survival or happiness lies in joining a carnival. From the mouth of young Cordy, the reader learns this reason for her unusual appearance:

> I used to wonder if it was because my mother was yellow with black hair, and my father was white with red hair, that I came out albino—without any color at all, as though all the color in my family had been used up. My hair is white and much of my face looks Oriental. Except my eyes are . . . well, they look pink, but that's because they have no color. . . I've been called Pinkie, Chinkie, Whitey, Bunny, Rare Bit, and Pale Face.
> (10)

This description is as matter-of-fact as the rest of this bizarre narrative. If Cordy is upset by the nicknames, we never see it. The racism in unquestioned; perhaps intended to be representative of the racial sentiments of the time. Nevertheless, Cordy's plight is portrayed as an inevitable consequence of *who she is*, not of the way society was. Cordy grows up without the company of other children—"I seemed to repel them," (31)—spending all her time in the woods. At one point she reflects that snakes are luckier than she is because they can shed their skin and "become someone new." (31) The literary liberties Platt took in creating Cordy this way are chilling in their adherence to ideas about socially maladjusted biracials[2] and warrants interrogation. If the intent was to create a character who stood out, simply making Cody albino *or* biracial would have been sufficient. By combining the two, it appears that Platt was invested in ensuring that no society would find her acceptable, echoing Stonequist's (1935) concern about "the peculiarities the mixed blood presents [as] a special problem for the community: what is to be his place in the social organization?" (10) The inevitable dysfunction of the biracial subject appears in several historical fiction novels discussed below.

Until the Supreme Court ruling against anti-miscegenation in 1967, twenty-nine states had laws that criminalized miscegenation. The term 'miscegenation' refers to the state of marriage, and the laws applied only to that legal institution. All twenty-nine states forbade black-white marriages, and some states included Indians, Asians and mestizos as groups forbidden from marrying whites. Some states went so far as to specify blood quantum in fractions up to 1/8 and third generation (Browning 1951). Penalties included prison time and/or heavy fines. In most states children from such unions were considered illegitimate. In an analysis of the purpose of such laws, Browning points out that a primary reason was the "desire in white groups to maintain economic and social advantages." (33) This was particularly necessary in states with larger populations of non-white people where the chances of mixed marriages were higher. According to Browning's analysis, at its highest, the number of such marriages in Boston over a twenty-four year period (1914–1938) was 0.13% of marriages involving whites, and 3.9% of marriages involving blacks. Another interesting statistic that Browning shares is that of about three thousand intermarriages in twenty-two states, four fifths involved white women marrying black men. These numbers suggest that the rigorous policing of miscegenation might be linked to an interest in policing (white) women's sexual freedoms as well as preserving white economic interests (34). Ultimately, miscegenation laws were maintained where the "social caste feeling" (34) i.e.: racism, was strong enough to warrant the creation and maintenance of legal statutes. Interracial relationships existed outside of marriage, and white male sexual dominance over black and Indian women was prevalent and known. The Loving v. Virginia decision overturned all these laws, and legally recognized unions and children. But social opinion took longer to change.

This context provides the backdrop for historical fiction that includes multiracial characters whose life experiences would necessarily have been shaped by legal and social perspectives about racial mixing. The books discussed in this chapter shed some light on the ways that authors include, avoid, or otherwise negotiate racial dynamics. The literary canons of African American, Native American, and some Latino/a authors, integrate multiracial characters as part of the complex cultural and historical narratives that involved white colonial power over individual lives and communities. Mildred Taylor's (2001), *The Land* is a superb account of the ways white privilege was secured through hypodescent and violence while black families resisted racism and built community despite tremendous odds. The protagonist, Paul Logan, is the son of a white plantation owner and a black-Indian slave. His origins are the premise of the story and a stark reminder of the impunity with which white men felt entitled to black women: "Now there were a lot of white men who fathered colored children in those days, even though the law said no white man could legally father a black child; that was in part so no child of color could inherit from his white daddy." (11) Taylor's decision to put these words in the mouth of her protagonist is reflective of a literary liberty she took: one that succinctly describes the racial tenor of the time in language that fits the character of Paul Logan. Throughout the novel Paul faces considerable difficulties stemming from the micro and macro operations of the Jim Crow south, all of which are designed to disenfranchise him and his family. Paul's light skin means that he is not always immediately read as black and therefore he is required to announce himself as a "man of color" lest he be accused of passing for white. Unlike the biracial characters in *Black Angels* (Murphy 2001), and *Say You Are my Sister* (Brady 2000), Paul is never allowed to forget about his racial identity.[3] This portrayal of a life shaped by institutionalized racism is far more historically accurate than the blasé depictions in other historical fiction novels in which passing for white is a preferable and possible option.

Historical fiction with multiracial characters serves to disrupt the misconception that multiraciality is a recent phenomenon, as post-Loving discourse might suggest. Given the vitriolic racism and accepted, institutionally-supported antagonism towards multiracial people, it is not surprising that contemporary publications about the past reflect that tone. The authors whose books are discussed in this chapter negotiate this tension with varying degrees of success.

Rejection

Given the prevalence of hostility towards interracial unions and multiracial offspring, it is contextually accurate for historical fiction to include stories of rejection and isolation. Readers can be guided to understand these texts as cultural artifacts that depict racial attitudes of the time and be encouraged to think about the ways in which attitudes have or have not changed. Among the few historical fiction books about multiracial experiences that appear repeatedly in searches, *The Likes of Me, Take Me With You* (Marsden 2010) and *Adaline Falling Star* (Osborne 2000) bear striking similarities to the In/Visibility novels discussed in Chapter 4 in the ways that multiracial identity is constructed as a literary device to establish the most abject of subjects. In/Visibility in novels of historical fiction is more closely connected to hypodescent than it is in contemporary fiction. The books are set well before Loving v. Virginia (1967), so the illegality of interracial relationships and the deep stigma of being mixed race weigh heavily on the characters. Readers are reminded of historical attitudes towards race issues and the impact on mixed race individuals. Characters are rejected by communities, and even by their own families, because their racial identity represents serious transgression of boundaries.

The Likes of Me is set in a lumber camp near Seattle in 1918. Cordelia (Cordy) Lu Hankins is the fourteen-year-old daughter of a white logger named Red Hankins, and a nameless Chinese woman who Red bought as an indentured servant and then married. As if to preclude the problem of having to represent a Chinese character, Platt conveniently disposes of her in a drowning accident before the novel opens. Furthermore, Red forbade the mother from teaching Cordy anything about her Chinese heritage, blatantly freeing the author from the responsibility of including any influence Cordy's mother might have had in her formative years. When the novel opens, Cordy's father is remarried, to a woman with no capacity to love a little mixed race albino child who is the target of cruel taunts and bullying by the people around her.

Having established Cordy as a social misfit with low self-esteem and little chance at happiness, Platt introduces the enigmatic Squirl, a new hire at the lumber camp whose momentary attention, so different from everyone else's captivates Cordy. Squirl is fascinated by Cordy: "You're so . . . strange, you're beautiful. Your eyes . . . they're dancing a jig. You're really amazing. You're almost ugly. But you're so beautiful." (48) Cordy's father spots them frolicking in the woods and warns her to stay away from the "no good half-breed." (68) Cordy takes the epithet personally and fires back: "one no-good half-breed deserves another . . . I am what you made me. Or at least *half* . . ." (68) This is the only time she defends her mixed identity, which is never mentioned again. The parents assume that Cordy and Squirl were having sex, and Squirl gets fired and leaves. Cordy is furious that the one person who noticed her has been sent away, so she runs away to Seattle to find him.

Incredibly, Cordy finds Squirl's sister, who runs a brothel in the city, and gives her a place to stay. She introduces Cordy to a Dr. Rideneour, who runs what was then known as a 'freak show.' At first Cordy resists becoming an exhibit item, but eventually gives in. She goes along with the performances and makes lots of money from in her role as "Cordelia—Daughter of the Orient, Mystic Child of the Ancients—who, by the power of her innocence and colorless eyes and the strength of her white hair, sees all, knows all and tells all." (158)

Cordy makes friends with other members of the show: a dwarf, a transvestite and several prostitutes. Events take dramatic twists and turns involving greed, murder and corruption. Ultimately the humanity of these socially marginalized characters trumps evil capitalism. Readers are never invited to criticize the systems that marginalize and exploit people. In fact, the characters' complicity in exploiting themselves reifies the idea that the "problem" of mixed race (or other unconventional) identity is inevitable and located in the subjects themselves. Furthermore, the novel suggests that multiracial people can only find companionship with other marginalized people and can never live in larger society, a state Stonequist (1935) calls "a problem of incomplete social assimilation as well as of incomplete biological amalgamation." (10) The conclusion suggests that Cordy has found a community and happiness allowing the reader to forget that she was pushed out of her home by the people who were supposed to take care of her. In this way *The Likes of Me* adheres to the Marginal Man theory suggesting that people who are atypical can only find community among other atypical people and will eventually die out.

The doomed-from-birth fate of the biracial is also borne out in *Adaline Falling Star*. Problematic depictions of (supposedly) Native American people permeate this novel, which is loosely based on the real-life frontiersman, Kit Carson. In the imagination of Mary Pope Osborne, being born mixed-blood was a child's worst fate. This is made clear on the very first page, when, at Adaline's birth, wolves howl, falling stars race across the sky and Arapaho warriors "put on red paint and did a death dance." (v) Had it not been for the presence of her father, Kit Carson, Adaline would have been put to death by her Arapaho grandfather. Her heroic father brings in the white doctor to explain to the furious grandfather that the falling stars are not the fire arrows of angry gods, but can be explained by a "special knowledge called Science," (vi) and the baby is allowed to live. This is the first of many instances in which Native knowledge is corrected by wise white men. Osborne makes no mention of Carson's long history of decimating Native populations and portrays him as an adventurous man of the times. Nor does Adaline's mother have a role in the story except as a wistful memory.

In the Author's Note, Osborne writes that she had read that Kit Carson had married an Arapaho woman with whom he had a daughter named Adaline, described by a historian as being a "wild girl." (iii) Feeling that the girl had been misrepresented, Osborne took it upon herself to set the record straight. Admitting that hardly anything is known about the real Adaline and that this story is entirely fictional, Osborne distances herself from her own creation with these words: "Soon a fictional Adaline was born and she provoked this imagined story." (iii) Reviewers describe the novel as being about self-discovery and realization of "true" identity that sheds light on the racist attitudes towards American Indians at the time, but it is hard to separate the racism of the white characters from the racist choices of the author.

The novel is told in the first person, inviting the reader to identify with Adaline. For most of the book, however, Adaline is silent, having vowed not to speak to her cruel relatives. Although this is presented as an act of resistance, the literal silencing of an Indian character by a white author weighs heavily in the realm of Native lives too often depicted by white authors. Thus the narrative is in the form of Adaline's thoughts, and the only sounds she makes are whoops and grunts. The story opens with her birth and then skips ahead eleven years. Carson returns from an expedition one day to find Adaline guarding her mother's dying body from wolves surrounding the teepee while her grandfather beats his tom-toms in the distance. As in the birth scene, the Arapaho are depicted as ignorant and foolish while the white man comes to the rescue. Carson takes Adaline to St. Louis to leave her in the care of his cousin Silas. It is immediately apparent that he has never mentioned his Arapaho wife to his family, and the shock is apparent on their faces when they see Adaline. She too is horrified, but only momentarily, and rather than critique Carson for this negligence, the reader is guided to view him through Adaline, as innocently unaware of the possibility that Silas would mistreat Adaline. After Carson leaves, Silas introduces Adaline to her new schoolmates with these words:

> Boys and girls, this is Adaline Carson. She's a mute, and none too smart, and I'm sorry to say that she has the devilish mixture of white and Indian blood. She's going to be working for us, so I ask you to kindly show her your Christian love. But always keep an eye out for her because she is and always will be part savage.
>
> (4–5)

Adaline is forced to work as a servant at Silas' house (with another servant girl who is Indian and Mexican). She decides to pretend she is mute in order to minimize interaction and because she fears her sassy talk will get her into trouble. Meanwhile she lingers in doorways, eavesdropping on conversations in which adults speak of "dirty Injuns," scalping, fleas, savages, and other racist fears. The taunts are all focused on Adaline being Indian and half-blood. Osborne clearly intends to reveal the family's racist cruelty, but in imagining Adaline's responses she reinforces racist notions about Native peoples. Adaline never speaks a word, nor does she show resistance in her behavior, and in this she comes off as a passive, powerless captive.[4] Furthermore, when she can bear the taunting no more, she lets out "bloodcurdling whoops," (17) leaps and chases, bares her teeth, snaps like a wolf, narrows her eyes and curls her lip, and dances "on the grass like a goat," (48) and in a moment of intense grief, slashes her body with a knife and slices off her hair. She has nightmares of a scalping she saw in the woods, and dreams of flying like a crow. Adaline's memories of living with her Arapaho kin are also of violence between tribes—poisoned arrows and senseless murders of sleeping innocents with no context. These images combine to reinforce all possible stereotypes of 'savage Indians.' Since the narrative does not provide any other images of Native Americans, readers have nothing with which to counter these depictions.

Thus, abandoned by her father, rejected by everyone around her, Adaline spends much of her time in her head, reliving memories, recalling conversations. Many of these are ones in which she asks her mother and father who she is. "What am I? What?" she demands of her father. "I can't tell you what you are. You're the one who's got to find that out." (20) Her mother's response is just as evasive "You cannot answer that question inside a house that does not love you, Falling Star. Ask your question to the fresh morning air." (21)

Unable to endure the racist cruelty around her, and longing to find her father and her identity, Adeline runs away into the wilderness. During the course of an adventurous sojourn in the outdoors, Adaline befriends a stray dog. He is described as an "ugly mongrel," (81) so it is no wonder he is alone. Heavy-handed parallels are drawn between girl and dog—"we two mongrels" (116)—who become inseparable. Adaline survives in the wilderness by drawing on skills (generic "Indian" abilities to hunt and fish) she supposedly learned while living with her Arapaho family. She narrowly escapes death when her father appears out of nowhere and rescues her. His abandonment is explained away with more heroism, and Adaline and the dog are assured of a happy life with him on a ranch in New Mexico. The novel ends with Adaline reflecting on her newfound happiness, resolved to spend her life talking about her mother and father, grandfather and dog, and all their adventures to anyone who will listen. Her alignment with a mongrel dog instills self-confidence and pride, "we're a match; we're both mongrels . . . I love him for his mix and he loves me for mine," (168) and so readers are left dubiously optimistic that when all else fails, mixed race people can find companionship with stray animals.

Mary Pope Osborne is a well-known and prolific author. Her *Magic Tree House* series is extremely popular among young readers. Furthermore,

Osborne's historical fiction has a niche in the My America series that is found in classrooms and libraries all over the country. *Adaline Falling Star* is one of her many historical fiction novels that is part of the Accelerated Reader, and Scholastic Reading Counts literacy programs. Her problematic portrayal of Native Americans is well known in scholarly realms, yet her popularity among publishers such as Scholastic ensures that her books are available and supported with teaching guides and resources.[5] Stewart (2013) reminds us that depictions of Native peoples in literature and film consistently recreate recognizable images, stereotypes, that serve a function of upholding a mythical rendition of a gruesome time in U.S. history. *Adaline Falling Star* maintains the idea that multiracial people are inherently lost and constantly seeking home which they can only find on the margins (with mongrel dogs) or in the protection of a patriarchal white savior.

Children of War

War brings people from different places into contact; often intimate contact that flouts social and cultural norms with impunity.[6] Antimiscegenation laws in the U.S. made sexual relationships between white and nonwhite people illegal. Yet many such relationships existed and the children of these unions bore the brunt; abandoned in orphanages, rejected by both racial groups, or abandoned to worse fates. American troops stationed overseas were even less bound by U.S. laws when it came to their personal behavior, and many children were born of war-time liaisons.[7] It is well known that a legacy of the U.S. occupation of Vietnam during the war was the children of U.S. soldiers and Vietnamese women. These children came to be known as Amerasians, and one fictional Amerasian's life is imagined in the novel in verse, *All the Broken Pieces* (Burg 2009). Biracial children born as a result of U.S. military operations in other parts of the world are an important part of American history, with life experiences that are shaped by matters of geography, nationality, language, culture and politics that are different from the lives of U.S. multiracials. The authors of *Take Me With You* and *All the Broken Pieces* invite readers to consider the experiences of children who live at the intersection of war and race in fairly credible ways.

Take Me With You is set in Naples, Italy, just after World War II. The mixed race character is Susana who lives in a home for unwanted girls. It is explained to her that she is part *nero*, her father likely being an American GI. She is the only dark skinned, dark haired girl in the home and Sunday visitors (potential parents) make it clear that they prefer the pretty blue-eyed blond girls. Susana is acutely aware of how her appearance sets her apart: "When the girls were being nice, they said she was the color of *cappuccino*. When they were mean, they said her skin was the color of unwashed brown potatoes." (4) To make matters worse, Susana has never seen another *nero*, only read about them as cannibals in *Robinson Crusoe*. Her low self-esteem and loneliness run deep. She knows that only dark-skinned parents will adopt someone like her and the likelihood of that happening is small:

> She wanted someone to love her for who she was. She wanted a parent to come looking for a dark child. Only a dark parent would want her. The people of Naples were browner than those of the north, but no Italian had skin as dark as hers.
>
> (16)

Miraculously, Susana's father appears. He is indeed an African American soldier and she is shocked at how dark his skin is. They spend some time together while he is stationed in Naples and as Susana grows to like him, their physical resemblance pleases her and she learns to like her own reflection for the first time in her life. Her father tells her that she looks like her mother, who was a beautiful woman with olive skin and dark curly hair. This validation in appearance shared with both parents is more than Susana could have hoped for. Unfortunately, in keeping with the stereotype of interracial relationships, Susana is the result of a one-night stand. This might not be surprising given the context, but in conjunction with all the other accidental mixed race births in this body of literature, works to normalize the anomaly of long-term interracial relationships and inevitable abandonment of multiracial children.

At the end Susana's future is unclear. Her father shows her pictures of his parents and siblings, but does not say anything about taking her home. It is implied that his work in the U.S. Navy will keep him in Naples for a while and that they will continue to develop their relationship, but nothing more. Given that America in the 1950s was a hostile place for African Americans and mixed race people, we might wonder how Susana would fare if he brought her home. Furthermore, how would his family react to him bringing home a biracial child from a one-night stand? Ultimately *Take Me With You* attempts to give voice to the stories of girls in that state of abandonment—one of the many sad consequences of war. Being an orphan is terrible. For a mixed race orphan the odds are seriously stacked against future happiness.

All the Broken Pieces is a novel in verse set in 1977. It is a deeply-moving story of the myriad ways in which the Vietnam War changed the lives of many people. *All the Broken Pieces* received starred reviews for its content and literary quality. Burg successfully weaves together the lives of adults and children, with ten-year-old Matt Pin as the thread that connects them. The story begins two years after Matt was airlifted from Vietnam and adopted by white American parents. His biracial identity is pivotal in a symbolic role as an outcome of the Vietnam War and the associations that carries for himself and others.

Matt identifies and is marked as Vietnamese rather than biracial. He is bitter about his white father who he believes abandoned him and his mother.

His anger is expressed right at the start, when he vows never to speak his father's name, "Though forever I carry his blood." (1) Matt has memories of his biological mother and a half-brother who was badly injured by a land mine. Matt was taking care of his little brother when the accident occurred and he blames himself. He has nightmares about the war and will not speak about it. His adoptive parents make an effort for him to stay connected to his Vietnamese heritage by taking him to cultural classes at the adoption agency where he makes dragons and lanterns and feels disconnected from everything he is taught there about Vietnam. Here again, he feels tainted by the legacy of his father that renders him different from other Vietnamese children: "Still, I am different. My face is part American." (24)

Matt's identity is shaped by memories of the family he left behind, and learning what it means to be Vietnamese in America in the 1980s. He is literally between worlds. Rob, a boy at school taunts him with racial epithets and blames Matt for the death of his own brother (a soldier in Vietnam). Matt is understandably withdrawn; wracked by the guilt he feels for his injured brother, the pain caused by his mother's betrayal in sending him away, and an inability to trust the love of his new family even though he wants to.

Recognizing Matt's inner turmoil, his parents and their friend Jeff, a war veteran, suggest that he attend Veteran Voices meetings where they hope he will be able to talk about his unspoken fears with people who are familiar with war. It is here that his biracial identity becomes instrumental in bridging past and present. Matt's Vietnamese features remind the veterans of the friendships and relationships they formed during the war, and his whiteness reminds them of children some of them (possibly) fathered. In an effort to assuage the complex guilt that the veterans feel, Jeff makes a speech about how if Matt's mother and other Vietnamese mothers could beg soldiers to take their children and trusted them, they must have done something good. This is a little farfetched, but it serves the purpose, which is to redirect the men's thoughts away from the horror in their heads towards something positive. It also casts Matt as the embodiment of that hope and humanity.

All the Broken Pieces is a critique of war, but for once this multiracial child is not cast as the unfortunate, accidental victim, but as opportunity that can come from tragedy. At school Matt and Rob have to face their demons together. Having spent time with the veterans and learned how the war damaged their lives, Matt develops empathy for Rob. He tells Rob the story of his brother's mine accident, articulating details he has never spoken of before. The realization that they share pain caused by the same war puts an end to Rob's racist taunts and we sense that they may become friends. Once again the mixed race subject's body is the sight of emotional baggage for other people, but readers may recognize that he is not alone in this conflict. The primary characters are all complicated. Rob's anger is understandable even if his racist attitude is inexcusable. Matt's father feels guilty that he went to medical school instead of Vietnam, causing Matt to wonder if his adoption is an effort to assuage that guilt—which it may well be. His mother is sad because she knows he misses his biological mother and feels she can't reach him. And while Matt is tortured by guilt about his brother in Vietnam, he adores his new adoptive brother with a fierceness that surprises them both. Eventually Matt talks to his parents about his nightmares and his fear that they won't love him completely. Everyone's emotional cards are on the table and the ending is an optimistic one. Biracial identity is never mentioned again, and we are left with the sense that when Matt will always view himself as Vietnamese, and when he encounters racism again, he will be able to draw on the love of his friends and family to respond appropriately, rather than withdraw in self-hatred. It is realistic that none of the issues are completely resolved: time will do the work of healing to the extent that it is possible.

Finding Home

In a heartwarming scene at the end of *Stealing Home* (Schwartz 2006), young Joey Sexton sobs "'Yes, Zeyda . . . I'll come home.'" (206) He is speaking of home as a physical place as well as an emotional one. The concept of "home" as Reimer (2011) reminds us, is almost ubiquitous children's texts, and no less so in multiracial children's fiction. Home takes a material and an emotional form–literally the dwelling place where one resides, and metaphorically the abstract space where people and associations create a sense of belonging. Some of the contemporary fiction discussed in other parts of this book feature protagonists who physically move from and between homes: Celia shuttles between parents' homes and eventually moves from Los Angeles to Napa; D Foster moves between foster homes and envies the stability of her friends' lives; Kai's home is destroyed by a tsunami and he is forced to recreate a new one with different people. Naomi, Kai, Jace, Clara, and Mark have to leave home to find it, while others, Tess, Rain, Ema have just to look a little more closely to see that home is all around them. For multiracial characters, home is split or doubled by the fact of their racial heritage.

This theme is evident in historical fiction as well. The finding, claiming, recreating, or transforming of home provides a framework through which readers can share the experiences of three very different multiracial protagonists in historical fiction. Richard Peck and Margarita Engle have won numerous awards in the genre, and Ellen Schwartz's books have received starred reviews. Their works are united here for the unique ways in which they strategically integrate multiracial protagonists to shed light on important times and places. All three novels include protagonists who negotiate their identity with believable agency and courage in contexts of tremendous odds. Their stories defy stereotypes of an inherent dissonance in biracial subjects who can never find home. Instead they shed light on racist social and legal institutions that operate to create that dissonance in people. Furthermore,

The River Between Us (Peck 2003), *Lion Island: Cuba's Warrior of Words* (Engle 2016), and *Stealing Home* (Schwartz 2006) connect readers with times and places rarely included in children's literature—unique windows into different eras.

The River Between Us comes at the issue of mixed race identity from an oblique angle that makes it the focal point of the novel, seamlessly integrated with many other themes. As with all of Richard Peck's historical fiction, readers are provided a nuanced, well-crafted literary look into a lesser-known aspect of American society. The story begins in 1916 with the young narrator, Howard Hutchings setting off with his father and brothers to visit his paternal grandparents in Grand Tower, southern Illinois. Upon their arrival, the narrative shifts to the voice of Howards' grandmother, Tilly Pruitt, telling the story of the arrival of Calinda and Delphine Duval, two young women from New Orleans. This part of the story takes place in Grand Tower, Illinois, in 1861, as the Civil War looms closer.

Delphine and Calinda arrive on a riverboat from New Orleans, displaced from their home by the advent of the war and resultant freeing of slaves. Later, readers learn that the end of slavery disrupted a long-established way of life unique to New Orleans, but the story is told from Tilly's perspective, so like her, readers are simply mystified by these astonishing, beautiful women. We also learn much later on, that Delphine is only fifteen when she arrives, which makes her fortitude and cognizance of society even more impressive. The Duval sisters are *gens de couleur*—free people of color, but Tilly has no knowledge of this, or even of the possibility of mixed race people. To her Delphine is simply exotic, an enigma with dark curly hair, "eyes large and darkly fringed" and "a mouth too dark to be as nature intended." (35) Tilly assumes that Calinda must be Delphine's slave since her complexion is darker. Perhaps out of maternal concern, or sheer kindness, Mrs. Pruitt offers the girls her home. They embrace their new surroundings with aplomb, stunning everyone with their beautiful clothes, spicy food, French-tinged accents and forthright manners. Noah quickly falls in love with Delphine, Cass and Calinda bond silently over their shared understanding of the occult, and Tilly and Mrs. Pruitt's circumscribed lives open up in ways they could never have imagined.

For the months that Delphine and Calinda live with the Pruitts, nothing is said about them being colored or black or Creole. With characteristic terseness, no one asks and nothing is offered. Tilly's only awareness of prevalent racial issues is that there was a law in effect that forbade black people from living in Illinois, but it was widely ignored and the black people who were there were free. Thus the sisters are in a precarious position that only they, and perhaps Mrs. Pruitt, understand. Delphine hangs a portrait of a white man above her bed, and later explains to Tilly that he is her father "of an ancient French family," (56) owner of luxurious mansions hung with Spanish moss. This may be a strategic move on Delphine's part and could be read as her effort to pass as white. If that is her intent, she does not need to try very hard as the ignorance of the townspeople make it simple for her to do so with minimal effort.[8] When the situation requires it, and mutual trust has been established between the Duvals and the Pruitts, Delphine shares everything about their former life. Meanwhile, the physical and social isolation that Mrs. Pruitt has established to protect her family from gossip makes their home an ideal place for the sisters.

The Duvals and Pruitts are the author's vehicle for writing about a complicated time and place. Descriptive language and compelling characterization make life in Grand Tower, Illinois vividly real. The Duvals were displaced from the only home they ever knew, and concern about the impact of southern cessation on the riverboat trade that sustains the settlement makes everyone tense. Noah is swept up in the fervor and joins the army.

The imminent war makes everyone suspicious. It also brings out surprising courage in some people. A group of women from town come to the Pruitt home to express their disapproval about the guests. They believe Delphine is a spy from the south. They call her "the white one" (77) and object to her being southern and attracting the attention of the men in the town. Mrs. Pruitt defends her decision to host the sisters and gets rid of the town women. She and Tilly are surprised at her boldness and Mrs. Pruitt acknowledges that it is because of Delphine's own outspokenness and confidence that she spoke up. Delphine, she decides, has "put some starch in my spine." (80) Delphine has this effect on Tilly and Dr. Hutchings too. Her uninhibited worldview and mild disdain for social mores slowly and subtly influences these otherwise provincial characters. Gradually, Delphine and Calinda transform their new home, essentially making it their own, by way of food, stories, attention to personal appearance, music and dance. Calinda and Cass share powers of prophecy and prediction. When Noah has to be rescued from the army camp Delphine rises beyond anyone's expectations. She and Tilly travel to the army camp in Cairo to find Noah. Having shared snippets of her New Orleans life with Tilly on the journey, she seems to have laid the groundwork to tell all. In Cairo, Delphine is confronted by a racist Irish guesthouse proprietor who makes a derogatory comment. This racist outburst is impetus for Delphine to explain the race and class dynamics between the Irish and the *gens de couleur*, the free people of color, in New Orleans. Delphine is very knowledgeable about the history of her people and their position in that city, which is simultaneously accepted and abhorred. Mrs. Hanrahan's attitude, she understands, is typical of the Irish immigrants who arrived in Louisiana poor and hungry and were exploited by wealthier residents even though they were white. Delphine is part of an old and established population responsible for the vibrancy of New Orleans. She sums up the fragility of the system very effectively:

'We were there before them. Our roots are in New Orleans mud. We people of color make the city work. It is like no other place because of us. We were there from the earliest times. They despise us for our ease, for our silken lives. They don't understand how people of color can be free . . . almost free . . . we free people of color live on a kind of island, lapped by a sea of slavery. Beyond that sea is this territory up here.'

(127–128)

Later Delphine explains what it was like to live under the system of *placage*, replete with wealth and luxury, but always aware of being inferior to the white families of their male protectors. Delphine grew up knowing that her survival lay in being the mistress of a white man, as her mother and grandmother were. She indicates that this was preferable even to marrying a quadroon like herself. Different standards for males enabled her brother to be sent to France where "he will become a Frenchman where people do not ask questions." (139) Between Delphine's description and the Author's Note, Peck provides a vivid picture of an intensely patriarchal system that was closely bound up in race and class interests. The Civil War left the free women of color in limbo, and many, like Delphine, were compelled to flee north and pass for white if necessary. Others, like Calinda, who were darker skinned, moved to California where they could live in relative anonymity in a more multicultural environment.

Eventually, Delphine makes Grand Tower her home; but a home on her own terms. The narrative switches back to 1916 and the second narrator, Howard, learns that Delphine is in fact, his grandmother. Adhering to the tradition that forbade her from marrying a white man, she refused to marry Noah though they lived as man and wife, and had a son: Howard's father. Howard is momentarily surprised by this news. His admiration and respect for his father having been established, and his own racial identity being completely secure, it is easy for Howard to claim to be proud of his heritage, of being Delphine and Noah's grandson, of passing on the legacy one day to his own child "with enormous violet eyes." (158)

Bold, charismatic and beautiful, Delphine cuts a striking figure who brings life and courage to the dull lives of the Pruitts. At the same time, her personal losses are tremendous. The war forces her to leave her mother and home in New Orleans, and invent a new identity in unfamiliar territory at a young age. Her sister Calinda, "too dark to pass" (152) left for California because of the risk her presence posed to Delphine. She had to pretend her child was not her own, and never knew her grandsons until that single summer visit when she was at the end of her life. Howard's mother's aloofness towards her husbands' family now makes sense; her racism kept the family apart. Like many people who had to pass as white in order to survive, Delphine had to give up everything to keep anything. In this she is reminiscent of the tragic mulatta figure. But tragedy is part of her life, not the entirety of it. Tilly, Dr. Hutchings, Noah and Delphine lived together as a family—a very unconventional family bound by secrets and loyalty and shared convictions about humanity. *The River Between Us* adds to the body of literature that tells the stories of people who resisted convention, social mores, religion and law, in the face of great danger. It shows how at a time when race relations were so deeply fraught with distrust and hostility, there were people like the Pruitts and Duvals, from completely disparate worlds, who could create homes and family when genetic ones were severed.

The concept of home is deeply rooted in texts about "settler societies" (Bradford 2007, 124) when displacement by colonial powers is closely tied to issues of identity. Bradford explicates the way children's literature depicts the intersections of identity construction in white colonial and Maori contexts. Carolyn Dunn (2006) reminds us that the relocation and dislocation of Native peoples from their lands has resulted in a fracturing of identity that so closely relies on a sense of home. In other colonial contexts, complex negotiations of power are inevitable and often literally connected to home in terms of land and occupation. So it is in *Lion Island*, the partly-fictionalized account of the early life of Antonio Chuffat. When the novel opens, Antonio is twelve years old, studying Spanish in Havana. The story sets the groundwork for his career as a labor activist and influential official in the newly-independent Cuban administration. In this remarkable historical novel in verse, Antonio uses his position as an Afro-Chinese Cuban to transform not only himself, but the lives of countless others.

Lion Island is set in Spanish-controlled Cuba between 1871 and 1874 when a treaty with China brought thousands of Chinese men to work on plantations. The men were forced to sign one eight-year contract after another, essentially making them powerless indentured workers. Many paired with or married Afro-Cuban women who were slaves or also indentured, forming blended Afro-Chinese-Cuban communities that merged language, traditions and values from each culture. Antonio Chuffat's father was a freed Chinese indentured worker and his mother was Afro-Cuban. When the novel opens, his father has sent him to Havana to perfect his Spanish. Antonio works for Señor Lam, carrying messages between Spanish and Chinese diplomats and officials. Antonio's Spanish and Chinese language skills make him an invaluable go-between, and afford him access to the political goings-on that fuel his activism. On one delivery mission he meets Wing, the second primary character in *Lion Island*. Wing and his twin sister, Fan, are Chinese American refugees from Los Angeles. Their family fled the anti-Asian mass lynchings in the mid 1870s. Wing and Fan's mother was white–a detail that matters because their integrated family was the target of anger from both sides when the violence erupted. It also meant that they were educated in English and Chinese. Multiracial identity is not the focus of this story, but it is the reason it exists. Antonio's Afro-Cuban-Chinese background enables him to relate to the similar ways in which all three communities (black, indigenous, and Chinese) were subject to Spanish colonial oppression. The same sense of injustice enflames Wing, who eventually joins a band of Chinese Cuban rebel fighters. Antonio, Wing and Fan band together to help Antonio's father hide and transport fleeing Chinese indentured workers. Their courage is powered by a personal knowledge of race-based economic policies and strategic use of their language skills and ability to cross social boundaries. *Lion Island* is rare among publications for children for the way Engle makes the dark truths of colonial history accessible to young readers without sugarcoating them. Antonio, Wing and Fan use their positions on the multiracial margins to effect social change. Antonio and Wing's comradeship is based on a shared vision of changing an oppressive system. Wing contributes his knowledge of the underground railroad as a successful form of resistance, and together with Fan, they hide runaways in the shadows of her theater rooms, using costumes and masks as disguises. Their work makes them feel useful, despite the danger. Eventually, they go separate ways, making their homes among like-minded people. Antonio works with his father to document the personal stories of hundreds of indentured workers all over the island, essentially transforming the future of his island home. Their stories, made public, are the stuff of quiet revolution, resulting in the Chinese government's withdrawal from the indentured worker treaty with Spain, which in turn, weakens Spain's colonial hold. Engle's well-crafted narrative integrates so many important issues that multiracial identity is just one of many on which *Lion Island* sheds light.

Delphine and Antonio were able to make homes where none existed before because of their inner fortitude and determination, but also because they spent their early lives in relatively secure contexts. Delphine's was a life of fragile privilege that granted her agency within certain social circles while denying it in others. Antonio had the advantage of being educated and bilingual, again within a narrow niche. The protagonist of *Stealing Home*, nine-year-old Joey Sexton, starts life in a significantly more precarious situation—orphaned—but no less courageous.

The novel begins in the Bronx, NY, in 1947 with a series of shocks for the young protagonist. Joey's mother died of a drug overdose, and he lives with a neighbor while a social worker searches for other family members. Her investigation reveals that Joey's father was also dead and had been living not far away, unbeknownst to anyone. She finds his maternal grandfather, an aunt and a cousin living in Brooklyn, eager to give Joey a home. He also learns that his mother was Jewish, and had changed her name from Greenberg to Green. In a scene prior to this, readers witness Joey being tormented by the neighborhood boys for being mixed race. Thus, abandoned by his African American father, and rejected by his black peers, Joey imagines his only hope lies in the possibility of starting his new life over–as white. This idea is introduced by a mixed race friend and an adult who tell him he could easily pass. Joey's plight may be tragic, but he is not a pitiable character. Rather, intelligence, wit, vulnerability and a streak of sheer fury at the world combine to make him immediately likeable.

Upon arriving in Brooklyn he is pleased to discover that his appearance is very similar to his cousin's, his aunt's and even his grandfather's. It seems that he might fit in after all. Some people in the neighborhood, however, are not willing to let him forget that he is part black. They remember the scandal caused by this mother when she left with a black man and then had a baby. In the community, Joey is received with warmth as well as hatred. Peers and adults alike taunt him with anti-black epithets. He can defend himself against the meanest racists, but what hurts him the most is that his grandfather does not stand up for him. Joey takes this silence to mean his Zeyda is also disgusted by him and considers his mother "a disgrace" (as one of the store owners described her). Joey finds himself in the hopeless position of being rejected because of his black heritage. The option of passing precluded, Joey has to come to understand what it means to be part black and part Jewish in ways that he never had to consider before.

In his new home in a Jewish neighborhood, Joey realizes he knows nothing about his Jewish heritage. He has vague memories of his mother lighting candles, but knows nothing of the customs and traditions that are part of daily life now. His cousin Bobbie and Aunt Frieda teach him, and he is eager to learn. Meanwhile, he finds himself cautiously interested in the Brooklyn Dodgers rookie, Jackie Robinson. Thus Joey's identity is being shaped by his family at home and by Robinson in the ball park. There are no other African American influences in his life and the shared experience of racism and Robinson's strength in the face of it inspires Joey. Interestingly, despite the time period, when a mixed race identity was not part of the cultural discourse, Joey identifies as mixed rather than black. Also, the most virulent racism he experiences comes from a storeowner who hates that Joey is mixed–a symbol of racial and moral transgression reflecting prevalent attitudes towards interracial relationships at the time.

Occasionally, *Stealing Home* is more about Joey's development of his Jewish identity, than his black or mixed race identity. What saves it from joining the realm of books about conflicted mixed race characters is that Joey ultimately turns out to be surprisingly self-assured about being both black and Jewish and identifies as mixed even though that feels anachronistic for the time. Though he is faced with heart-breaking racist cruelty from adults around him, Joey stands up for himself bravely and with convincing self-confidence. Zeyde's rejection matters more than the attitudes of strangers, and it is his approval that Joey seeks.

Joey bonds with his cousin who loves baseball as much as he does, and his aunt who is loving and kind (and resembles his mother). But Joey yearns for his grandfather's approval. He is convinced that the reason the old man is nasty to him because he is part black. Eventually he learns that the situation is more complicated. Joey's mother was a rebellious teenager and her relationship with her father was always fraught after her own mother died. She became more and more adversarial and the last straw was running away with Joey's father and then becoming a drug addict. Joey's pranks remind Zeyde of his disobedient daughter and make it hard for him to love his grandson. Like every other racist character who rejected their child for being with a person of color, Zeyda's behavior is excused by circumstance or social norms.[9] Before he learns about this, Joey has no way of understanding Zeyda's hostility except as a function of racism.

Ultimately it is Aunt Frieda who is instrumental in letting Joey know he is loved and has a home. One day Zeyde spanks Joey and his cousin after they break into a ball game illegally. Frieda defends the children, especially Joey, when Zeyde threatens to send him away saying he is as troublesome as his mother had been. Frieda reminds her father that his aggressiveness was very much a part of Becky's rebellious behavior: she holds him accountable. Joey is overwhelmed at his aunt's bold defense, though the fragility of his situation is made all the more evident. She also tells him stories about his mother and her relationship with Zeyde so that he starts to understand that things were complicated even before he was born. In this way Joey learns that being biracial is *not* the reason his life has been difficult. In a final show of loyalty and love, Frieda confronts the bigoted shopkeeper when she insults Joey in the store, "'That boy, Mrs. Yanofsky, is my nephew. My sister's son. My flesh and blood . . . there is nothing shameful about him . . . nor about my sister . . . nor about my family.'" (191)

Emboldened by his aunt and a few tiny moments of kindness by Zeyde, Joey is prompted to give his grandfather a photograph of his mother thinking that he would be impressed that Joey was giving him something so cherished. But the plan backfires. Zeyde is furious and tells Joey to get out. The boy runs away to his old home in the Bronx. Zeyde comes after him and admits that Joey's departure scared him the same way Becky's had and he didn't want to lose his grandson after all. The conclusion of *Stealing Home* is a happy one. The penultimate chapter shows Zeyde taking Joey to the synagogue with him and proudly introducing him as his grandson "'Becky's boy. Isn't he the image of her?'" (209) In the final chapter we see the family going to the 1947 World Series game at Ebbet's Field wearing Dodgers caps and loudly rooting for Jackie Robinson. New-found security in a home with family that will love him for who he is leaves us with the hope that Joey will grow up with a healthy sense of self rather than inner turmoil.

Power and Agency in Multiracial Historical Fiction

Many of the most prominent voices of multicultural education (Sleeter and McLaren 1995; Nieto 2002; Banks and Banks 2010) urge educators to examine the ways power operates in society, school, curricula, classroom environments. It is through such examination that transformation of injustices can begin. In children's literature, critical analysis allows the reader to investigate operations of power in text. From inception to reception, children's literature is replete with ideological manifestations of power that communicate messages about the world that young readers absorb. Thinking critically about multiracial historical fiction, we are prompted to ask questions about why an author might have chosen to create a biracial character and what implicit ideologies are embedded in the constructions of these characters. As a whole, *The Likes of Me* can be understood as a story of people on the fringes of society: lumber camp laborers, circus entertainers, and a biracial albino protagonist who serves as a vehicle to guide the contemporary reader through this strange world. Cordy's albinism is the reason her parents cannot or will not love her, but finds her a place in the circus community. Although her plight invites our empathy, it does not invite our critique of a prejudiced society. A character with a different point of view, or an act of resistance on Cordy's part would have thrown her marginalization into relief, but the absence of any such perspective normalizes her situation, leaving readers to believe that's just the way things were. An "exotic" appearance afforded by her Asian features adds another level of anomaly that Dr. Ridenour seizes for his own financial gain when he recognizes that she will draw crowds. Cordy's willingness to go along with his plans signals her lack of agency within the only system that accepts her. Adaline, on the other hand, rejects the oppression she experiences at her uncle's home. We can understand her act of running away as an act of resistance against a society that rejects her for being half-Indian. On the other hand, placing Adaline alone in the wilderness removes the reader from the need to think about racism any further. Scenes of Adaline's attempts to rely on hunting and fishing skills supposedly learned when she lived among the Arapaho are reminiscent of the iconic ways literature, art and film position Indians as inherently able to survive in nature—"relentlessly ecological"—rather than recognizing the balance between humans and nature (Slapin, Seale, and Gonzales 1996, 20). Adaline's power exists only in her motivation to find her father, the white man who will save her. In preparation for her new life, her father tells her they will be living in New Mexico but that she will have no contact with her Arapaho family as they are all dead: "'Ain't no Arapaho livin' on Horse Creek anymore. Cholera got 'em.'" (166) This use of passive language removes any human involvement in the spread of cholera among Native peoples, and relegates the Arapaho population to the realm of "vanished" Indians. Adaline's quiet acceptance secures a passive reader's implication in the scenario. Mixed-race Adaline will presumably assimilate into her father's world and her Arapaho heritage will become the stuff of stories she will tell to "anyone who'll listen." (168)

By contrast, historical fiction such as *The River Between Us*, *Lion Island* and *Stealing Home* integrate commentary on racist social and legal systems by showing how they affected the multiracial protagonists. Delphine and Calinda Duval negotiate the racial terrain in Grand Tower by captivating the residents with their food and talents while remaining selective about revealing their black heritage. This don't ask, don't tell arrangement suits everyone. However, when Delphine is confronted by a racist, she responds with candor and courage. Tilly Pruitt's narrative voice changes from naïve awe to deep admiration, providing readers with a perspective that highlights the small but significant ways white and nonwhite people negotiated social mores about race, family, and society. Delphine and Calinda's presence transformed the Pruitt family, and together they were complicit in forming and protecting a family arrangement that was against the law. Stuart Ching (2005) makes an important distinction between multicultural children's books that include and exclude manifestations of power. Those that celebrate diversity and a common humanity fall into the realm of cultural pluralism, and those that affirm racial and cultural difference with a recognition of power in terms of equity and inequity embody "pluralism that manifests power." (132) The historical fiction about multiracial experiences described here can be read critically with a focus on exploring the degrees to which they embody multiracial pluralism and power.

Notes

1 Scholarship in multicultural children's literature examines liberties taken by authors whose writing perpetuates harmful stereotypes of people of color:
    McNair, Jonda. "The Representation of Authors and Illustrators of Color in School-Based Book Clubs." *Language Arts* 85, no. 3 (2008): 193–201.
    Chaudhri, Amina, and Nicole Schau. "Imaginary Indians: Representations of Native Americans in Scholastic Reading Club." *Children's Literature in Education* 47, no. 1 (2016): 18–35.
    Koss, Melanie D. "Diversity in Contemporary Picturebooks: A Content Analysis." *Journal of Children's Literature* 41, no. 1 (2015): 32–42.
    Stewart, Michelle Pagni. "Judging Authors by the Color of Their Skin? Quality Native American Children's Literature." *MELUS* 27, no. 2 (Summer 2002): 179–96.
2 The uncritical depiction of multiracial identity conflated with social and emotional dysfunction is similar to the same pattern discussed in Chapter 4, Multiracial In/Visibility.
3 See Chapter 8 for an analysis of the ways authors represent the experience of passing in these texts.
4 Slapin, Seale, and Gonzales (1996) write that one of the most harmful stereotypes about Native Americans in literature is the one of a passive people who collude in their own downfall, and resistance cast as senseless violence.
5 Scholastic's website provides a teaching discussion guide for *Adaline Falling Star*. Questions assume that readers trust that depictions of the Arapaho are realistic, and that the book presents a trustworthy account of white and Arapaho lives so that they can respond to questions such as: "Do you think that there is an unbridgeable gap between the science of the white folk and the spiritual beliefs of the Arapaho? Why or why not?" http://www.scholastic.com/teachers/lesson-plan/adaline-falling-star-discussion-guide
6 Although not technically set in the context of war, all the novels with Indian and white biracial characters take place at the time of westward expansion and violent colonial contact: *Crossing the Panther's Path* by Elizabeth Alder (2002), *Call Me the Canyon*, by Ann Howard Creel (2006), *Trouble at Fort La Pointe*, by Kathleen Ernst (2000), and *Battle Cry*, by Jan Neubert Schultz (2006).
7 Although exact numbers are hard to find, The Mixed Heritage Center (www.mixedheritagecenter.org) reports that there are thousands of Amerasians, children of American soldiers stationed in Korea, Japan, the Philippines, Laos, Cambodia, and Thailand.

8 Chaudhri, Amina. "Mixed Race Identity and Power in YA Fiction." *VOYA* 39, no. 2. (June 2016): 32–33.
9 *Gray Baby* by Scott Loring Sanders (2009), *Brendan Buckley's Universe and Everything In It*, by Sundee Tucker Frazier (2007), *Border Crossing* (Cruz 2003)

References

Alder, Elizabeth. 2002. *Crossing the Panther's Path*. New York: Farr Straus Giroux.
Banks, James A., and Cherry A. McGee Banks. 2010. *Multicultural Education: Issues and Perspectives*. Hoboken: Wiley and Sons.
Bradford, Clare. 2007. *Unsettling Narratives: Postcolonial Readings of Children's Literature*. Waterloo, Ontario: Wilfrid Laurier University Press.
Brady, Laurel. 2000. *Say You Are My Sister*. New York: HarperCollins Publishers.
Browning, James K. 1951. "Anti-Miscegenation Laws in the United States." *Duke Bar Journal* 1, no. 1: 26–41.
Burg, Ann E. 2009. *All the Broken Pieces: A Novel in Verse*. New York: Scholastic Press.
Ching, Stuart H. D. 2005. "Multicultural Children's Literature as an Instrument of Power." *Language Arts* 83, no. 2: 128–36.
Creel, Ann Howard. 2006. *Call Me the Canyon*. Weston: Brown Barn Books.
Dunn, Carolyn. 2006. "Playing Indian." In *Cultural Representation in Native America*, edited by Andrew Jolivétte, 139–58. Lanham: Altamira Press.
Engle, Margarita. 2016. *Lion Island: Chinese Cuba's Warrior of Words*. New York: Atheneum Books for Young Readers.
Ernst, Kathleen. 2000. *Trouble at Fort La Pointe*. Middleton: Pleasant Company Publications.
Fox, Dana L., and Kathy G. Short. 2003. *Stories Matter: The Complexity of Cultural Authenticity in Children's Literature*. Urbana, IL: National Council of Teachers of English.
Frazier, Sundee Tucker. 2007. *Brendan Buckley's Universe and Everything In It*. New York; Random House.
Marsden, Carolyn. 2010. *Take Me with You*. Somerville, MA: Candlewick Press.
Murphy, Rita. 2001. *Black Angels*. New York: Delacorte Press.
Nieto, Sonia. 2002. *Language, Culture, and Teaching: Critical Perspectives for a New Century*. Mahwah, NJ: L. Erlbaum.
Osborne, Mary Pope. 2000. *Adaline Falling Star*. New York: Scholastic Press.
Peck, Richard. 2003. *The River Between Us*. New York: Dial Books.
Platt, Randall Beth. 2000. *The Likes of Me*. New York: Delacorte Press.
Reimer, Mavis. 2011. "Home." In *Keywords for Children's Literature*, edited by Philip Nel and Lissa Paul. 106–109 New York: New York University Press.
Russell, David L. 1997. *Literature for Children: A Short Introduction*. New York: Longman.
Schultz, Neubert Jan. 2006. *Battle Cry*. Minneapolis: Carolrhoda Books.
Schwartz, Ellen. 2006. *Stealing Home*. Plattsburgh: Tundra Books of Northern New York.
Slapin, Beverly, Doris Seale, and Rosemary Gonzales. 1996. *How to Tell the Difference: A Guide to Evaluating Children's Books for Anti-Indian Bias*. Berkeley: OYATE.
Sleeter, Christine E., and Peter McLaren. 1995. *Multicultural Education, Critical Pedagogy, and the Politics of Difference*. Albany: State University of New York Press.

Stewart, Michelle Pagni. 2013. "'Counting Coup' on Children's Literature about American Indians: Louise Erdrich's Historical Fiction." *Children's Literature Association Quarterly* 38, no. 2: 215–35.
Stonequist, Everett V. 1935. "The Problem of the Marginal Man." *American Journal of Sociology* 41, no. 1: 1–12.
Taxel, Joel. 2003. "Multicultural Literature and the Politics of Reaction." In *Stories Matter: The Complexity of Cultural Authenticity in Children's Literature*, edited by Dana L. Fox and Kathy G. Short, 143–164. Urbana: National Council of Teachers of English.
Taylor, Mildred D. 2001. *The Land*. New York: Phyllis Fogelman Books.
Zusak, Markus. 2005. *The Book Thief*. New York: Alfred A. Knopf.

8 Hidden Identities
Whiteness and Passing

When Nancy Larrick critiqued the "all white world of children's literature" in 1965 she was calling attention to the acute dearth of books by nonwhite authors, and about nonwhite experiences. She was not, however, commenting on the construction of whiteness as a racial identity in the many stories containing white characters, families, heroes, and role models. As a racial identity, whiteness is unnamed and invisible. It is the default race that tends to be conflated with being American while 'other' Americans require an additional adjective: African American, Native American, Asian American, Arab American, and so on. Race and whiteness studies scholars (McIntosh 1990; Doane and Bonilla-Silva 2003; Haney-Lopez 2005; Omi and Winant 2015) have written extensively about the nuanced social and discursive manifestations of unearned white privileges that permeate every niche of society. They call attention to the ways in which race-based scholarship and social movements have failed to examine the construction of whiteness along with the construction of Other racial issues, and thereby maintain a silence, a neutrality, that downplays the role of white racial identity beyond racist acts. Feminist and anti-racism scholar and activist, Peggy McIntosh's (1990) article "White Privilege: Unpacking the Invisible Knapsack" is a timeless work that is often read in colleges, high schools and even some middle schools. In it, she lists ways in which she, as a white person, can go about her life without having to think about her identity in ways that people of color cannot. Among the "daily effects of white privilege" (np) are the assurances of knowing that she will always find people like herself represented in curricula, cultural traditions, the media; that she can flout social mores without being held representative of her entire race; that she can "worry about racism without being seen as self-interested or self-seeking;" and so on. McIntosh's list could easily be used as a rubric against which to measure the ways white literary figures (and authors and illustrators) operate with what she calls an "obliviousness about white advantage" (np) compared to the hyper-awareness with which many people of color live. Sociologist Ashley Doane (1997) describes the same concept in different language, calling the lack of white awareness of an ethnic identity "hidden" (378) because of the way it is kept in the background.

Needless to say, whiteness in children's literature is rarely named unless there is a context of racism as in (to name a few) *Brendan Buckley's Universe and Everything In It* (Frazier 2007), *Gray Baby* (Sanders 2009); and *Soldier Sister, Fly Home* (2016).[1] External white racism is something multiracial characters must accept as part of their reality, and combat with a secure sense of self, and supreme inner strength: being part white does not offer protection from racism. Some authors describe their characters' white parents as "American" (Yep 2001; Lorenzi 2012; Parry 2016) or do not racially identify them at all, so that readers must presume. The question of what it means to be part white is moot because white-non-white biracials are otherized based on their nonwhite element. In some multiracial fictional depictions, protagonists appear to live free of racial prejudice, for the most part, however, the inevitable public scrutiny of their non-white heritage is a constant reminder that they are Other.

The absence of any other markers of difference suggests a raceless and cultureless identity, an all-American identity that is essentially white. In a study with second grade students, Rebecca Rogers and Melissa Mosely (2006) observed that young children noted that characters must be white when authors did not provide any descriptive information, and based on characters' speech and actions. Complicated questions do not arise in children's literature of any multicultural stripe. Thus whiteness in multiracial children's literature is visible in two ways: as racism, or as ethnicity (Irish, Scottish, Swedish, Italian, Jewish), and critical readers might be guided to notice how whiteness is consistently rendered invisible unless associated with one of these labels.

In the research for this project I found two ways in which whiteness played a significant role in multiracial identity construction: as Scottish, and as Jewish.[2] In both these cases, the biracial protagonists try to learn about their Scottish and Jewish heritage in the ways characters in other books learned about their non-white heritage. These learning experiences have a distinctly celebratory tone. In *Half and Half* (Namioka 2003), Fiona Cheng is Chinese and Scottish, and in *The Whole Story of Half a Girl* (Hiranandani 2012), Sonia Nadhamuni is Indian and Jewish. Both characters' identities are questioned by others because they are phenotypically ambiguous. Fiona and Sonia seek information about what it means to be part Scottish and part Jewish. Here whiteness is associated through participation in cultural practices, and distanced from the power dynamics inherent to racial construction. In other words, although there are moments when Sonia and Fiona are made to feel they don't belong, those moments are fleeting and their identity-journeys do not involve thinking or learning about prejudice. Rather, they are about collecting enough cultural knowledge about their heritage so that they can feel better about themselves. Unfortunately, both books rely heavily on replicating stereotypes that readers will recognize but are not invited to critique.

Ethnic Whiteness

The terms "race" and "ethnicity" are often conflated so it is necessary to differentiate how I am using them here. In the context of analyzing the role of whiteness, I find Stuart Hall's definition useful: "the term ethnicity acknowledges the place of history, language, and culture in the construction of subjectivity and identity" (cited in Hintz and Tribunella 2013). Since whiteness as an identity in the hegemonic paradigm is typically devoid of these elements unless specified, it makes sense to refer to the explicit constructions of Scottish and Jewish identity in children's fiction as "ethnic whiteness." In the books analyzed here, whiteness is distanced from privilege and a legacy of prejudice. Instead, readers learn alongside the protagonists about customs, food, traditions and other celebratory aspects of their white heritage.

As the title announces, *Half and Half* (Namioka 2003) brings attention to an identity crisis. The cover depicts a girl divided, literally, by a line down the middle of the page. In one half she is Chinese: represented by long dark braided hair and traditional clothing. In the other half she is Scottish, indicated by her red hair and tartan hat and vest. *Half and Half* foregrounds the problem faced by many children when asked to check a racial box on a form. Eleven year-old Fiona Cheng is confounded when she is told that her application for a folk dancing class is incomplete because she did not check a box for race. The form requires that only one box be filled in. Fiona wants to choose White and Asian, but cannot, and choosing Other "would make me feel like an outsider, a weirdo who didn't belong anywhere . . . Why didn't they have a box for people like me, who were half and half?" (3) Fiona appeals to her parents who urge her to do what feels right to her. Fiona's dilemma is grounded in a political reality rarely mentioned in children's fiction; that racial identification on forms is tied to allocation of funds, "It's just that I have to be accurate . . . The recreation center has to report the number of kids they have in each race to get money from the government." (6) Fiona turns to her brother, Ron, to ask which box he chose. It turns out that he was perfectly happy choosing "other." This does not sit well with Fiona, but Ron sees his choice as a small act of resistance: "I kind of like it when they can't fit me in a box so easily." (8) Fiona, however, is more concerned with the idea of belonging, which is symbolized by the choosing of the correct box on a form. Such larger questions of group affiliation are short-lived. Ultimately Fiona's negotiation of her biracial identity focuses on whether or not she looks the part: specifically, the part of a Scottish folk dancer in the summer festival. In *Half and Half* whiteness is described in terms of Scottishness.

Even while *Half and Half* seems intended to affirm biracial heritage by exposing the ways people are undermined by social processes, it also reinforces stereotypes. Once she has resolved the matter of the application form, Fiona's identity crisis revolves around her concern that her Chinese appearance will render her unsuitable for the Scottish dance performance at the Folk Fest. She addresses this with the absurd idea that dying her hair red will make her look more Scottish (ie: less Chinese). She believes that her efforts to fit in will be successful if her appearance matches her identity (for the dance). Fiona's Scottish grandparents arrive, bringing with them the unspoken disappointment that it is Fiona, not Ron, who is carrying on the male family tradition of folk dancing. Their presence is also an opportunity for Fiona and the reader to learn about all things Scottish. It is a heavy-handed, exhaustive list of references that includes a history of the kilt, a description of the family tartan, haggis, Bonne Prince Charlie, and traditional folkdance customs. Fiona's mother claims she owes her tendency to be frugal to her Scottish ancestry "since the Scots have a reputation for being great savers," (31) and at several points the grandparents' dialog includes long, drawn-out *r-r-rs* to indicate their accent. Descriptions of Chinese cultural tropes are equally present (and stereotypical), establishing that Fiona's identity rests on knowledge of both sets of traditions that she demonstrates can coexist despite the competition created by the sets of grandparents. Grandpa's offensive greeting "Well if it isn't Fu Manchu himself!" (27) is treated as harmless joke shared between Grandpa and Ron. The racism embedded in the reference is dismissed by the clarification that Ron looks nothing like Fu Manchu. A critical reader can note that Grandpa's comment perpetuates ideas about all Asians looking alike, and/or looking like martial arts heroes. Critical race theory reminds us to note that racism appears "natural and ordinary" (Delgado 1995, xiv). Ron's acceptance of the 'joke' permits the reader to chuckle along with Grandpa who may be forgiven because of his age, thus casting a racist joke as natural and ordinary, part of their banter.

Ultimately, Fiona resolves the conflict of having to choose between her Scottish and Chinese 'halves' by participating in two events at the folk fest: dressing as the traditional Chinese heroine of her father's picture book, and dancing in the Scottish dance performance organized by her grandfather. Being able to embody these two identities through costume and performance are satisfactory resolutions to Fiona's earlier identity crisis and she concludes "I realized I was probably the only person in the whole Folk Fest who'd gotten to participate in two programs for two different cultures. And it had happened because I don't fit into a box or a category. I wasn't 100% anything—except myself . . . I got to be both: half and half." (136) The celebratory cultural pluralism embedded in the manifestations of identity through costumes and dance are quite evident. Furthermore, identity is cast as something one can literally put on and take off like a costume. The initial idea of government forms used to determine racial membership appears to have been resolved by Fiona's ability to "be both"—and at a stretch, her actions can be read as a form of resistance to social impositions.

Participation in traditions, or rather the lack of participation in traditions, forms part of the learning experiences of eleven year-old Sonia Nadhamuni in *The Whole Story of Half a Girl*. The rupture in Sonia's life comes when a change in the family finances means she has to move from her progressive private school to the neighborhood public school. At her old school, Sonia was part of a racially and culturally diverse student body where her racial identity was not a point of difference, rather one of cultural pluralism. Early in the novel she notes that what she knows about her Indian heritage is from memories of a trip to the Taj Mahal and of colorful saris spread out on a field to dry. Of her mother's Jewish heritage, she notes that she knows very little: "Mom only makes Shabbat dinner if my grandparents are visiting . . . I don't even know if we count as a real Jewish family any more than we count as an Indian one." (13) As the title implies, this dubious amount of knowledge will change. Slightly.

Like Fiona's parents, Sonia's have done little to teach her about her cultural history, much less about race and power. She is unprepared for the racial dynamics of her new school and does not know where to place herself. At lunch she notices that the white kids sit together and the black kids sit together "where were you supposed to sit if you were too dark to be white and too light to be black?" (43) Phenotype defines the social groups and Sonia sees herself between light and dark skin tones and grapples with where to belong. Hiranandhani sets up the dichotomy in the form of two potential friendships: one with a white girl named Kate, and the other with an African American girl named Alisha. Sonia is drawn to Alisha's warmth and friendliness, but is pulled by the allure of Kate and her cheerleader friends. These girls are painted with familiar shades of all-American girl brushstrokes so that the reader learns to mistrust them before Sonia does. They dress alike, talk about crushes, and look down on kids who are different, especially Alisha. In this and other unflattering ways, Kate and her clique are posited as the antagonists who favor conformity over difference. They include Sonia but only up to a point; the point when someone brings up her Indian heritage, which makes them visibly uncomfortable. Thus with these white peers, Sonia is never allowed to forget that she is not like them. On the other hand, Alisha and her group are mildly curious, friendly, and ultimately indifferent to her presence as anything other than a new peer. Sonia notes that no one at the black kids' table seems to care that she's there, but she is struck by how pale she feels by comparison. She is used to being the darker skinned one at her old school. These first-day observations prompt Sonia to start asking questions about her racial identity at home. She asks her father if he would call himself black or white. The brief conversation that follows provides the reader with a brief treatise of the complications of racial labels in the U.S. It ends inconclusively with the parents telling her she can define herself any way she wants.

Sonia frames her identity in terms of skin color—neither light nor dark—which renders her different from everyone else. When asked or prompted, she replies that she is Jewish and Indian, describing herself through labels of religion and nationality or geography. She knows so little she cannot relate to either. She reflects that her friend Sam's family belonged to a temple and cooked Shabbat dinner while hers does not. Meanwhile, her friend Kate represents all things cool and American (i.e.: white). Kate and Alisha pull Sonia in opposite directions on many levels, including thinking about her identity. Kate is part of a clique of girls who conform to each other's perspectives and interests. Kate seems to like Sonia but is embarrassed by her. When classmates ask questions or tease Sonia, Kate stays silent, distancing herself. Alisha is friendly and interested in Sonia and asks her questions about being Indian and Jewish, and is, in fact, a catalyst to Sonia's identity exploration. She goes so far as to ask Sonia which side she would choose if she had to. This leads Sonia to consider the limits of her cultural knowledge:

> Maybe it would be easier to just be Indian and not have to explain the Jewish part. Mom doesn't seem to think being Jewish is important, otherwise she would have done all the things Sadie does—belong to a temple, have Shabbat dinner every Friday night, and send me to Hebrew school. Why didn't she do those things for me? Why couldn't she have raised me really Jewish like Sam, so I wouldn't have to think so much about it? Now it's too late.
>
> (85)

Identifying as "half Jewish" distances Sonia from Kate and the other white girls. Sonia struggles with wanting to spend time with Alisha with whom she feels comfortable but relegated to the social margins with the other black girls, and with Kate and the popular cheerleaders with whom she gains a larger social stamp of approval. Kate's gentle but persistent efforts to pull Sonia away from Alisha are tacitly racist. Kate takes Sonia shopping and suggests clothes and make up like her own, to the extent that Alisha points out that Sonia is starting to look like Kate. Molding Sonia to be more like her is, in fact Kate's goal, so much so that she insists Sonia attend church with her. It is not surprising then, when Kate's mother registers some disapproval at this idea, reminding Sonia that she is Jewish: "Something flickers across her eyes. Normally she's excited when I join them in anything." (115) Ultimately, Sonia's participation in this family is conditional upon her being invisible. This, and the possibility of Kate and her friends being racist are the two instances of identity-related prejudice in *The Whole Story*, and it is significant that they both come from the same source.

Sonia's knowledge about her Jewish heritage takes a turn when her maternal grandparents come to stay during a family crisis. Sonia takes it upon herself to ask her Grandma many questions, such as why she keeps kosher, why her mother doesn't, if Grandma objected to Mom marrying an Indian man (i.e.: out of her faith). Grandma's explanations are tender and pragmatic, explaining that there are various ways of practicing the faith, and that ultimately "you were born to a Jewish mother, and that makes you completely Jewish, not barely," (189) and loved unconditionally by her Grandma. It is doubtful how much this assurance registers with

Sonia because she looks down at her brown hands in her Grandma's white ones and wonders how they can be related: skin color still holds sway over customs, beliefs and practices. Nevertheless, with this new knowledge, Sonia's preoccupation with her identity is suddenly dropped, resolved by the promise of security with family and friends.

Multiracial identity in *The Whole Story of Half a Girl* is constructed through a process that begins with a fracture in the protagonist's 'normal' life that sends her on a journey of social and emotional dissonance. Sonia's need to make friends and find a place to belong at her new school sparks the series of questions about her Indian and Jewish heritage, none of which are answered with much depth. At the end, rather than understand these aspects of who she is, Sonia has prompted her parents into considering the role they play in proving her with the tools and information she needs to navigate the world as a biracial parent. Critical readers will observe the ways internal and external forces work in tandem to provoke responses from Sonia that make her unhappy, but ultimately more actively engaged in determining her own identity.

Passing

A small part of the corpus of historical fiction featuring multiracial characters includes the topic of passing as part of the life experiences of the characters. Racial passing is a not a topic many elementary school teachers are likely to address, and currently it is not as fraught an issue as it was in the past. The authors of *Say You Are My Sister* (Brady 2000), *Black Angels* (Murphy 2001), and *Hidden Roots* (Bruchac 2004) take up the issue of passing in very different ways, providing opportunities for readers, supported by teachers with the adequate background knowledge, to explore the concept of racial passing in a historical context. Richard Peck's historical fiction novel, *The River Between Us* (Peck 2003) can also be considered a commentary on a kind of passing and is discussed in Chapter 7. These opportunities allow readers to think critically about the social and political constructions of race and racial identity in complex ways.

Conceptually, passing is as difficult to pin down as race since to use the term means to ascribe to discrete racial categories even while disputing them. Furthermore, passing as a state of being can apply to various behavioral practices: to those moments when we let others believe something about us that we know to be untrue. In her book, *Passing: When People Can't Be Who They Are,* Brooke Kroeger (2003) offers this definition of passing:

> In the most general way, it is passing when people effectively present themselves as other than who they understand themselves to be. *Effectively* is key because an ineffectual effort to pass is just that, a failed attempt. Passing means that other people actually see or experience the identity that the passer is projecting, whether the passer is

telegraphing that identity by intention or by chance ... Passing never feels natural. It is a second skin that never adheres.

(7–8)

Passing can be intentional or unintentional. Unintentional passing happens all the time, when people read other people and assume they have identified their race, class, gender, sexual orientation, nationality, legal status, age, ability etc. In this case the observer makes decisions over which the observed has little or no control unless they have intentionally prepared their appearance to be a certain way. Intentional passing is a more complicated practice. Both can be short term or long term. Passing only exists because social paradigms have made it so there is an undesirable kind of identity that makes a person feel the need to pretend to be something else in order to avoid negative repercussions. In other words, people from low social statuses pass for higher social statuses because of the safety and privileges afforded. Any population that has historically experienced institutional oppression includes members who have or do pass as something else: gay for straight, old for young, poor for rich, nonwhite for white, undocumented for legally documented.

In this analysis my focus is on racial passing, specifically nonwhite passing for white. Historically, laws of hypodescent that vigilantly policed racial identity with rules such as the 'one drop rule' put in place identity practices that nonwhites had to negotiate, often with little or no agency. Thus, while white men often fathered children with black women, the children were considered black and were raised and loved in black families. Many African Americans today take the likelihood of some white ancestry for granted. The one drop rule required people who appeared phenotypically white but had known black ancestry to identify as black, and as a consequence there is often an acceptance of a range of phenotypes and skin tones in the African American community. Some African Americans who chose to pass as white may be considered 'traitors' as they are viewed as rejecting the cultural and historical elements of their identity for the privileges of living as white. It is beyond the scope of this project to explicate the multifarious nuances and tensions surrounding passing. Essentially, passing is a personal and political act that, as Kroeger reminds us "takes guile" (8) and involves a lifetime of secrecy.

Set as they are in the Jim Crow south, the historical fiction novels analyzed below include characters who intentionally and unintentionally pass for white in a perilous context. Critical examination of the construction of multiracial identity and the protagonists' ability to choose to "be" white lays bare the liberties authors take in recreating this period in history. In *Say You Are My Sister*, *Black Angels*, and *Hidden Roots*, the reader is guided towards the surprise revelation that a character, presumably white, turns out to have black or Native American ancestry—information that rendered survival dependent on secrecy.

The Element of Surprise

A lifetime of secrecy is well-known to Georgie Keddrington, a primary character in *Say You are my Sister*. The novel is set in Georgia, Alabama in 1944. A number of tragedies befall Georgianna (Georgie) and her younger sisters, Mony and Keely Faye, leaving them orphaned in a small town to fend for themselves. The story is told from Mony's point of view and is essentially her *bildungsroman*. She learns about the dark side of human nature and the power of love beyond biology.

Halfway through the book, Mony and the reader learn that Georgie has a black grandparent. Mony accidentally comes across a file with her family's last name on it while working at the town doctor's office. She reads the contents, and Dr. Fellowes explains what she does not understand: mainly, that Georgie and Mony are not biologically related. Georgie's parents were a white man named Richard, and a "half Negro" (114) named Lynette, who were married in Pennsylvania. Richard was killed, leaving Lynette pregnant with Georgie. Shortly after, Mony's father met and fell in love with Lynette and married her. When she died giving birth to Georgie, Pa returned to Georgia with the baby and remarried, raising Georgie as white in his white family. Through the doctor's explanation readers will learn some general information about anti-miscegenation laws and the violent reality that befell some interracial couples: it is possible that Richard was murdered for marrying Lynette despite their marriage being legal in Pennsylvania. They will also learn of the bravery of individuals like Mony's father who violated the Jim Crow laws by protecting Georgie at his own peril. Furthermore, Dr. Fellowes' father also knew of Georgie's heritage and protected her secret. According to the laws of the state at the time, interracial marriages were "utterly void." (Browning 1951, 27). Revelation of this family secret would most certainly have landed Georgie in prison if not worse.

Mony's shock at this discovery is understandable: "'Now I had lost another person, and this time it was Georgie. 'Cause from what Doc Wallace wrote in that there file, I had just learned that Georgie's not my sister. Not a half, not any other fraction. She's not my sister at all. And on top of that, she's part Negro.'" (113) Mony has no way of conceiving of her relationship with Georgie outside of biology. To learn that there is no biological connection, and that there is a racial secret is a double blow. Part of what she learns over time is that none of these factors diminish their ability to care for each other and live as sisters.

Dr. Fellowes' lengthy explanation of the racist mores of some of the townspeople remind Mony that racism runs deep in the town. He insists that she keep this new information a secret. Mony argues that people who know and like Georgie would never hurt her. Fellowes reminds her of the barber who was thrown out of his own window for allowing a colored man into his shop. Mony's insistent denial is consistent with the fact of her being young and white and never having to think about race. Of all the hardships that have befallen the family, this one is the hardest for her to contemplate. Mony is shaken from her disbelieving attitude and forced to realize the far-reaching effects of racism. It is from this point that the reader, through Mony, views Georgie through a racial lens, as someone who is passing, unknowingly. The depiction of the racial attitudes in town is believable and provides the context for Georgie's vulnerability.

Georgie, Mony and the baby live alone and fend for themselves against bitter odds. They are penniless and starving, and have to prove to the authorities that Georgie is a fit guardian. Their biggest fear is that they will be separated. The racism of some powerful people in town has already been established so it is clear that if word gets out that Georgie is "colored" that fear would surely be realized. At this point the complexity of the one-drop rule and its effects on families is painfully evident: for all intents and purposes Georgie has lived as a white girl, part of a white family. Public knowledge of her black ancestry could ruin her life.

Georgie is a strong, creative, responsible sixteen-year-old with the maturity and resolve to take on the role of both parents in caring for her sisters. That she is passing for white is nothing more than a factor of her innocence. She dreams of going to Europe to become a fashion designer and when the impossibility of this is precluded by her new role as caretaker, she determines to put her dress-making skills to use by buying the shop and serving the wealthy women of the town. Her determination is admirable. Eventually the strain of their life and having to keep the secret from her sister is too much for Mony and in an impassioned outburst, tells Georgie that they are not biologically related and that her mother was "half a Negro." (189) The shock is Mony's when Georgie replies that had known for years.

It is with this revelation that Brady's portrayal of a black girl passing for white loses some integrity. Georgie has known about her biological parents since she was very young. Though she lived secure in the love and protection of her adoptive parents, she also knew first hand, the sting of racism. The young man she loved proposed to her, and in the interest of full disclosure, she told him about her racial heritage. His response was one of disgust, and he spit in her face. She also witnessed racism in the town towards blacks and their white allies. So it seems somewhat incredible then, that her outrage is directed at the doctor for precluding her opportunity to be open about her identity. With indignation she announces that she felt smothered by her secret and was ready to let it out:

> When Adam took off, I was glad. I wanted folks to know the reason. Wanted folks to see how foolish all this was. I wanted to be proud of who I was, wanted people to see it didn't make no difference. I may be part colored, but I'm still Georgie, still can run a dress shop, still can make up dresses fit for queens. I could have faced them all, like Pa did at the barbershop. I wanted to. I was ready to, finally, after what Adam did.
> (196)

Georgie's idealism here is both uncharacteristic and feels anachronistic in the way she is citing a modern kind of mixed race identity unlikely to have been part of the discourse of the Jim Crow south. By this point in the novel, enough has been established about the town to ensure that Georgie would not have been accepted and it is surprising that she could imagine she would have been. On the other hand, we can read Georgie's entitlement as a function of her being raised white. She has none of the racial analysis or experience that an African American in their town would have, and cannot imagine the depth of racial hatred because it never applied to her. Wanda Brooks (2009) ascribes a similar kind of entitlement to Paul-Edward Logan, the biracial protagonist of *The Land* (Taylor 2001). Having been raised by his white father as if his black heritage was not of concern, he is deeply shocked when he learns that his being mixed prevents him from owning land. Brooks contrasts Paul-Edward's perspective about landownership with that of another former slave, who rather than own land, wanted to be free of it. Georgie's desire to be honest with Adam about being part colored stemmed from a naiveté born of not having had to think about race before.

Since this is Mony's story, it is she who is transformed by the events in their family. She has learned many hard lessons about human nature and power. She learns how being white can literally save your life in a town like theirs. She now regards her sister "as something more than what I always thought she was" (206) and admits that now she views the black people she passes by as possible kin. Couched in this positive language, we can appreciate Mony's perception of her sister as "more" rather than less or half. In this aspect *Say You Are My Sister* is similar to Bishop's social conscience books in which white children learn about acceptance and tolerance via a black catalyst. Georgie has passed for sixteen years and can continue to do so, if she chooses, but she and Mony now live in fear of this secret being discovered. The racist context in which they live strips them of any agency and renders them helpless in the face of it. The Keddrington family is a microcosm in which values are based on humanity and love, not biology, social conventions, religion or law. Mony's momentary regard of Georgie as being vastly different, with the blood "of another whole people" (125) rather than part of *her* family is replaced by the reminder that she had other ancestors who were not biologically related to her either. Thus, she realizes family does not have to be constrained by biology.

Knowing now that Georgia has been passing intentionally rather than innocently changes how readers must understand her situation and gives us pause to wonder about her sheer lack of fear considering all that is at stake. Georgie is unfazed by the ramifications of being multiracial in Jim Crow Georgia, and plans to merge into her newly-public identity with pride. It is unclear, however, how she plans to do this. Love trumps all else in their little home, but outside is a different reality. At the end, when all the secrets and lies are cleared up, Georgie expresses her guilt at having lived a lie, and while she and Mony resolve to "change the world, one barber shop at a time," (207) we are given the impression that Georgie does not intend to be too public about her identity:

> 'It isn't fair: I went to a white folks' school. I can sit wherever I want on a bus or the trolley. I can buy my lunch at the white's only place. And when I die, my picture will be in the front part of the newspaper, not the back where the colored folks are. It isn't right. It isn't fair.'
>
> (204)

This is an unsubtle but explicit articulation of some of the privileges of passing. What is not expressed is the knowledge that her life is constantly shadowed by a perilous secret. This is a misleading representation of a reality that would be much more complicated. In *Say You Are my Sister,* passing for white is presented as a choice that Georgie can practice and control, which is unrealistic. A more credible depiction is the earlier need for secrecy given her context.

Rita Murphy's (2001) *Black Angels,* also explores the issue of passing in Georgia (in the 1960s). This novel hinges on one central question: What does it mean for a young girl who thinks she is white to suddenly learn that she has a black grandmother, which would, according to the law of the times, make her black too? Celli Jenkins, the protagonist of Rita Murphy's *Black Angels* is not immediately recognizable as a mixed race character. She presents as white and her life is marked by the privileges of whiteness in the stark ways that characterized the social context in Georgia in the early 1960s. Half way through the book Celli meets her African American grandmother and learns that her father was biracial. This results in a brief internal, emotional turmoil, after which Celli throws herself into heroic efforts to help the black residents in town when a riot breaks out upon the arrival of the Freedom Riders. In effect, the story suggests that a white girl can only really care about racism towards blacks when it affects her personally.

In *Black Angels* it seems necessary for protagonist and reader to be prepared for the information about Celli's racial identity. Murphy establishes Celli as different from her peers in a number of strange ways. The title comes from the three fairy-like creatures, "three naked black girls with creamy white wings" (1) that Celli sees whenever she is by herself in the garden. Perhaps these are meant to be a metaphor for her unknown self, since they do, in fact, disappear once she comes to terms with the new information about her identity. Celli calls herself "a freak of nature" (15) because she is the only girl on the paternal side of her family. Her only friend is the black housekeeper, Sophie, (and the angels). She is lonely for the father she never knew and spends most of her time alone. Celli and her brother often go to church with Sophie and afterwards play with the children there, who they call their secret, "Sunday friends." (13) Celli is aware of the fact that her love for Sophie and occasional friendships with black children would not be approved of by people in her white world. She thinks of herself as different, as non-racist, but likely to be ostracized for it. In the context of literary insistence that multiracial people must necessarily be isolated, *Black Angels* adheres to the paradigm that isolation is due to inherent flaws rather than social prejudice.

The novel focuses on the racial tension that is building in anticipation of the arrival of the Freedom Riders. The town of Mystic is described as fairly typical for a small town in the Jim Crow south. For most of the novel Celli does not care a bit about the growing excitement. She is bored when Sophie takes her to church to listen to speeches and resentful that Sophie is more caught up in the movement than in spending time with her. The point of the story is that Celli has to grow out of this self-centeredness and start to care about the world in which she lives.

As the focal point of the novel, Celli's mixed race subjectivity is handled rather clumsily. She meets her African American grandmother (named Pearl) half way through the story, and everything builds to this moment. The first half of the novel is laden with problematic language and images. Told in first person, Celli's description of Sophie is replete with degrading stereotypes. Very much a traditional 'mammy' figure, Sophie is described as large, "sassy", "shiny" (15), smelling of food and unrelentingly loyal to her white family, in Celli's words:

> . . . a big, black, bossy woman with sturdy arms that could wrap around me twice. A woman who will wipe the dirt from my face with her own spit, scold me for forgetting my manners and then gather me in her lap and sing me gospel songs until I fall asleep.
>
> (14)

This problematic description might be read as being in keeping with the character who later has to confront her own racism (but the degree to which she interrogates her own biases is superficial). References to dark and frizzy or wavy hair are frequent descriptive clues to hidden multiracial identity in children's books. Several references to Ellery's frizzy hair dot the narrative—giving it undue significance—until Celli learns that their father was half black, and Ellery's hair suddenly makes sense to her. It is an ineffective epiphany. Other comments about appearance feel like authorial afterthoughts or awkward attempts at foreshadowing: "I'm lucky. Mama says I have enough pigment in my skin so I'll probably never burn," (56) and an odd remark for a mother to make to her children about why she fell in love with their father, because "he had a fine set of lips." (20) Again, we may read these offensive comments as being in character, but a more critical reading would be to understand that the author chose to use problematic stereotypes as literary devices with no regard for consequence.

As if to prolong and prepare for the news Celli is to receive upon meeting her grandmother, we are given a long description of a young man named Fergus who greets Celli as she waits for Pearl at the hotel. Fergus is black and (white) Jewish. His mother worked as a maid for a wealthy family whose son "took a liking" (66) to her. According to Sophie, Fergus represents an unforgivable transgression for the racists and some blacks in Mystic "hard enough being of mixed blood and mixed faith without being illegitimate on top of it." (66) It is difficult to ignore that "took a liking" is a euphemism that dismisses the sexual abuse suffered by countless black domestic workers in white homes. To put the words in the mouth of a black character is even more problematic as it renders such practices acceptable. Fergus' good looks and sweet nature endear him to both black and white women who love to spoil him while he does their chores. Celli is acutely aware (through Sophie) of the fact that Fergus is most threatening to white men specifically because he is mixed and his body is evidence of a serious transgression of boundaries. Fergus is a minor character with a small but significant role later on, but his primary purpose seems to be to get Celli thinking about mixed race identity. Shortly after the description of Fergus, Celli and the reader meet Pearl and learn that Celli is "no longer vanilla." (69)

Celli is physically ill at the discovery. She throws up in the bathroom, sickened at what it means to have her "world turned upside down." (70) Her reaction is believable. She thought that loving Sophie, attending her church and being friends with Rosa and Tilly marked her as non-racist. Yet she is surrounded by racism of the deepest kind so how can she have escaped internalizing it? In this emotional moment what seems to hit the hardest is the fact of her grandmother sitting on back porch of the hotel, in the part reserved for African Americans "like she doesn't matter. Like I don't matter. Like neither of us is good enough." (70) The systemic devaluing of African Americans becomes clearer to Celli in this moment than ever before: it pertains to her and that is why it suddenly matters.

As the knowledge of her ancestry sinks in, Celli is gripped by the fear of how her life will change if word gets out. The word 'passing' is never mentioned, but for all intents and purposes, Celli has unknowingly passed as white while her family kept the secret safe from public knowledge. Suddenly the racism of her environment, the reality lived by Sophie and the other black residents of Mystic means something because she might have to live it too. Celli even wonders, with dread, if the warmth and welcome she experienced at the church was because people there somehow knew: "I'm just like them now. But I don't want to be like them, I want to be me. Like I've always been." (79) Given the context in which she was raised, this is a believable reaction, as it reveals her own prejudice and confusion. Her next reaction is one of denial. Celli decides that the activism around civil rights has nothing to do with her, and that it is more important to maintain her identity as a white girl:

> I've decided it's not my battle. Just because Pearl may be my grandmother doesn't mean I have to be part of this. There is no need for me to

get involved with any Freedom Riders. Sophie can go off and get herself in trouble if she wants to, but I don't have to stand around and watch. My skin is white and that's all that matters in Mystic. I can just go on living like I've always done and no one will ever find out about Daddy.
(89)

Again, this is a believable reaction in that she has been given to think this way by everything and everyone around her. But she can't stay away and follows Sophie to the rally in front of the courthouse and later finds herself involved in helping Fergus escape a racist mob that thinks he is a symbol of everything that is wrong in Mystic.

Celli's bike ride to the church to get help for Fergus can be read metaphorically. The irony of her situation becomes clear and helps her in the upcoming reconciliation about her identity. While on the east side of town, the white side, she is terrified of being seen by the racists she knows live there. Once she crosses the geographical divide, her relief is tangible:

Every muscle in my body relaxes. There is no one on this side of town who would hurt me. I've never thought of it like that before, but it's true. On the east side there are plenty of folks ready to do you harm if you think different than they do, but not here. It strikes me funny all of a sudden that Katie Blanchard is afraid of walking down Sophie's road at night 'cause she thinks she'll turn black and I can hardly wait to get there.
(113)

This sudden switch in racial allegiances is highly romanticized as it suggests that mere knowledge of ancestry ensures group membership and security. It may be true that multiracial Celli's body is safer in the black part of town, but that would be due to stringent racial power dynamics, not kinship. Celli assumes that if known, her mixed race heritage will automatically grant her a place in the black community. We can read this assumption, like Georgie's naiveté, as a function of being raised with the privilege of being ignorant about the depths of Jim Crow racism. The realization brings some peace to her inner turmoil and she shifts her attention to the idea that what she is really afraid of is losing the people she loves, like she lost her father. A little later Pearl explains that the reason for Celli's father's disappearance is that he was never at ease with himself as a mixed race person, wearing that identity as a "second skin that never adheres" (Kroeger 2003):

He passed for white, but he knew he was also black and that was too much for him to bear at times, so he did some drinking to forget his pain ... he's still running from the pain ... it would be better if he could turn around and face it, feel that pain through and through and be free from it instead of letting it eat him up inside.
(126)

This description accurately reflects the inner turmoil created by living a lie and one can empathize with the character in this moment (although we have no context for his need to pass). Passing is presented as a matter of individual choice, and it raises questions about the context in which a person would make such a choice, and live in pain, rather than claim his African American heritage: was it worse to be black? For Celli, this information explains why she has been lonely all her young life, as if some mysterious genetic force was at work within her.

At the end, Celli and Ellery's new knowledge of their father's identity, and their own, seems insignificant. Celli's angels vanish since she no longer needs them. There is nothing to suggest that Pearl will figure any more prominently than as the sender of letters from Cleveland. Fergus is safe, living with Pearl in the supposedly racially-accepting north and life seems to go back to normal in Mystic but for an undercurrent of racial tension. Celli is remarkably quick to accept the information about her heritage, which if publicly known, would destroy her life. Empathizing with Celli, readers might understand why she must now knowingly pass because not to would be dangerous. Her decision is made in isolation and ignorance. There are no adult characters to guide her, and readers are left to believe that passing was a matter of individual choice and little consequence. Ultimately, Celli's understanding of the racial dynamics in the town are a little altered and she understands Sophie's desire to be an agent of change rather than a bystander. She admits that she "feels different on the inside" (158) in that she is less afraid of losing loved ones and that her father and grandmother's racial identity doesn't seem unusual. She says this from the safety of a life she continues to live as a white girl albeit with some slight anxiety about the reality of her racial identity becoming known.

Passing and Survival

One of the darkest events of U.S. history was the eugenics project. In his comprehensive documentation of racializing practices, *Almost All Aliens,* Paul Spickard (2007) explicates the emergence of "pseudoscientific racial thinking" (262) that began during the Enlightenment in Europe with Karl Linne's systems of taxonomy of all living things. The Linnaeus system organized all living beings into species–discrete categories with impermeable boundaries. This system was eventually applied to humans to create the racial categories by which we are still bound. Eugenicists such as Francis Galton were interested in "directing human evolution" (269) with the goal of perfecting the human species through selective breeding. Eugenics gained popularity in the U.S. in the early 1920s, and this branch of pseudoscience crossed disciplines to argue that heredity could provide information about a person's metal and physical 'perfection.' Among other groups, women of color were targeted for sterilization in a legally supported effort to decrease populations. In the Author's Note at the end of *Hidden Roots,* Joseph Bruchac (2004) informs readers of the thirty-three states where bills were passed to allow doctors and nurses to perform sterilizations on Native Americans, people of color, and vulnerable populations such as the mentally ill or weak, without their full consent. Bruchac brings this gruesome topic to young readers in a remarkably palatable way without mitigating the heinous consequences on families and communities.

It is almost absurd to talk about multiracial identity when it comes to indigenous populations since it is such a clear imposition of a colonial racial paradigm on a vast array of peoples for whom identity has completely different and diverse meanings. Tribal membership and identity were and continue to be determined by tribal systems that predate white colonization. Dunn (2006) explains that the term "mixed-blood" is an identity complication that is a consequence of white and indigenous intermixing as well as cross-tribal intermarriages (145). The U.S. policy of federal recognition of tribal sovereignty essentially imposed a way of constructing identity. Perceptions of race and discourse about racial identity that makes use of concepts of blood quantum are part of this legacy. Currently, Native tribes follow, adapt, reject, and negotiate this policy in a variety of ways befitting the communities' needs and wants. The limitations of language are made abundantly clear in the difficulty of writing about something without reascribing it.

In *Hidden Roots*, Bruchac creates a family that is passing for white and living in relative isolation as a consequence of the forced sterilization policy. As in *Say You Are My Sister* and *Black Angels*, readers are guided, via the protagonist, to learn of his racial identity through a gradual process. *Hidden Roots* is set in a town called Sparta in the Adirondack hills outside Vermont in 1954. Eleven-year-old Howard (Sonny) has always lived in fear–fear of his father's temper, fear of being noticed in school, and fear of "being crept up on." (9) He does not understand who or what will creep up on him, just that his mother is very serious about their need to be vigilant—just in case. Like many other multiracial characters in the corpus, Howard is a lonely boy who keeps to himself. He recalls several factors that set him apart from his peers. One is that his refusal to fight another boy in third grade earned him the nickname "Howard the Coward" and the derision of his peers. He determines that the other kids must not like him and keeps to himself. The other is that there are so many secrets in his family that he thinks it is best to avoid friendships lest anyone ask questions. Howard's parents teach him to "watch my back and keep quiet" (8) but do not say why. There are suggestions of domestic violence and topics Howard learns he must never ask about: World War II, his mother's bruises, and Uncle Louis' past.

Thus secrecy is normal in his world. The novel builds up to the revelation of information that he could not have guessed—that he and his parents are Abenaki Indians and Uncle Louis is his grandfather. They fled the eugenics efforts in Vermont before Howard was born, and shed all markers of their tribal heritage so that they could blend into their small rural community.

But before he learns his, Howard begins to relearn what he knows about Indians through Uncle Louis.

Howard's mild curiosity about Indians dots the first half of the novel and reveals the ubiquity of stereotypes. Despite his distance from peers and adults—sources of conventional knowledge, Howard has absorbed paradigmatic notions about Indians. When his mother tells him he must watch his back, his immediate thought is that she means he must protect himself from Indians. Bruchac makes clear that Howard has learned this fear from a movie in which sleeping cowboys are attacked. Later when he asks his mother about Uncle Louis' family, she snaps at him, telling him never to ask again. He understands that something tragic had happened and assumes "it had something to do with Indians." (31) Howard reflects that he doesn't know much about Indians, only what he has learned from school and the movies, and about the "dirt-poor half-Indians on the other side of the mountain, but they weren't real Indians from what I heard. They lived in shacks, not teepees, and they didn't ride horses; they rode about in old jalopies. They didn't even wear feathers." (32) Thus, his understanding is shaped by stereotypes that most readers would probably recognize.

Howard spends more and more time with Uncle Louis, impressed with the older man's knowledge about trees, soil, animals and the connectivity of all living things. Louis' view of the world makes sense to Howard, and incites his curiosity about the Indians on the other side of the mountain. He is confused when Uncle Louis tells him that they "used to be" (57) Indians, and proceeds to explain racism and how the Indians had no way to survive but by blending in to the white community and shedding all traditions and markers of who they really were. Survival, Louis explains, sometimes means hiding "even if we have to do it in plain sight." (39) This is all that is needed to explain the need to pass as white.

When school resumes in the fall, Howard's world is opened up even further by an unexpected mentor, the school librarian, Edith Rosen. Rosen gives him books to read, including *The Last of the Mohicans*. Uncle Louis knows Rosen and Bruchac describes a poignant scene in which the two acknowledge each other's tragic histories: "it was as if the two of them were talking a language that only they knew." (106) Louis explains the Holocaust to Howard, telling him how Ms. Rosen's parents were not able to escape. Talking about prejudice in the context of anti-Semitism provides an opening for him to tell Howard the truth about his own family. He shows Howard the medical form that authorized his wife's sterilization, drawing the parallel between Nazi and U.S. eugenics, "they done what they done because it was the law and because she was Indian. Just like me." (114) He also tells Howard that he is his grandfather.

The novel ends with Louis and Jake (Howard's father) explaining the 1931 Vermont law that established forced sterilizations of Indians and the devastating effects that had on tribes and families. The reader, now aligned with Howard, learns alongside him. Howard learns that both his parents are of Abenaki, Mohawk and perhaps some French ancestry, and that their secrecy about it was meant to protect him, and themselves. After Louis' wife died, leaving behind their first child (Howard's mother), Louis was terrified that the Vermont government would take the child to a boarding school and he found her a home with a white couple who raised her as their own. The family's isolated, secretive life now makes sense and echoes Kroeger's articulation of the complexity of passing: "Passers stay in character no matter what. When the passing is intentional, the passer also needs stealth and gumption, cunning, agility, and social conceit." (8) Louis explains that Jake felt that hiding their Indian roots would mean Howard would have "more of a chance in life," (117) that racism and injustice would otherwise destroy their family. He, on the other hand, believes ancestry provides the foundation, strength even in the face of terrible adversity: " . . . roots is what helps a tree to stand up against the wind. Your family is always your family." (118)

The juxtaposition of Jake and Louis' views about passing provide readers with opportunity to think about the difficulty of the decision to do so, and the difficulty of experiencing racism all the time by choosing not to. Both characters are empathetic and drawn with equal complexity. Although Bruchac clearly favors the family embracing their Abenaki heritage, Jake is not demonized for choosing to pass. He has internalized shame and is twisted up inside with anger and pain that weakens him emotionally and physically. Jake needs Louis to tell him to be as proud of himself as he is before he can start letting go of years of pain. *Hidden Roots* provides one picture of how American Indians with white ancestry used phenotype (when possible) to assimilate in order to survive. Bruchac is not only deeply knowledgeable about this complex negotiation, he is also a skilled writer who makes clear the devastating effects of legally sanctioned racism on American Indian populations, families and individuals. Furthermore, *Hidden Roots* provides a critique of assimilation and its underlying fallacy within the rhetoric of the American melting pot. As a counterstory, it exposes stereotypes and replaces them with a more authentic picture of an American Indian life. Although *Hidden Roots* is one of the many novels of historical fiction identified for this study, it is vastly different from other novels rooted in the "settler-meets-Indian genre." Furthermore it is a refreshing example of a story in which author and characters "name [their own] reality." (Delgado 1995)

Counterstories and Counting Coup

A tenet of critical race theory (Delgado 1995; Brooks 2009) is the creation and validation of counterstories. Simply put, these are stories that counter the dominant narrative in which the experiences of people of color have been "written about" rather than "written by." Counterstories are less concerned with authorial subjectivity than with perspective. In children's literature studies, Jonda McNair (2008) and Wanda Brooks (2009) posit texts such as *The Watsons Go to Birmingham-1963*, *Roll of Thunder Hear My Cry* and *The Land* as counterstories because the authors, Christopher Paul Curtis and Mildred Taylor, reclaim narratives of black childhood and retell them from their perspectives. In these historical fiction novels, racism is exposed not just for the violence it inflicted on families and individuals, but for the ways in which white supremacy permeated legal institutions, social norms and everyday ways of being to uphold whiteness as a privileged, secured, albeit precarious construct. Michelle Pagni Stewart (2013) draws on Catherine Rainwater's application to literary analysis of a similar concept of reclamation in the Native American tradition of counting coup. They describe counting coup as " . . . the means by which some American Indian warriors would measure their success in war. If a warrior could get close enough to an enemy to touch him or seize his belongings, the warrior could earn a coup, an honor for his bravery and cunning." (216) In the context of literary analysis, Rainwater and Stewart posit, a Native author can count a coup if he or she reclaims a position from a Western perspective and presents it from an insider perspective. We can read Bruchac's *Hidden Roots* as counting coup because the author has chosen to bring the topic of the 'vanishing Indian' to the fore, and expose it as a myth. Daniel Francis (1992) and Paul Spickard (among others) have argued that the narrative of the vanished or vanishing Indian served the colonial project of land acquisition: if there were no Indians, there would be no need to justify their decimation. The myth of the vanished Indian is sustained today because it supports the paradigmatic refusal to recognize the decimation of millions of people's lives. *Hidden Roots* explicitly addresses the role of the government sponsored eugenics efforts to forcibly sterilize and thereby eliminate Native populations, contributing to the "vanishing." At the same time, the myth of Native people's erasure is evident in Uncle Louis's explanation about hiding in plain sight–passing. The identities may be hidden, but the people are still here.

Notes

1 In "'What Could I Say?' A Critical Discourse Analysis of the Construction of Race in Children's Literature." Rebecca Rogers and June Christian (2007) analyze the literary construction of whiteness in children's fiction using critical discourse, hermeneutical and literary analysis. Their study discusses ways in which texts recenter whiteness at times, and at other times, disrupts the privileging effect of whiteness. *Race Ethnicity and Education* 10, 1, 21–46.
2 Several multiracial characters make brief mention of the ethnicity of their white parent. Jace, in *Stringz* mentions that his father was Irish. Cameron, in *Off-Color* and Connor in *American Ace* assumed their darker features were due to Italian ancestry. Albie, in *Absolutely Almost* comments he is "half Swiss." Novels in which protagonists name their whiteness through their Jewish identity include much more developed, albeit stereotypical, depictions of what being Jewish means to the characters. *Stealing Home*, *My Basmati Bat Mitzvah*, *I Wanna Be Your Shoebox*, *The Whole Story of Half a Girl* are discussed in Chapters 5, 6, 7, and 8.

References

Brady, Laurel. 2000. *Say You Are My Sister*. New York: HarperCollins Publishers.
Brooks, Wanda. 2009. "An Author as a Counter-Storyteller: Applying Critical Race Theory to a Coretta Scott King Award Book." *Children's Literature in Education* 40: 33–45.
Browning, James. 1952. "Anti-miscegenation Laws in the United States." *Duke Bar Journal* 1, no 1: 26–41.
Bruchac, Joseph. 2004. *Hidden Roots*. New York: Scholastic.
Delgado, Richard. 1995. *Critical Race Theory: The Cutting Edge*. Philadelphia: Temple University Press.
Doane, Ashley W. 1997. "Dominant Group Identity in the United States: The Role of 'Hidden' Ethnicity in Intergroup Relations." *Sociological Quarterly* 38: 375–97.
Doane, Ashley W., and Eduardo Bonilla-Silva. 2003. *White Out: The Continuing Significance of Racism*. New York: Routledge.
Dunn, Caroline. 2006. "Playing Indian." In *Cultural Representation in Native America*, edited by Andrew Jolivette, 139–158. Lanham: AltaMira Press.
Flood, Bo Nancy. 2016. *Soldier Sister, Fly Home*. Watertown: Charlesbridge
Francis, Daniel. (1992). *The Imaginary Indian*. Vancouver, BC: Arsenal Pulp Press.
Frazier, Sundee Tucker. 2007. *Brendan Buckley's Universe and Everything in It*. New York: Delacorte Press.
Hintz, Carrie, and Eric L. Tribunella. 2013. *Reading Children's Literature: A Critical Introduction*. Boston: Bedford/St. Martin's.
Hiranandani, Veera. 2012. *The Whole Story of Half a Girl*. New York: Delacorte Press.
Kroeger, Brooke. 2003. *Passing: When People Can't be Who They Are*. New York: PublicAffairs.
Larrick, Nancy. 1965. "The All White World of Children's Books." *Saturday Review* 11: 63–85.
Lopez, Ian Haney. 2005. "Hispanics and the Shrinking Majority." *Deadalus*, Winter, 42–52.
Lorenzi, Natalie Dias. 2012. *Flying the Dragon*. Watertown, MA: Charlesbridge.
McIntosh, Peggy. 1990. "White Privilege: Unpacking the Invisible Knapsack." *Independent School* 49, no. 2 (Winter): 31–33.
McNair, Jonda. 2008. "'I May be Crackin', but Um Fackin': Racial Humor in the Watsons Go to Birmingham-1963." *Children's Literature in Education* 93, no. 3: 201–12.
Murphy, Rita. 2001. *Black Angels*. New York: Delacorte Press.
Namioka, Lensey. 2003. *Half and Half*. New York: Delacorte Press.
Omi, Michael, and Howard Winant. 2015. *Racial Formation in the United States*. New York: Routledge.
Parry, Rosanne. 2016. *The Turn of the Tide*. New York: Random House.
Peck, Richard. 2003. *The River between Us*. New York: Dial Books.
Rogers, Rebecca, and June Christian. 2007. "'What Could I Say?' A Critical Discourse Analysis of the Construction of Race in Children's Literature." *Race, Ethnicity and Education* 10, no 1, (March), 21–46.
Rogers, Rebecca, and Melissa Mosely. 2006. "Racial Literacy in a Second-Grade Classroom: Critical Race Theory, Whiteness Studies, and Literacy Research." *Reading Research Quarterly* 41, no. 4: 462–95.
Sanders, Scott Loring. 2009. *Gray Baby: A Novel*. Boston: Houghton Mifflin.
Spickard, Paul R. 2007. *Almost All Aliens: Immigration, Race, and Colonialism in American History and Identity*. New York: Routledge.
Stewart, Michelle Pagni. 2013. "'Counting Coup' on Children's Literature about American Indians: Louise Erdrich's Historical Fiction." *Children's Literature Association Quarterly* 38, no. 2: 215–35.Taylor, Mildred D. 2001. *The Land*. New York: Phyllis Fogelman Books.
Yep, Laurence. 2001. *Angelfish*. New York: Putnam's.

9 Teaching and Learning with Multiracial Fiction

The current corpus of easily-accessible fiction depicting multiracial experiences is limited in too many ways. There are too few books, too little variety in terms of racial diversity (not to mention other types of diversity), and too few books that merit the literary recognition that will springboard them into the limelight and subsequently into classrooms and libraries. In the realm of multicultural children's literature, mixed race experiences are infrequently given the same prominence as other racial identities. Yet the multiracial population is growing rapidly, and 2017 marks the 50th anniversary of Loving v. Virginia—a national milestone, the reminder of which is likely to reopen discussions of race relations in the U.S. Recently, the Black Lives Matter (BLM) movement in response to the killing of black men by the police, and the range of public and private reactions to BLM's calls to end the violence have forced us to reckon with the persistence of brutal racism all over the country. This discussion is being extended by initiatives such as the Say Her Name campaign that asserts the need to include violence against black women to this national effort. Indeed, racism takes many forms, and must be exposed and dismantled in all its manifestations—even those that may not be recognized as such.

In the Introduction to this book I shared the anecdote of one of my 4th grade students who pointed out that she did not know of any books that mirrored her Asian American and white heritage. When I shared this observation with colleagues, several were surprised that the student identified as biracial, assuring me that they didn't see her as such, rather as "just American." They suggested that the problem of there being no published stories about children like her was a minor one that could be redirected by not calling attention to race, rather to connections she could make with other themes in literature. The subtext of this response is deep and multilayered. It represents a colorblindness that erases difference—specifically nonwhite racial difference. My colleagues did not mean that they saw the student as Asian American or Chinese: "just American" meant white. This, despite the fact that her mother, who is Chinese American, was an active member of the school community and an advocate for multicultural diversity in that predominantly-white context. The student and her mother's racial identity was erased by colorblindness. There is ample research to support the assumption that the teachers' refusal to see her racial Otherness would not have occurred if the student had been part Latino or black, and there is also research to support the reality that some Asian American groups are more easily and quickly assimilated into white social norms than other populations of color. Nevertheless, this scenario reflects a form of racial microagression that is symptomatic of a society that has historically avoided, and continues to avoid, talking about race, racial identity, and racism.

Microagressions: Subtle Reminders of Difference

Multiracial fiction for children is well-suited to facilitating classroom discussions of microagressions, assuming teachers and parents are knowledgeable and supportive—and there is a precedent for doing so. Classroom teaching and learning about race typically involves reading about notable figures who overcame tremendous odds and left behind legacies of courage and fortitude. Harriet Tubman, Martin Luther King, Anne Frank, Rosa Parks, for example, are curricular icons. Similarly, significant events such as the Civil Rights Movement, the Trail of Tears, the Underground Railroad, the Japanese internment, women's suffrage, struggles for fair labor laws and so on can be learned about through a number of remarkable fictional and informational texts. Historical fiction and nonfiction play an important role in conveying the vitality and grit of those times in our national past with tangible immediacy to a contemporary readership. Where racism and prejudice are relegated to the past with historical fiction, contemporary fiction by writers such as Kekla Magoon, Rita Williams-Garcia, Jewell Parker Rhodes, and Jacqueline Woodson (to name a few) are shining a light on the ways racism still operates, similar in spirit though different in form. Through their stories, elementary school-age children come to recognize overt forms of prejudice in emotional, physical, and social violence as it operates currently.

Less easy to recognize, and for some, to accept as discriminatory, are the subtle, though perhaps more ubiquitous microaggressions. Psychologist Derald Wing Sue (2007) and his colleagues describe microaggression as a modern form of racism that operates subconsciously alongside social values that consciously champion egalitarianism (273). Microaggressions, according to Sue et al., are "brief and commonplace daily verbal, behavioral, and environmental indignities, whether intentional or unintentional, that communicate hostile, derogatory, or negative racial slights and insults to the target person or group." (273) In other words, microaggressions are the subtext behind questions such as "what are you?" or "where are you from?" which imply difference and not-belonging. The underlying power dynamic is hierarchical and the questions or comments seek to establish high and low social status. The mixed race person who is repeatedly asked "what are you?" or told she or he does not "look (fill in the racial blank)" is being held to an expectation of discrete, phenotypically-consistent racial standards that only exists in the imagination of the beholder. Multiracial books such as *The Whole Story of Half a Girl* (Hiranandani 2012), *Somewhere Among* (Donwerth-Chikamatsu 2016), *Bird* (Chan 2014), *The Other Half of My Heart* (Frazier 2010) and many of the Mixed Me picturebooks described in Chapter 3, Multiracial Stories in Picturebooks, are replete with examples of such racial microaggressions that leave the protagonists in the position of having to defend themselves as legitimate members of their families and/or communities.

Virginia Huynh (2012) reminds us that the popular belief that racism is considerably diminished and fast-declining makes it difficult for some people to accept microaggressions as a form of discrimination. (833) Indeed, discourse about the country being in a post-racial time, and the insistence on color-blindness symbolized by the success of public figures such as President Obama and celebrities such as Tiger Woods, Mariah Carey, Derek Jeter and so on, feed our national reluctance to confront the ubiquity of racial prejudice. Huynh points out that often subjects who experience racial microaggressions are made to feel they are too sensitive. Over time, being repeatedly undermined by public perceptions that seem well-intentioned or innocently curious results in feelings of low self-worth. Huynh's research highlights connections between repeated experiences of racial microaggressions among Asian American and Latino adolescents and psychological stress (842) that parallel the findings of mixed race studies by Rockquemore, Brunsma, Root, Nakashima, and the other scholars and theorists referenced in earlier chapters.

In some respects, teachers are already involved in the work of teaching about microaggressions, even if they are not using this specific label. Nation-wide, state standards require curricula to include opportunities for children's social and emotional development, and address issues of bullying. Even without mandates, teachers play a significant role in socializing children, modeling and scaffolding empathetic behavior and upstander responsibility. Teachers in the early grades could incorporate books such as *Mixed Me!* (Diggs and Evans 2015) and *Marisol McDonald Doesn't Match* (Brown and Palacios 2011) as read alouds and prompt students to consider how the protagonists are being made to feel by peers who point out their differences frequently. Through role play, students might practice standing up for Mike and Marisol, or even pretend to be in their shoes, and reflect afterwards on what it felt like to be the perpetrator, recipient and defender in situations that may seem harmless but can be hurtful over time. Such learning experiences can be extended by having everyone share all the ways they are different from each other, from their siblings and parents, and how that difference is valuable and interesting. Since the point is not to shut down conversation but to open it up and share safely, teachers can guide students to think of ways to be inquisitive in nonjudgmental ways. The novels mentioned above offer older readers the same opportunities to conceptually understand microaggressions as they occur in the literary lives of multiracial characters and the real lives of children. The transformational possibilities are endless.

Teaching about the Constructedness of Race

Readers in upper elementary and middle grades can start to understand race and identity as social constructs rather than biological facts through some of the books that make this concept explicit and are of good literary quality. All three of Sundee Frazier's novels; *Brendan Buckley's Universe and Everything in It* (2007), *The Other Half of My Heart* (2010), and *Brendan Buckley's Sixth-Grade Experiment* (2012), have engaging plots and well developed characters that will appeal to readers. The books include universal themes about family and friendship, as well as the specific content that addresses the protagonists' multiracial identity. Frazier places her protagonists in situations in which they are directly called to explain their racial identity, allowing readers to share the experience of constructing themselves through language and context. The transparency of this process lays bare the myth of biological race and the paradoxical need for labels and categories. *Flying the Dragon* (Lorenzi 2012), *My Basmati Bat Mitzvah* (Freedman 2013), *Becoming Naomi León* (Ryan 2004), *Angelfish* (Yep 2001) and other contemporary fictional novels analyzed in earlier chapters in this book offer opportunities for readers to consider how the protagonists negotiate racial and cultural labels in multiple ways and prompted by multiple circumstances. For example, Skye in *Flying the Dragon*, had only a tangential sense of herself as Japanese until her cousin and grandfather arrived from Japan and she learned—through art, language, values, interests and other familiar or new factors—that her life was all the more richly complicated for being symbiotically connected to people from across the world. Tara Feinstein, in *My Basmati Bat Mitzvah* wears her biracial identity proudly, even when peers mock her Indian heritage and question her membership in the Jewish community. Skye and Tara dismantle, negotiate, and rebuild their identities before our eyes, enabling readers to clearly see their agency and the layers of internal and external power at work in identity construction. Through these examples, readers can easily see how racial identity is shaped in response to external expectations to conform while protagonists resist, adapt and consider the extensive palette of options available to them.

Some of the multiracial novels analyzed in Chapter 4, Multiracial In/Visibility, may be problematic in their perpetuation of mixed race identity as unstable and dysfunctional, however, they can be used in classrooms to promote critical thinking that interrogates the narratives. Jaime Adoff's *Jimi & Me* (2005), *The Death of Jayson Porter* (2008), and *Names Will Never Hurt Me* (2004) tell grim stories of deeply damaged characters. Adoff's use of blank verse to describe stark experiences will resonate with adolescents for whom these books will be mirrors and windows that capture reality without sugarcoating it. Readers can question the ways the protagonists experience their multiracial identity as oppressive, and think about the myriad messages that the protagonists must have internalized in order to feel the way they do. Matt de la Peña's (2008) *Mexican WhiteBoy* has already been incorporated into literature curricula and it too, offers opportunities for layers of analysis and examination. Danny Lopez feels like an outsider in the white suburbs where he lives with his mother, and in the *barrio* where he spends the summer getting to know his Latino family. He is a smart, thoughtful teen whose loneliness is characteristic of adolescence and will resonate with teen readers.

Onward

As the population of American children grows more multiracial, it makes sense that they are reflected in the literature they and their peers read—that literature adds to their visibility, recognizing difference, celebrating the blurring of racial, cultural and social boundaries without erasing the elements that make them unique. Bishop (2007) reminds us that "literature educates the heart as well as the head." (xiv) Every time people like Matt de la Peña remind the public that he never thought "people like me" could win a Newbery Award, it should be a signal to publishers, marketers, librarians, teachers and all the other adults along the chain of children's literature production that we need to do a better job of making today's children feel their lives are worth being in books. Multiracial literature needs to become visible in the discourse of childhood and children's lives and it has the potential to enable recognition rather than neglect of difference in positive and transformative ways.

References

Adoff, Jaime. 2004. *Names Will Never Hurt Me*. New York: Dutton Children's Books.
———. 2005. *Jimi & Me*. New York: Jump at the Sun/Hyperion.
———. 2008. *The Death of Jayson Porter*. New York: Jump at the Sun/Hyperion Books for Children.
Bishop, Rudine Sims. 2007. *Free Within Ourselves: The Development of African American Children's Literature*. Westport, CT: Greenwood Press.
Brown, Monica, and Sara Palacios. 2011. *Marisol McDonald Doesn't Match*. San Francisco: Children's Book Press.
Chan, Crystal. 2014. *Bird*. New York: Atheneum Books for Young Readers.
de la Peña, Matt. 2008. *Mexican Whiteboy*. New York: Delacorte Press.
de la Peña, Matt. 2016. "Newbery Medal Acceptance Speech." *The Horn Book Magazine*, July, 56–64.
Diggs, Taye, and Shane Evans. 2015. *Mixed Me!* New York: Feiwel and Friends.
Donwerth-Chikamatsu, Annie. 2016. *Somewhere among*. New York: Atheneum Books for Young Readers.
Frazier, Sundee Tucker. 2007. *Brendan Buckley's Universe and Everything in It*. New York: Delacorte Press.
———. 2010. *The Other Half of My Heart*. New York: Delacorte Press.

———. 2012. *Brendan Buckley's Sixth-Grade Experiment*. New York: Delacorte Press.
Freedman, Paula J. 2013. *My Basmati Bat Mitzvah*. New York: Amulet Books.
Hiranandani, Veera. 2012. *The Whole Story of Half a Girl*. New York: Delacorte Press.
Huynh, Virginia W. 2012. "Ethnic Microaggressions and the Depressive and Somatic Symptoms of Latino and Asian American Adolescents." *Journal of Youth Adolescence* 41: 831–46.
Lorenzi, Natalie Dias. 2012. *Flying the Dragon*. Watertown, MA: Charlesbridge.
Ryan, Pam Muñoz. 2004. *Becoming Naomi León*. New York: Scholastic Press.
Sue, Derald Wing, Christina M. Capodilupo, Gina C. Torino, Jennifer M. Bucceri, Aisha M. Holder, Kevin L. Nadal, and Marta Esquilin. 2007. "Racial Microaggressions in Everyday Life." *American Psychologist* 62, no. 4 (May): 271–86.
Yep, Laurence. 2001. *Angelfish*. New York: Putnam's.

Appendix A
Multiracial Picturebooks

Author	Illustrator	Title	Date	Racial Mix
Ada, Alma Flor	Savadier, Elivia	*I Love Saturdays y domingos*	2002	Latina and white
Alko, Selina	Alko, Selina	*I'm Your Peanut Butter Big Brother*	2009	Black and white
Atinuke	Tobia, Lauren	*Anna Hibiscus* (series)	2010	Black and white
Averbeck, Jim	Ismail, Yasmeen	*One Word From Sophia*	2015	Black and white
Baek, Matthew	Baek, Matthew	*Be Gentle With the Dog, Dear!*	2008	Asian and white
Barkow, Henriette	Brazelle, Derek	*That's My Mum*	2001	South Asian and white, black and white
Beauvais, Garcelle and Sebastian Jones	Webster, Janice	*I Am Mixed*	2012	Black and white
Becker, Shari	Wong, Nicole	*Maxwell's Mountain*	2006	Asian and white
Benjamin, Floella	Chamberlain, Margaret	*My Two Grannies*	2007	Black and white
Benjamin, Floella	Chamberlain, Margaret	*My Two Grandads*	2011	Black and white
Brown, Monica	Palacios, Sara	*Marisol McDonald Doesn't Match*	2011	Latina and white
Bullard, Lisa	Basaluzzo, Constanza	*Emma's Easter*	2012	Black and Jewish
Catledge, Tiffany	Riviere, Anissa	*Mixed Me*	2012	Black and white
Cheng, Andrea	Ange Zhange	*Grandfather Counts*	2000	Chinese and white
Crosman, Marsha	Kendall, Kyra	*Mixed Blessing*	2012	Black and white

Author	Illustrator	Title	Date	Racial Mix
Diggs, Taye	Shane Evans	*Mixed Me!*	2015	Black and unclear*
Edmonds, Lyra	Wilson, Anne	*An African Princess*	2004	Black and white
Evans, Shane	Evans, Shane	*Olu's Dream*	2009	Black and white or Asian
Golliday-Cabell, Gina	LeMaire, Bonnie	*Mixed Like Me*	2012	Unclear*
Graham, Bob	Bob Graham	*Oscar's Half Birthday*	2005	Black and white
Juster, Norton	Raschka, Chris	*The Hello, Goodbye Window*	2005	Black and white
Juster, Norton	Raschka, Chris	*Sourpuss and Sweetie Pie*	2008	Black and white
Kallok, Emma	Bower, Joel	*Gem*	2001	Black and white
Krishnaswami, Uma	Jamel Akib	*Bringing Asha Home*	2015	Indian and white
MacLachlan, Patricia	Graegin, S	*You Were the First*	2013	Black and white
Meshon, Aaron	Meshon, Aaron	*Take Me Out to the Yakyu*	2013	Japanese and white
Monk, Isabell	Lee, Janice	*Family*	2005	Black and white
Monk, Isabell	Porter, Janice Lee	*Blackberry Stew*	2005	Black and white
Nichols, Grace	Taylor, Eleanor	*Whoa, Baby, Whoa*	2011	Black and white
Quarmby, Katharine	Grobler, Piet	*Fussy Freya*	2008	Indian and white
Ryan, Leslie	Soliz, Adolph	*I Am Flippish*	2011	Filipino and white
Say, Allen	Say, Allen	*The Favorite Daughter*	2013	Japanese and white
Shin, Sun Yung	Cogan, Kim	*Cooper's Lesson*	2004	Korean and white
Stehlikc, Tania Duprey	Vanja Vuleta Jovanovic	*Violet*	2009	"violet"
Wahl, Phoebe	Phoebe Wahl	*Sonya's Chickens*	2015	Unclear*
Wong, Janet	Chodos-Irvine, Margaret	*Buzz*	2000	Asian and white

*These books come up repeatedly in searches as being about racially mixed people as the protagonists have one light-skinned and one dark-skinned parent.

Appendix B
Contemporary and Historical Fiction with Asian and White Multiracials

Author	Title	Date	Genre	Racial Mix
Balliet, Blue	*Chasing Vermeer*	2004	Contemporary fiction	Indian & white, Jordanian & white
Balliet, Blue	*The Wright 3*	2006	Contemporary fiction	Indian & white, Jordanian & white
Balliet, Blue	*The Calder Game*	2008	Contemporary fiction	Indian & white, Jordanian & white
Burg, Ann E.	*All the Broken Pieces*	2009	Historical fiction	Vietnamese & white
Chang, Margaret Scrogin	*Celia's Robot*	2009	Contemporary fiction	Chinese & white
Dione, Erin	*Ollie and the Science of Treasure Hunting*	2014	Contemporary fiction	Vietnamese & white
Donwerth-Chikamatsu, Annie	*Somewhere Among*	2016	Contemporary fiction	Japanese & white
Easton, Kelly	*Hiroshima Dreams*	2007	Contemporary fiction	Japanese & white
Engle, Margarita	*Lion Island*	2016	Historical fiction	African, Chinese & Cuban
Freedman, Paula	*My Basmati Bat Mitzvah*	2013	Contemporary fiction	Indian & Jewish
Graff, Lisa	*Absolutely Almost*	2014	Contemporary fiction	Korean & Swiss
Headley, Justina Chen	*Nothing but the Truth: (and a Few White Lies)*	2006	Contemporary fiction	Taiwanese & white
Hiranandani, Veera	*The Whole Story of Half a Girl*	2012	Contemporary fiction	Indian & Jewish
Kadohata, Cynthia	*Outside Beauty*	2008	Contemporary fiction	Japanese & white

Author	Title	Date	Genre	Racial Mix
Lamba, Marie	*What I Meant*	2007	Contemporary fiction	Indian & white
Lorenzi, Natalie Dias	*Flying the Dragon*	2012	Contemporary fiction	Japanese & white
Lowitz, Leza	*Up From the Sea*	2016	Contemporary fiction	Japanese & white
Namioka, Lensey	*Half and Half*	2003	Contemporary fiction	Chinese & Scottish
Parry, Rosanne	*The Turn of the Tide*	2016	Contemporary fiction	Japanese & Swedish
Platt, Randall Beth	*The Likes of Me*	2000	Historical fiction	Chinese & white
Werlin, Nancy	*Black Mirror: A Novel*	2001	Contemporary fiction	Japanese & Jewish
Wong, Janet	*Minn and Jake's Almost Terrible Summer*	2008	Contemporary fiction	Korean, Norwegian, German & French
Yee, Lisa	*Bobby the Brave*	2010	Contemporary fiction	Chinese, English, French & German
Yee, Lisa	*Bobby v. Girls*	2010	Contemporary fiction	Chinese, English, French & German
Yep, Lawrence	*Angelfish*	2001	Contemporary fiction	Chinese & white

Appendix C
Contemporary and Historical Fiction with Black and White Multiracials

Author	Title	Date	Genre
Adams, Jewel	Elise's Heart	2001	Contemporary fiction
Adoff, Jaime	Names Will Never Hurt Me	2004	Contemporary fiction
Adoff, Jaime	Jimi & Me	2005	Contemporary fiction
Adoff, Jaime	The Death of Jayson Porter	2008	Contemporary fiction
Brady, Laurel S	Say You Are My Sister	2000	Historical fiction
Carbone, Elisa	Last Dance on Holladay Street	2005	Historical fiction
Chan, Crystal	Bird	2015	Contemporary fiction
Curry, Jane Louise	The Black Canary	2005	Contemporary fiction
Edwards, Nicholas	Dog Whisperer: The Rescue	2009	Contemporary fiction
Finotti, M. C.	The Treasure of Amelia Island	2008	Historical fiction
Frank, E. R.	America	2002	Contemporary fiction
Frazier, Sundee Tucker	Brendan Buckley's Universe and Everything in It	2007	Contemporary fiction
Frazier, Sundee Tucker	The Other Half of My Heart	2010	Contemporary fiction
Grimes, Nikki	The Road to Paris	2006	Contemporary fiction
Magoon, Kekla	Camo Girl	2011	Contemporary fiction
Marsden, Carolyn	Take Me with You	2010	Historical fiction
McDonald, Janet	Off-color	2007	Contemporary fiction
McMullen, Margaret	Cashay	2009	Contemporary fiction
Murphy, Rita	Black Angels	2001	Historical fiction
Myers, Walter Dean	Riot	2009	Historical fiction
Nelson, Marilyn	American Ace	2016	Contemporary fiction
Peck, Richard	The River Between Us	2003	Historical fiction

Author	Title	Date	Genre
Rinaldi, Ann	*The Education of Mary: A Little Miss of Color, 1832*	2000	Historical fiction
Rinaldi, Ann	*Numbering All the Bones*	2002	Historical fiction
Rodowsky, Colby F.	*That Fernhill Summer*	2006	Contemporary fiction
Sanders, Scott Loring	*Gray Baby: A Novel*	2009	Contemporary fiction
Schwartz, Ellen	*Stealing Home*	2006	Historical fiction
Schwartz, Virginia Frances	*Send One Angel Down*	2000	Historical fiction
Taylor, Mildred D.	*The Land*	2001	Historical fiction
Wenberg, Michael	*Stringz*	2010	Contemporary fiction
Willis, Meredith Sue	*Billie of Fish House Lane*	2006	Contemporary fiction
Wilson, Diane L.	*Black Storm Comin'*	2005	Historical fiction
Woods, Brenda	*The Blossoming Universe of Violet Diamond*	2014	Contemporary fiction
Woodson, Jacqueline	*The House You Pass on the Way*	1997	Contemporary fiction
Woodson, Jacqueline	*If You Come Softly*	1998	Contemporary fiction
Woodson, Jacqueline	*Behind You*	2004	Contemporary fiction
Woodson, Jacqueline	*After Tupac & D Foster*	2008	Contemporary fiction

Appendix D
Contemporary Fiction with Latino/a and White Multiracials

Author	Title	Date
Anderson, Jessica Lee	*Border Crossing*	2009
Cruz, Maria Colleen	*Border Crossing: A Novel*	2003
Frank, Lucy	*Just Ask Iris*	2001
Haslam, Gerald W. and Janice E.	*Manuel and the Madman*	2000
Osa, Nancy	*Cuba 15*	2003
Peña, Matt de la	*Mexican WhiteBoy*	2008
Peña, Matt de la	*We Were Here*	2009
Resau, Laura	*What the Moon Saw: A Novel*	2006
Ryan, Pam Muñoz	*Becoming Naomi Leon*	2004
Wilson, Barbara	*A Clear Spring*	2002

Appendix E
Contemporary and Historical Fiction with Native and White Multiracials

Author	Title	Date	Genre
Alder, Elizabeth	Crossing the Panther's Path	2002	Historical fiction
Bruchac, Joseph	The Dark Pond	2004	Contemporary fiction
Bruchac, Joseph	Hidden Roots	2004	Contemporary fiction
Creel, Ann Howard	Call Me the Canyon	2006	Historical fiction
Ernst, Kathleen	Trouble at Fort La Pointe	2000	Historical fiction
Flood, Nancy Bo	Soldier Sister, Fly Home	2016	Contemporary fiction
Hesse, Karen	Aleutian Sparrow	2003	Historical fiction
Hughes, Dean	Missing in Action	2010	Historical fiction
Ketchum, Liza	Where the Great Hawk Flies	2005	Historical fiction
Little, Kimberley Griffiths	The Last Snake Runner	2002	Historical fiction
Osborne, Mary Pope	Adaline Falling Star	2000	Historical fiction
Raffa, Edwina, and Annelle Rigsby	Escape to the Everglades	2006	Historical fiction
Schultz, Jan Neubert	Battle Cry	2006	Historical fiction
Smith, Cynthia Leitich	Rain Is Not My Indian Name	2001	Contemporary fiction
Sommerdorf, Norma	Red River Girl	2006	Historical fiction
Spooner, Michael	Last Child	2005	Historical fiction
Vanasse, Deb	A Distant Enemy	2004	Contemporary fiction

Appendix F
Contemporary Fiction with Nonwhite Multiracials

Author	Title	Date	
Cardenas, Teresa, and David Unger	*Letters to My Mother*	2006	Afro-Cuban
Garcia, Cristina	*I Wanna Be Your Shoebox*	2008	Japanese/Cuban/Jewish
Flake, Sharon	*Money Hungry*	2001	Korean and black
Flake, Sharon	*Begging For Change*	2004	Korean and black
Lynch, Janet Nichols	*Messed up*	2009	Cheyenne and Mexican
Maldonado, Torrey	*Secret Saturdays*	2010	Black and Puerto Rican
Nye, Naomi Shihab	*Going Going*	2005	Mexican and Lebanese
Pierce, Nora	*The Insufficiency of Maps: A Novel*	2007	Quechan and Mexican
Robinson, Gary	*Son Who Returns*	2014	Mexican, Filipino, Chumash and Crow
Woodson, Jacqueline	*Miracle's Boys*	2000	Black and Puerto Rican

Index

activism around multiracial identity 16, 69–70
Adaline Falling Star (Osborne) 39, 96–100, 112n5
Adoff, Arnold 3, 23
Adoff, Jaime 3, 39–40, 44–5, 48, 139
African American characters in multiracial fiction 25, 40, 53, 56, 58, 59–62, 66, 84, 86, 91n3, 95, 101, 108–9, 119, 122, 125–30
All the Broken Pieces (Burg) 100–3
Alko, Selina 24–6
America (Frank) 45–6
American Ace (Nelson) 83–4, 86
American Indians: in children's literature 6, 8, 98, 133
Anderson, Jessica 42
Angelfish (Yep) 66n2, 71–3, 91n4, 139
antimiscegenation laws 3, 18, 100
Asian American 19
Asians 18, 24, 54, 94; Amerasians 100, 112n7; characters in multiracial fiction 118; racially mixed 71
Atinuke 32
Averbeck, Jim 31

Balliett, Blue 2, 52, 54–5
Beatty, Patricia 1
Beauvais, Garcelle 26
Becker, Shari 32
Becoming Naomi Léon (Ryan) 2, 66n2, 139
Begging for Change (Flake) 61–3, 66n2
Benjamin, Floella 28–9
binary caste system 4
biological basis for racial identity 12, 37–9, 44, 97, 123, 125, 139

biracial baby boom 15
Bishop, Rudine Sims ix, x, 1, 6, 24, 51, 57, 65, 70, 125, 140
Black Angels (Murphy) 95, 121, 122–7, 131
Black Mirror (Werlin) 41–2
blood quantum 14, 15, 37, 94, 131
Border Crossing (Anderson) 42–4
Border Crossing (Cruz) 76–80
Botelho, Maria Jose 7, 19, 90
Brady, Laurel 95, 121, 124
Brendan Buckley's Sixth Grade Experiment (Frazier) 139
Brendan Buckley's Universe and Everything in it (Frazier) 73–6, 77, 116, 139
Brooks, Wanda 125, 133, 134
Brown, Monica 6, 8n3
Bruchac, Joseph 39, 73, 121, 130–4
Brunsma, David 15, 19, 26, 39, 54, 58–9, 66, 138
Burg, Anne, E. 100–1
Buzz (Wong) 32

Camo Girl (Magoon) 51, 59, 91n4
Case for Loving: The Fight for Interracial Marriage, The (Alko) 26
Cashay (McMullen) 51, 58–61, 63
Catledge, Tiffany 24, 25
Census *see* U.S. Census
Cheng, Andrea 23
Chinese: Afro-Chinese 107; Chinese American 1, 136; identity in multiracial fiction 45, 53, 71–3, 93, 96, 116–18; indentured workers 107, 108; language use 24, 53, 107
Clear Spring, A (Wilson) 51, 56–7, 64
Colonialism x, 12, 14, 15, 38, 95, 107–8, 131, 134

152 Index

colorblind 17, 19, 136–7
Cooper's Lesson (Shin) 28, 33
Cosman, Marsha 24, 25
counterstories xi, 7, 25, 90, 133–4
Critical multicultural analysis 3, 7
Critical race theory 7, 23, 118, 133
Cuban identity in multiracial fiction 26, 38, 64–5, 107–8
Cultural pluralism 112, 118, 119
Curtis, Christopher Paul 1, 4, 73, 134

Death of Jayson Porter, The (Adoff) 39, 44–5, 139
Deldago, Richard 7, 23, 47, 90, 118, 133
Diggs, Taye 27, 138

Easton, Kelly 88
Engle, Margarita 103, 104, 108
ethnicity 85, 116, 117, 134n2
eugenics 14, 130, 131, 132, 134
Evans, Shane 27, 32, 138

family: broken interracial 38, 40, 41, 43, 45, 98, 101, 102, 103, 108, 126; intact interracial 2, 23, 25, 26, 28, 29, 31, 32, 56, 58, 62, 64, 73, 76, 78, 87, 89, 107, 110, 118, 119; multiracial 29, 32, 53, 55, 57, 60, 64, 80, 104, 124, 131
Flake, Sharon 19, 59, 61, 62
Flying the Dragon (Lorenzi) 61, 139
foster children as characters in multiracial fiction 45, 54
Frazier, Sundee Tucker 73, 91n3, 138, 139
Fulbeck, Kip *see* The Hapa Project

Garcia, Christina 65
Gaskins, Pearl Fuyo 57
Going, Going (Nye) 18, 56, 66n2
Grandfather Counts (Cheng) 23

Half and Half (Namioka) 91n4, 116, 117
Hapa Project, The 57, 65
Hidden Roots (Bruchac) 39, 121, 122, 130–4
Hiranandani, Veera 116, 138
Hiroshima Dreams (Easton) 88
historical fiction with multiracial content 2, 5, 38, 48, 94–112, 121–34

hypodescent 15, 18, 40, 53, 54, 58–61, 95, 96, 122

identity: cultural 29, 32, 33, 80; ethnic 115; racial x, 2, 4, 5, 11–19, 137, 139
Ifekwunigwe, Jayne, O. 13, 16
immigrant characters in multiracial fiction 55, 57, 71, 78, 84, 105
I'm Your Peanut Butter Big Brother (Alko) 24, 66n2
Indian *see* My Basmati Bat Mitzvah; Native American; *The Whole Story of Half a Girl*
indigenous 12, 13, 82, 107, 131
interracial marriage *see* family
I Wanna Be Your Shoebox (Garcia) 64–5, 134n2

Japanese and Japanese American characters 28, 41, 46–7, 58, 59, 61, 64–5, 89–90, 139
Jewish identity in multiracial fiction 2, 41–2, 63–5, 82, 108–10, 116–21, 128, 134n2
Jim Crow 1, 84, 95, 112, 123–9
Jimi & Me (Adoff) 39–40, 139

Kadohata, Cynthia 1, 73
Korean American identity in multiracial fiction 19, 28, 30, 52, 59, 61–3
Krishnaswami, Uma 2, 6, 8n3, 24

Land, The (Taylor) 95, 125, 134
Larrick, Nancy 5, 115
Last Stop on Market Street (de la Peña) 23, 31
Latino characters in multiracial fiction 24, 28, 51, 52, 57, 59, 64–5, 140
Likes of Me, The (Platt) 48, 93–4, 96–7, 111
Lion Island (Engle) 66n2, 104, 107–8
Lorenzi, Natalie 61, 116, 139
Loving v. Virginia 3, 15, 26, 95, 96, 136
Lowitz, Leza 46, 59

Magoon, Kekla 51, 137
Marginal Man theory 13, 39, 41, 42, 97
Marisol McDonald Doesn't Match (Brown) 24, 28, 29–30, 33, 66n2, 138

Marsden, Carolyn 96
Maxwell's Mountain (Becker) 32
melting pot paradigm 51, 57, 133
Mexican WhiteBoy (de la Peña) 38, 40–1, 66n2, 140
microagressions 137–9
Missing Half paradigm 38, 40, 43
Mixed Me! (Diggs) 17, 30, 138
Money Hungry (Flake) 19, 61–2, 66n2
mulatto 12, 13, 45, 47
Murphy, Rita 95, 121, 126
My Basmati Bat Mitzvah (Freedman) 2, 63–4, 134n2, 139
My Two Grandads (Benjamin) 28, 66n2, 91n4
My Two Grannies (Benjamin) 29, 66n2, 91n4

Nakashima, Cynthia 17, 138
Names Will Never Hurt Me (Adoff) 39, 139
Namioka, Lensey 116, 117
Native American 12, 14, 19n2, 38, 48, 76, 81, 82, 97–100, 122, 131–4
Nelson, Marilyn 83
Newbery award 23, 140
Nye, Naomi Shihab 18, 56

Obama, Barak 11, 17, 138
Off-Color (McDonald) 83–6, 134n2
One-drop rule 5, 14, 19, 54, 84, 122, 124
One Word from Sophia (Averbeck) 31–2
Osborne, Mary Pope 39, 96–100

Parry, Rosanne 59, 116
passing 121–34
Peck Richard 103, 104, 106, 121
Peña, Matt de la 23, 38, 40–1, 52, 140
phenotype 28, 31, 56–9, 76, 77, 82, 85, 119, 122, 133
Platt, Randall 48, 93, 94, 96
post-racial era 17, 66; *see also* colorblind
power 19, 30, 34, 53, 66, 69–70, 83, 87, 107, 110–12, 116, 119, 125, 137, 139

quadroon 12, 106

racial categories 3, 5, 8, 12, 16, 69, 95, 121, 130

Rain is Not my Indian Name (Smith) 76, 80
Resau, Laura 87
Reynolds, Nancy 1, 2, 3, 4, 38, 44
River Between Us, The (Peck) 104–7, 111, 121
Rockquemore, Kerry Ann 15, 19, 26, 39, 54, 58, 66, 138
Root, Maria, P. P. 4, 15, 19, 19n3, 69, 138

Say You Are My Sister (Brady) 95, 121, 122–6, 131
Schwartz, Ellen 75, 103
Slapin, Beverly 111, 112n4
slavery 12, 19, 84, 104
Soldier Sister, Fly Home (Flood) 19n1, 116
Son Who Returns (Robinson) 19n2, 66n2
Sonya's Chickens (Wahl) 31
Spickard, Paul 18, 19, 130, 134
statistics about multiracial people: in literature 3, 118; population 5, 18, 19, 33, 54, 69, 94
Stealing Home (Schwartz) 75, 103, 108–10, 134n2
Stonequist, Everett 13, 39, 47, 48, 94, 97
Stringz (Wenberg) 51, 59–60, 134n2

Take Me With You (Marsden) 96, 100–1
Taylor, Mildred 95, 134
tragic mulatto *see* mulatto
tribal membership 15, 131
Turn of the Tide, The (Parry) 59, 61

Up from the Sea (Lowitz) 46, 59, 61
U.S. Census ix, 3, 5, 12–18, 69, 74
U.S. Supreme Court *see* Loving *v.* Virginia

Vietnamese characters in multiracial fiction 100–3; *see also All the Broken Pieces*
Vietnam War 100, 101

Werlin, Nancy 41
What the Moon Saw (Resau) 66n2, 87–8
whiteness as racial identity xi, 14, 16, 71, 75, 79, 82, 84, 90, 102, 115–35;

Irish 26, 59, 76, 80, 84, 89, 105, 116, 134n2; Italian 83, 84, 101, 116, 134n2; Scottish 116, 118; *see also* Jewish identity in multiracial fiction

Whole Story of Half a Girl, The (Hiranandani) 116, 118, 121, 134n2, 138

Wong, Janet 32
Woods, Tiger 11, 17, 84, 138
Woodson, Jacqueline 2, 51, 53–4, 73, 137

Yep, Lawrence 71, 73, 91n1, 116, 139
Yokota, Junko 3, 23